A New Vision of God for the 21st Century

A New Vision of God for the 21st Century

◆

Discovering the Essential Wesley for Pastors and Other Seekers

Stanley A. Fry

iUniverse, Inc.
New York Lincoln Shanghai

A New Vision of God for the 21st Century
Discovering the Essential Wesley for Pastors and Other Seekers

Copyright © 2005 by Stanley Aaron Fry

All rights reserved. No part of this book may be used or reproduced by any means, graphic, electronic, or mechanical, including photocopying, recording, taping or by any information storage retrieval system without the written permission of the publisher except in the case of brief quotations embodied in critical articles and reviews.

iUniverse books may be ordered through booksellers or by contacting:

iUniverse
2021 Pine Lake Road, Suite 100
Lincoln, NE 68512
www.iuniverse.com
1-800-Authors (1-800-288-4677)

ISBN-13: 978-0-595-34656-1 (pbk)
ISBN-13: 978-0-595-79401-0 (ebk)
ISBN-10: 0-595-34656-1 (pbk)
ISBN-10: 0-595-79401-7 (ebk)

Printed in the United States of America

With Gratitude and Love
To Anita
and
Our Three Sons
Peter, Andy, and Kip

Contents

Preface: Wrestling with the Angel xi

Part I

CHAPTER 1	He Lived by Preaching 3
CHAPTER 2	Deep Were the Roots 32
CHAPTER 3	Saved by Grace 54
CHAPTER 4	In Search of a New Vision 79
CHAPTER 5	Spirit Is God 102
CHAPTER 6	Things of the Spirit 127
CHAPTER 7	Addressing the Universal Needs 149

Part II

CHAPTER 8   More than Natural—Sermons on Prevenient Grace 177
- *Sermon 1 In the Beginning God* *178*
- *Sermon 2 Where No One Stands Alone* *184*
- *Sermon 3 Free at First* *191*

CHAPTER 9   Turning the Corner—Sermons on Justifying Grace 198
- *Sermon 4 Be Honest with Yourself* *199*
- *Sermon 5 Coming Home* *205*
- *Sermon 6 The Day the Glass Shatters* *211*

- Sermon 7 I, If I Be Lifted Up 217

Chapter 10 Growing Up—Sermons on Sanctifying Grace . . 224
- Sermon 8 Pray without Ceasing.......................... 225
- Sermon 9 Tomorrow Is Another Day..................... 232
- Sermon 10 Sitting Loose 238
- Sermon 11 The Greatest of These......................... 244

Chapter 11 Choosing the Future—Sermons on Glorifying Grace..250
- Sermon 12 Fear Not....................................... 251
- Sermon 13 The Flower of Hope........................... 257
- Sermon 14 Joyful, Joyful 263

Endnotes 269
Index 293

Acknowledgments

Among those to whom I owe a debt of gratitude are my parents, Glenn and Clara Fry, who taught me more about religion than I was ready to learn, and the following friends, who have read diverse chapters at various stages of composition and stimulated me with their critiques and comments: Bob Ross, Shirley Oskamp, Tom Peterson, Jim Farrell, Royal and Roberta Fishbeck, and D. A. Riley. I have benefited greatly from lengthy discussions with assorted people, friends, and acquaintances alike, about many of the issues with which I have dealt. Among them are Dick and Carol Johnsen, Marilyn Peterson, Nancy Tims, Helemar Reis, Érico Georg, and Edith Schisler. The last four named are Brazilian Methodists indebted to John Wesley, each in his or her own special way. I thank all of them for their gifts. John Wesley would certainly have approved of all of those challenging exchanges, because he believed one of the means of grace was spiritual conversation.

My three sons, Peter, Andrew, and Kevin (Kip), and my sisters, Evelyn, Doris, and Agnes, have given indispensable encouragement to me. Not all of them have read or discussed with me material appearing in the book, but all have supported me with their love and interest. My son, Kip, a freelance writer and editor, has contributed uniquely and generously with his liberal editorial pen. However, no one of those to whom I am indebted can be held responsible for the conclusions I have expressed in this book.

I am also indebted and deeply grateful to Janet Noddings, my Publishing Services Associate at iUniverse, for her prompt and patient responses to all my questions and publishing needs, to Jessica Barringer for her skilled and helpful editorial guidance, and to the other people at iUniverse for their many contributions.

Finally, my gratitude overflows when I remember the congregations I have served and the patience and love with which they received my ministrations and struggled with me to find our way into a closer communion with the Spirit who is God.

To all, my profound appreciation.

Preface
Wrestling with the Angel

My mama died when I was eight years old. She went to the hospital a couple of towns away to give birth to my youngest sister. The baby was nearly a week old, and my father had returned to the hospital that day, leaving my other sisters and me at home with a lady named Mary who lived across the alley. Sometime that evening, the telephone rang and Mary left the room to go answer it. When she returned, she gathered us at her knee and told us all about the golden streets of heaven where angels flew about and where good people go when they die.

Without telling us our mama had died, she was doing the best she could—but I knew. Even then, I thought, "She's telling us these stories to make us feel better, but I don't believe them."

A hundred times since, I have disbelieved religious things I have heard proclaimed or read. Even so, the time came when I decided to become a preacher myself because there was much I did believe. Plus, there were many things I wanted to say and do as a pastor.

After I became a pastor, whenever I was asked questions formulated in traditional theistic terms, my affirmations and responses were often contorted and even irrational, failing to make much sense. They were ultimately unsatisfactory—both to me and those I wanted to help.

Therefore, I constantly struggled to reconcile my own views with the ordinary images and doctrines of Protestantism. This struggle has always plagued my preaching, teaching, and even counseling.

In order to reorient myself, I often turned to John Wesley, the founder of the Methodist movement, because I was a Methodist preacher myself. But not until I began digging more thoroughly into his writings did I discover that the root of my struggles—both in life and in answering my congregation's questions satisfactorily—was the unquestioned doctrinal presuppositions that lay at the root both of his thought and mine. These presuppositions dealt with the concept of God and the associated doctrinal corollaries I shared with Wesley and, in fact, with most Christians since the fourth century.

Even so, Wesley's doctrine of grace continued to say to me, "There is something here. Look for it, identify it, isolate it, and use it in every part of your ministry." In order to do that, I needed to remove the troublesome theological presuppositions that were often the source of serious existential and theological questioning—both by me and by the members of my congregation. This required a careful look at Wesley's preaching message, because it is there one finds both the implications of his image of God and a model or framework for the development of a new vision, a new way of thinking about and talking about salvation.

As I considered my effort to abandon his theological presuppositions and reformulate his message about salvation by grace, the image that sprung to my mind was of Jesus, who was reported to have said, "One does not put new wine into old wineskins." Wesley's assumptions about God and its corollaries—the Trinity, the Incarnation, and the Atonement—constitute the old wineskins holding his doctrine of grace. They needed to be replaced by the new wineskin of a fresh vision of God.

Initially, my purpose in writing this book was not to make any claims, but only to present some of the results of the last twenty years or so of my struggle to preach in a manner both faithful to my inherited Wesleyan tradition and in lively communication with my own times.

However, I soon found I had to make some moves that I had not clearly anticipated when I began. That is, I had to find that new wineskin. Thus, *A New Vision of God for the 21st Century* became much more than a report on what I had learned. Writing it became an exciting learning experience. It also became a witness to my own personal theological journey.

I know there are pastors who are satisfied with the traditional explanations. They are usually unwilling to ask troublesome questions because their beliefs are settled and comfortable. Those who are satisfied will likely find this book to be an unwelcome stirring of the waters. I also know there are many people sitting in our pews for whom theological questions are of little conscious concern.

The contemporary mind-set, however, is not conducive to careless thought. Thoughtful people are increasingly confused or simply alienated by the incoherence of traditional Christian thought about who God is and what God does. They have become accustomed to the rigorous disciplines of the physical and social sciences. Stories about miracles, the efficacy of prayer, and the claims of providential occurrences require something more than blind faith. Therefore, what I have written here is not only a personal quest and testament; it is also a recommendation addressed directly to discontented preachers seeking a more coherent message for these new times. Of course, I also believe that the message I recommend will speak meaningfully and persuasively to those who listen to preachers but are disillusioned or even alienated by what they are hearing. I hope many of them will be listening in as I talk to their pastors.

Most preachers, however, are still seekers because they sense their preaching could address their congregations with more power if they could just discover a more coherent, persuasive message for these times. Moreover, they are unclear about the universal human needs that only such a message can address and that must be addressed if we are not to leave ourselves and our people unfed. In general, I am simply sharing here my struggles and conclusions with other seekers who are dissatisfied with the state of their present spiritual and theological understanding.

In Part I, I use the first three chapters to discuss the evolution of Wesley's preaching in the context of his life and ministry, to identify the major sources that fed the development of his mature message and to set forth that message within the framework he developed. The fourth chapter is an analysis and critique of his message, along with a case for the development of a new theological perspective that can speak more adequately to the contemporary mind-set than his orthodox theism can.

The last three chapters of Part I describe an alternative vision of God for the twenty-first century; what that vision means for the ideas of the Trinity, the Incarnation, and the Atonement; its implications for a new understanding of salvation ordered by Wesley's doctrine of grace; and, finally, the universal human needs that his message met in his time and that our message must meet in the twenty-first century.

It is this revised view of salvation that I think of as "the essential Wesley." I am calling it that because I believe it satisfies both the spiritual instincts of the early Christian movement and those of Wesley. In both cases, I believe there was an almost inarticulate desire for a more relational understanding of the faith. However, Wesley could not adequately develop his true spiritual instincts, because he was constrained by his inherited orthodoxy, an orthodoxy that took shape three to four hundred years after the Christian movement had begun but which continues to hold so much of the church in thrall.

In Part II, I take a deep breath and boldly set forth a group of sermons in which I attempt to articulate a nontheistic message of salvation for the twenty-first century. I introduce each sermon with a brief statement about its relation to Wesley's theological content, its biblical references, and the universal needs that are the targets of the sermons. The use of printed sermons for this purpose employs Wesley's customary means of educating his people.

Thus, I intend to offer a new perspective on the content of our preaching and teaching for those who are willing to search for a better understanding, a clearer hope, and a surer purpose for these new times.

Whenever I look back upon my struggles, I often think of Jacob wrestling with the angel, hip out of joint, anguished about the future, but exhilarated by the assurance that the angel is somehow the presence of God himself. Now is the time of hope.

PART I

1

He Lived by Preaching

In recent years, John Wesley's reputation as a lightweight theologian has been dissipating rather rapidly. Both scholars in the various Wesleyan denominations and theologians in other communions, including the Roman Catholic Church, have rediscovered him.

It is true he was not a systematic theologian, but he was an ingenious "folk-theologian" whose primary interest was in understanding and teaching what salvation can mean for ordinary folks. Neither did his reputation as a preacher begin to compare with that of George Whitefield, his friend and rival from college days, whose funeral sermon he preached on November 18, 1770. But his preaching formed the foundation of the Wesleyan movement of the eighteenth century because it prompted the formation of the classes and societies in which his converts were nurtured and held accountable.

Our new vision of God for the twenty-first century arises out of an examination of the preaching message of John Wesley in which we find both his theological presuppositions and his doctrine of salvation. I have also illustrated and filled out his teaching from other sources in his voluminous writings.

The story to be told in this chapter is that of John Wesley as a preacher.

Wesley's Story

John Wesley grew up in a family of preachers. His two grandfathers, his father, and two brothers were all preachers in the Church of England. However, his grandfathers had both been Nonconformists. More than that, his mother was well read in the religious literature of the day and had a profound influence upon him, both as a child and an adult. One could say preaching was both in his blood and in the air he breathed.

He was the thirteenth or fourteenth child of eighteen or nineteen born to Samuel and Susanna Wesley (Samuel lost count of the numbers) on June 17, 1703, at Epworth, England.

One night when he was six years old, the rectory in Epworth, where his father was rector of the local church, burned nearly to the ground. At the last moment, John was saved when he leaped from an upstairs window into the arms of a waiting parishioner. The origin of the fire was suspicious because the elder Wesley had alienated a number of his parishioners. But nothing was ever proved. In any case, both his mother—and later John—came to believe he had been providentially spared for some great purpose that only God knew. What actually happened was that he became the founder of a spiritual movement that has spawned a multitude of denominations throughout the world.

In 1714, following homeschooling at his mother's knee, he was sent at the age of eleven to attend the well-regarded Charter House School in London. He did well in school, and, in 1720, he went to Oxford University to attend Christ Church College. There, he was broadly educated in the classics. In his time, both Locke and Aristotle loomed large in the college's curriculum. This background undoubtedly influenced Wesley's practical empiricism. While the High Church values of the Church of England provided the religious context there, the Tories dominated politics.

Wesley himself became a tutor and began holding get-togethers with serious-minded students, initially for study purposes. Because such colleges as Christ Church commonly served as seminaries for holy orders in the church, it was natural this group should attract a number of young men considering priesthood in the Church of England.

Wesley took his bachelor's degree in 1724. In 1725, he was ordained a deacon at the university. At this time, he determined to make religion the business of his life. His ordination at the university also formed the basis for his later claim that the world was his parish. It was then he began keeping his diaries in code. Only in recent years have they been deciphered.[1]

The following year, he was elected a fellow of Lincoln College at Oxford. The position provided a stipend, teaching responsibilities, and entitlement to occupy a place in the succession of preachers invited to preach regularly at the university. In 1728, again at the university, he was ordained a priest.

He took his ordination as a member of the Lincoln College of Divines to be warrant for his access to all places in what he came to call his "extraordinary ministry." In fact, by tradition, it was the university chancellor's prerogative to license any clergyman ordained at the university to preach in any diocese. Though Wesley never received such a license, he nevertheless presumed to have that authority because he had been ordained at the university.

Therefore, his earliest preaching was—understandably—traditionally High Church in content and style. According to Dr. Outler, a leading Wesley interpreter, "He was a High Church Tory who made it a point to wear his clerical vestments whenever he preached, even in the field."[2]

In 1728, his father persuaded him to become his curate at the churches in Epworth and Wroote. He stayed for less than two years, but, during these months, he began reading the literature of "the mystical writers," which he discussed at great length with his mother.

In 1729, he was recalled to the university to assume his role as a fellow. There, he was reunited with his younger brother, Charles, who had begun to meet with a group of students called the Holy Club. However, the club would be called a variety of less favorable names by other students, including the name Methodists. Beginning as a study group, the students had developed a system of spiritual disciplines and had finally undertaken social work with widows, orphans, and prisoners.

During the ten-year period following his first ordination in 1725, Wesley wrote sixty-eight sermons and preached many of them repeatedly. We now know this from the diaries he wrote during that period. Wesley only published one of these sermons, which suggests his own dissatisfaction with most of his early efforts.

The first sermon Wesley ever wrote and preached was found in his papers. It has been given the title "Death and Deliverance." Using Job 3:17 for its text, he first preached the sermon in Fleet Marston on October 3, 1725, just two weeks after his ordination. He wrote his second sermon, based on Matthew 6:33, the following month. The third was a funeral sermon, which he preached on January 15, 1727, for a young friend of his at Bradbury. He wrote and preached his fourth sermon in Wroote in 1728 while he served as his father's curate. The manuscripts for a number of the sermons he preached during his curacy there have survived. But not one that has survived was ever published by Wesley. This suggests any published manuscript was also destroyed.

He preached his first university sermon as a fellow of Lincoln College at St. Mary's Church in Oxford on November 15, 1730, after returning to the university following his service with his father. Using Genesis 1:27, he called it "The Image of God." Outler says of it, "After fifty mediocre sermons, here is finally one with a touch of genius."[3] Wesley preached this sermon at least four more times in nearby churches.

Throughout these years and until he and Charles left for Georgia in 1735, John was a lecturer in logic (1726–1730), Greek (1726–1727; 1729–1734), and philosophy (1730–1735). He was also invited regularly to preach at the university, usually at St. Mary's Church.

On January 1, 1733, he preached again at St. Mary's Church, delivering a sermon called "The Circumcision of the Heart." Outler calls it a landmark sermon "in Wesley's entire theological development thereafter."[4] In it, Wesley set forth what would be the basic form of his doctrine of grace. It was the first sermon in Wesley's second volume of published sermons. In fact, Wesley himself wrote of it in 1778: "I know not that I can [even now] write a better sermon on 'The Circumcision of the Heart' than I did five-and-forty years ago."[5] According to John's brother, Charles, he spent the entire month of December preparing it.

It is quite amazing this sermon should so well articulate the idea of salvation through faith nearly three years before Wesley met his first Moravians in Georgia and nearly five-and-a-half years before his much-commented "warm heart" experience at the Aldersgate Street meeting on May 24, 1738. Beginning at least with this 1733 sermon at St. Mary's Church and until Aldersgate, he had believed and preached the doctrine of salvation by grace through faith, but it very often met with negative results.

Fifteen years later Wesley modified this important sermon by inserting a description of the way in which holy living is a fruit not simply of faith but of justifying faith, rather than the cause of justifying faith.

"Justification," as it appears in Paul's letters, is a legal (or forensic) concept in which one stands convicted before the bar of God's justice, but is nevertheless acquitted or pardoned because of Jesus' death. It was this pardon or justification by the grace of God that put one into a new relationship with God. "For by grace you have been saved through faith, and this is not your own doing; it is the gift of God."[6]

In spite of resistance to his focus on faith, the records show he preached at the university more frequently than any other preacher did, both before his trip to Georgia and afterward. He preached there six more times before leaving for Georgia at the end of 1735.

That year, he began to keep a journal, a discipline he maintained for the rest of his life. In it, he recorded his adventures and theological journeys for posterity. The encoded diaries, however, remained private until recently.

One of his significant journeys involved his ill-fated sojourn with Charles to Oglethorpe's Georgia from 1735 to 1737. Not only did he fail to evangelize the native inhabitants, which was his desire when he left England, but he also failed in his courtship of Sophy Hopkey, a young confirmand of his. Through the vacillations of his courtship he allowed her to give up on him and marry another man. Her new husband became angry with him and brought charges against him. He charged Wesley, among other things, with improperly refusing to give the sacrament to Sophy after she had married against his wishes. Rather than face the charges, he returned to England. His brother had returned earlier.

The following year, 1738, was a year of transition for John Wesley. Together, it may be said the experiences of this crucial year formed the turning point in his ministry and, thus, in his preaching. Through it, he moved from being a floundering seeker to being a driving force.

Of course, he already believed salvation was by God's grace. This is known because, nearly four years earlier on January 1, 1733, he had preached his landmark sermon in which he had credited grace through faith with the gift of holiness, a subject which, at that point in his life, was his obsession.

He had also been preaching salvation by faith for some time as a guest preacher in many other churches of the area, but he was forbidden to preach again in at least half of them. The message of salvation by faith rather than good works was new and unwelcome.

He had met a group of Moravians aboard the ship to Georgia, and their peaceful demeanor during a storm at sea duly impressed him. While in Savannah, he engaged them in numerous conversations. They persuaded him that he could not find peace in his spirit without the "witness of the spirit that he was a child of God,"[7] the assurance that Christ had died for him. One could find that peace only by the free gift of God. They pointed out he must be personally assured he had been accepted by grace through faith in the Atonement. Because he had not felt that assurance, he believed he had no faith. So he fell into despondency.

This life-changing year would bring a series of emotional lows and highs. He went to America to convert the Indians, but returned to England, believing it was he who needed to be converted. His failure, both in ministry and in love, had disillusioned him. That is how the year started.

After returning from America, he met and held many conversations with another Moravian, Peter Boehler, who was spending time in England. Peter fully persuaded him that belief in salvation by faith alone was not good enough. He must experience an assurance of his own personal salvation before he could receive peace with God.

Then, on the evening of May 24, he attended a Moravian meeting in Aldersgate Street in London. His heart was "strangely warmed," and, briefly, he felt he had found the peace he had been longing for. He had received the assurance that

God accepted him. The impact on Wesley of his experience of assurance at Aldersgate had been immediate. In his journal, he describes it in these familiar words:

> In the evening, I went very unwillingly to a society in Aldersgate Street, where one was reading Luther's Preface to the Epistle to the Romans. About a quarter before nine, while he was describing the changes which God works in the heart through faith in Christ, I felt my heart strangely warmed. I felt I did trust in Christ, Christ alone for salvation; and an assurance was given me that he had taken away my sins, even mine, and saved me from the law of sin and death.[8]

As early as June 11, following his return from Georgia and just days after Aldersgate, he was once again invited to preach at St. Mary's Church.

However, the turnaround in his life did not happen overnight. The famous Aldersgate experience was probably not the most significant in his mind because it seemed to very quickly recede from his memory. The peace of heart and the joy he immediately experienced in Aldersgate Street did not last for long.

In this new time of depression, he determined to journey to Herrnhut and Marienborn in Germany so that he could spend more time with the Moravians. However, they became frustrated with him and he with them. At last, he broke with them over their refusal to recognize that, following justification, a person had the responsibility to use the "means of grace" in order to grow spiritually. His objection to them was over their insistence that justification was to be followed by no action at all. Instead, one needed only be "quiet" before the Lord. He saw them as antinomians, that is, those who ignore the law of God.

So, the "great reversal" continued to work itself out in his life. That is, he was learning how union with God and the holy life were not the result of good works, right beliefs, or devotional work. Instead, they were the fruit of justification. They followed from justifying faith. Nevertheless, there was more to come in this fateful year of 1738.

Soon after returning to England from Germany, he read the account of the Great Awakening in New England in the American colonies. Written by Jonathan Edwards, this story of great successes served only to further discourage him because his preaching had no such spectacular results.

Near the end of 1738, he finally returned to his home base in the Church of England. There, among its ancient documents, he made a quite remarkable discovery. He found the *Book of Homilies*. A long-ignored text, it provided a very satisfying response to the teachings of the Moravians. In the homilies, he found the framework for his doctrine of grace and the theological rationale for his experience of assurance. Actually, of course, the homilies had been there all along; however, the church had largely forgotten them.

In November of that same year, he compiled an abstract of the first five homilies and had it published.[9] In fact, it may well have been these homilies, which had been so important during an earlier period in the history of the English church, that later encouraged him to take the sermon as his preferred form for the education of his people.

The homilies had been prepared in 1542 when former members of the Roman clergy were required to preach in their churches without proper training for a Protestant ministry. Twelve model homilies were prepared for their instruction. Wesley used the first five, which were probably written by Thomas Cranmer, archbishop of Canterbury and principle author of the *Book of Common Prayer*. Neither at this time nor later did Wesley hesitate to borrow and use others' writings. Outler notes:

> The significance for us of such borrowing is their indication of Wesley's instinctive dependence upon typical Anglican authors for his doctrine of holy living. They also remind us that at this stage of his career Wesley felt no special need to establish himself as an original preacher in his own right; the practice of adapting and using this material from others was a common place in his time.[10]

He also highlights the importance of this event:

> It is very important to notice this conscious self-identification with the English reformers. It marked the final stage of Wesley's maturation as a theologian and it continued to serve as the basic datum-plane for all subsequent developments in his thought.[11]

The result of this discovery was that Wesley came to see salvation as including both justification by grace through faith and the ongoing process of sanctification or holiness of life by grace through faith. His "Circumcision of the Heart" sermon had not originally included the explicit recognition of the need for justification. It focused on holiness of life as though that were the whole meaning of salvation. But, before it was actually published in 1746, Wesley inserted the following:

> Every true believer is enabled to bear witness, "I know that my redeemer liveth," that I "have an advocate with the Father," that "Jesus Christ the righteous" is my Lord, and "the propitiation for my sins." I know he "hath loved me, and given himself for me." He hath reconciled me, even me, to God; and I "have redemption through his blood, even the forgiveness of sins."[12]

Thus, the sermon now included justification and the assurance of justification as well as the doctrine of holiness. In 1765, Wesley was able to write, "I preached a sermon on 'The Circumcision of the Heart,' which contains all that I now teach concerning salvation from all sin, and loving God with an undivided heart."[13]

Nearly a year after Aldersgate, several months after his visit to Germany, and a half year after his discovery of the homilies, Wesley's preaching suddenly began to work. That is, it began producing dramatic results.

George Whitefield, a former member of the Holy Club, had begun some work in Bristol, England, but he wanted to preach in the colonies. So, in 1739, he invited John to come to Bristol to continue his work preaching to the coal miners and peasants in the fields. Wesley went fearfully to the task, and the Wesleyan movement was born with power.

At last, his preaching began bearing results. From 1739 to 1760, the Wesleyan movement spread all across England. It also spread to Scotland, Wales, Ireland, and the colonies.

Dr. Outler says of this event, "...finally he had found his unique calling, and his sermons (early, middle and late) are mirrors to that."[14] Peter Boehler, his Moravian friend, had told him to preach faith until he had it. Then he would preach faith because he had it. Outler suggests, however, he preached faith until others began to find it. Then he preached it because others had found it.

Thus began his unique ministry, even though he had already learned to preach extemporaneously at Oxford. So, it was not the extempory character of his field preaching that accounted for his new effectiveness. Rather, it was the message itself in combination with hearers who were honest enough to recognize in themselves the needs he addressed.

William Webb recorded one report of that first outdoor sermon in Bristol:

> I went to the place appointed, out of curiosity, and heard that great and good man; but with much uneasiness all the time, not knowing what was the matter with me; nor could I relate any part of the sermon, being much confused in my mind and filled with astonishment at the minister. For I had never seen such proceedings before, it being quite a new thing to preach in the open air and not in a church or chapel. This was the first sermon Mr. Wesley preached in Bristol. When it was ended I was induced to follow him, but, at the same

time, knew not why I did so, being shut up in ignorance and gross darkness through the multitude of my sins and the hardness of my heart…But O!, how great was the goodness of God to me, who drew my heart with love to follow that dear minister of Jesus Christ, whose name I revere and esteem![15]

In this case, the sermon's impact was to draw young Webb to the preacher himself and, apparently, belatedly to Christ. That day the "third rise of Methodism," as Wesley himself called it, was launched. The first was the period of the Holy Club at Oxford; the second was the formation of small groups in the churches in Georgia.

His success as an evangelist has often been attributed to his work with the classes and societies he established, not to his preaching. Without a doubt, the movement he initiated would have never occurred without such organizational efforts. But, there was something that touched the massive crowds Wesley often addressed. It caused the manifestations of spiritual ecstasy to which charismatics and Pentecostals (those who make much of the gifts of the Spirit such as speaking in tongues) often point. It led many of his hearers to ask for the kind of personal contact and mutual support the classes and societies afforded. Unless he had been preaching with power, it would never have happened.

In spite of this, historians of the period have repeatedly ignored Wesley. He is not listed among the great English preachers or among preachers of the Great Evangelical Revival.[16] Surely, part of the reason is that "Wesley was by no means the most exciting or eloquent preacher of his time."[17] Nevertheless, his "influence was the greatest of them all because of the 'Methodist Connexion.'"[18] The missing connection of classes and societies in their ministries explains the reason he could call his fellow evangelists "ropes of sand."[19] They left no lasting product. He used this expression to characterize them—only after he had written to a large number of them suggesting they support one another rather than wrangling and after he had only received responses from three of them.

But, it is clear to my mind that the societies and classes in themselves could not have produced a lasting product unless the preaching that prompted their formation had been able to address the people's needs with a responsive message. Moreover, the genius of his message was that he was always working in his preaching and teaching for a synthesis of disparate focuses. It can be no surprise—in view of the paradoxical character of John Wesley himself—that his actions and even the theology that gave form to his preaching were a constant struggle to keep opposing forces in balance. One example is the apparent conflict between the roles of faith and works in the process of salvation.

Actually, the syntheses he strove for—in both his actions and his theology—were apparent to some of his contemporaries. An anonymous correspondent of John Wesley, calling himself John Smith, recognized the following personality pattern in Wesley:

> Hard-driving, yet also sensitive; intense, yet also patient; detached, yet also charming; self-disciplined, yet also intensely emotional; opinionated, yet also curious; open to counsel, yet impervious to pressure; brusque with bad faith, yet also tolerant of contrary opinions. The "character," once identified, is discernible in every aspect and context of his entire career.[20]

Though he was temperamentally traditional and would not preach outside the churches during the hours of regular worship, he was a radical underneath the vestments and the external proprieties in the sense that he was striking at the roots of contemporary faith and practice. It was difficult for him to enter the fields to preach at the behest of his friend George Whitefield. But he did so and thrived. He was not content to gather huge crowds to hear him preach, but, without the approval of the local priests, he dared to organize what we might call "house churches." He refused to leave the Anglican Church, but he was able to facilitate the formation of the Methodist Episcopal Church in the colonies in 1784.

So, Wesley's radicalism was not due to any real extremism on his part because he sought, even in his early years, to maintain a balance in all things. Rather, the rejection he experienced early on at St. Mary's Church as well as in the parish churches was because he probed deeply at the roots of the spiritual malaise of the English Church and English society. That is, his preaching was unwelcome because of his stress on the sinfulness of all persons, including the student body and the social elites to whom he spoke, both early and late in his career.

By the time he preached at St. Mary's Church again on July 25, 1741, the Wesleyan revival was well underway. His sermon that day is not extant, but it was based on an earlier sermon called "Almost Thou Persuadest Me." He ended it with some rather pointed words directed at Oxford University.

In 1744, he preached in St. Mary's Church in Oxford for the last time. He was never invited to preach there again, even though he remained a fellow of the university until his marriage in 1751.

His problems at Oxford had begun much earlier, but a description of the last sermon he preached at St. Mary's Church on August 24 will clarify why he would never be invited—nor did he expect to be—to preach there again.

Dr. Benjamin Kennicott, a well-known Hebrew scholar, had been a student at Oxford when Wesley preached his final sermon called "Scriptural Christianity." He wrote, in part:

> On Friday last, being St. Bartholomew's Day, the famous Methodist, Mr. John Wesley, fellow of Lincoln College, preached before the university; which being a matter of great curiosity at present, and may possibly be greater in its consequences, I shall be particular in the account of it...On Friday morning, having held forth twice in private, at five and at eight, he came to St. Mary's at ten o'clock...When he mounted the pulpit, I fixed my eyes on him and his behavior. He is neither tall nor fat; for the latter would ill become a Methodist. His black hair quite smooth, and parted very exactly, added to a peculiar composure in his countenance, showed him to be an uncommon man. His prayer was soft, short, and conformable to the rules of the university. His text, Acts iv 31: "And they were all filled with the Holy Ghost." And now he began to exalt his voice. He spoke the text very slowly and with an agreeable emphasis...(there follows a summary of the major part of his message)..."Now," he says, "where is this Christianity to be found. Is this a Christian nation? Is this a Christian city?" asserting the contrary to both. I liked some of his freedom; such as calling the generality of young gownsmen "a generation of triflers," and many other just invectives. But considering how many shining lights are here that are the glory of the Christian cause, his sacred censures were much too flaming and strong, and his charity much too weak in not making large allowances. But so far from allowances, that, after having summed up the measure of our iniquities, he concluded with a lifted up eye in this most solemn form, "It is time for Thee, Lord, to lay to Thine hand," words full of such presumption and seeming imprecation, that they gave an universal shock. This, and the assertion that Oxford was not a Christian city, and this country not a Christian nation, were the most offensive parts of the sermon, except when he accused the whole body (and confessed himself to be one of the number) of the sin of perjury. Had these things been omitted, and his censures moderated, I think his discourse, as to style and delivery, would have been uncommonly pleasing to others as well as to myself...However, the vice-chancellor sent for the sermon, and I hear the heads of college intend to show their resentment.[21]

William Blackstone, the famous lawyer, who had also attended Charter House School in London, was present in St. Mary's Church for the same sermon.

> We were last Friday entertained at St. Mary's by a curious sermon by Wesley, the Methodist. Among other equally modest particulars he informed us; first, that there was not one Christian among all the Heads of Houses; secondly, that pride, gluttony, avarice, luxury, sensuality and drunkenness were the

characteristics of all Fellows of College, who were useless to a proverbial uselessness. Lastly, that the younger part of the University were a generation of triflers, all of them perjured, and not one of them of any religion at all. <u>His notes were demanded by the Vice-Chancellor, but on mature deliberation it has been thought proper to punish him by a mortifying neglect.</u>[22]

One may well understand why Wesley was never invited to return to preach at St. Mary's Church again. But he was a realist. Better than anyone else, he understood why he had preached that sermon. In his journal entry on that same day, he wrote:

> I preached, I suppose, the last time at St. Mary's. But if so, I am now clear of the blood of these men. I have fully delivered my own soul. The Beadle came to me afterward and told me the Vice-Chancellor had sent him for my notes. I sent them without delay, not without admiring the wide providence of God. Perhaps few men of note would have given a sermon of mine the reading if I had put it into their hands; but by this means it came to be read, probably more than once, by every man of eminence in the university.[23]

It was no wonder he was seen early as a rambunctious radical. In fact, he seemed to glory in the fact he was forbidden pulpit after pulpit during those earlier years. Even after he began finding great success with the poor and hopeless following Whitefield's challenge in Bristol, it was many years before he was again welcomed in the parish churches of England.

He published the first four volumes of *Sermons on Several Occasions* in 1746. They became the standard texts for the movement. He wrote in his "Preface" to those volumes that they were to set forth "the substance of what I have been preaching for between eight and nine years last past." Outler suggests the indefinite reference to "eight and nine years" is a self-conscious attempt on Wesley's part to identify the somewhat extended period of approximately one year during which he had undergone the aforementioned radical reversal in his views.[24] One might even suggest the period of reversal reached back, perhaps, as far as his sermon on "The Circumcision of the Heart" in 1733 before his sojourn in Georgia.

If he was seen as rambunctious, it was primarily because of the radicalism of this probing. Secondarily, it was due to the irregularity of his practices. Outler asserts:

> In Wesley's break with eighteenth century taboos against field preaching, extempore prayer, and lay leadership (including his own), he was appealing to larger precedents than those currently being set...Actually he was reclaiming a

longer, richer tradition that reached back into medieval times and the English Reformation...We have...the fascinating story of the "lewd" (i.e., popular) preachers and the wandering friars, pardoners, and almoners of the fourteenth and fifteenth centuries...They, too, had been itinerants, and had "preached abroad" at the numerous "preaching crosses" scattered across the land...That Wesley stood in their line is clear, and this is important in any interpretation of his self-chosen role as a folk-theologian.[25]

Once his field preaching had begun, his ecclesiastical irregularities were more troublesome to the authorities than his theological message. It was unacceptable to preach extemporaneously, pray extemporaneously, and preach outside the churches. It was unacceptable to use lay preachers in his ministry, including women. It was unacceptable to preach expository sermons in which each word of a text was analyzed separately. Many of these practices were already in use, especially among the Puritans. Many of the Methodist chapels adopted the Puritan practice of placing the pulpit in the center with a large Bible positioned on a red, velvet cushion. This style reflected the view that preaching the Word was a chief means of grace.

Wesley, of course, was a sacramentalist. That is, he believed in the centrality of the sacraments of Baptism and the Eucharist in the life of the church. He personally adopted the practice of communicating daily whenever possible. However, the chapels were not considered to be churches. Instead, they were considered to be preaching places. He was not a Separatist, one who sought separation from the Church of England. Thus, he could both adopt the Puritan architecture for his chapels and yet remain an Anglican communicant.

A typical Methodist chapel service has been described as follows:

> From the beginning the men and women sat apart, as they always did in the primitive church. And none were suffered to call any place their own, but the first comers sat down first. They had no pews, and all the benches for rich and poor were of the same construction. Mr. Wesley began the service with a short prayer; then sung a hymn and preached (usually about half an hour), then sang a few verses of another hymn, and concluded with prayer. His constant doctrine was salvation by faith, preceded by repentance, and followed by holiness.[26]

For all these reasons, many people saw him as a rebel. However, Wesley:

> never saw himself as a rebel, even though the blithe irregularities in his churchmanship left the impression that, although he was certainly in the

Church of England as defined by her tradition, he was never altogether of it, as defined by her eighteenth century self-understanding.²⁷

Over the next four decades, John Wesley continued preaching. Often times, he would preach three or more times in a day. Nearly every summer was spent traveling. Wherever he traveled, he preached.

Finally, Mary Vazeille, a widow, became his wife in 1751. However, it was a marriage that fell apart rather quickly. He was traveling when she died years later.

Sometimes, his preaching was received with demonstrations of great emotion. Some persons fell to the ground in anguish over their sins; others cried out for salvation. Such demonstrations, of course, brought about much criticism. Wesley was called an "enthusiast." That is, his critics usually meant he appealed to the emotions and not to reason. He did not take these criticisms lying down. Instead, he wrote vehemently to refute the charges and to affirm his respect for the use of reason. In fact, the demonstrations that sometimes punctuated his preaching seemed to embarrass him. These phenomena were irregular for a relatively staid Anglican clergyman, but they have also made it possible for charismatic Christians to claim him as one of their own.

He was frequently harassed—and sometimes beaten—by mobs that local priests and other authorities had often stirred up. Nevertheless, he was never seriously injured:

> He had also faced mobs in Bristol and violent disruptions in London (including an ox being driven through his outdoor congregation at Charles Square). But these incidents did not prepare him for the violence of the opposition that had been aroused by the once-friendly vicar of Wednesbury when Wesley arrived there in October 1743. The story of that riot, told in great detail in Wesley's Journal, became the epitome of God's providential protection in the face of brutal opposition. Dragging the Oxford don (at times by the hair) through the countryside at night through a heavy rain, the mob soon was confronted by a rival gang from a neighboring village. The custody of Wesley was their common excuse for the fighting that ensued.²⁸

Wesley attributed his survival to God's providence, but, when he told the story to his younger brother the next day, Charles simply remarked that John's short stature had protected him from all except a couple of the blows the mob had aimed at him.

Through all the years of his career, he engaged in sporadic controversies with the followers of John Calvin, the French reformer. He formed classes and societies for mutual spiritual support and thus stabilized the results of his preaching.

He built preaching houses or chapels designed to revitalize the spiritual life of the people. (It was not the purpose of these buildings to replace the churches.) He recruited and trained preachers from all corners for the solidification of the movement. Some were, like him, priests of the Church of England. Others were laymen. Some were even laywomen, even though they had somewhat restricted roles.

During the last three decades of his ministry from 1760 to 1791, the movement was consolidated and placed on a firmer foundation. He started schools. He anthologized religious materials. He wrote a book on health and Latin and Greek grammars. He also composed thousands of letters. A new edition of his sermons was published, and new emphases in his preaching appeared as his people became second- and third-generation Methodists.

He started the *Arminian Magazine* in 1778. In this publication, he proposed publishing additional sermons, one in each monthly issue. Thus, forty-three sermons were published in the magazine by 1788 when a new set of *Sermons on Several Occasions* (volumes V–VIII) came out. Thirteen more sermons were added to the forty-three already published in the magazine. (All in all, a total of fifty-six sermons were published.)

In spite of being called an Arminian by his Calvinist detractors because he taught that human beings had been given free will, Wesley had never read the writings of Arminius. When he named his magazine, he called it the *Arminian*. It was possibly an act of defiance against the Calvinists. But his insistence upon human freedom did not come from Arminius. Instead, it came from the influence of the Greek Fathers' doctrine of the Holy Spirit and his own refusal to forego responsibility for his own spiritual life in the face of the Calvinists' insistence upon irresistible grace, the notion that no one can do anything either to earn God's grace or to resist it.

For many years, Wesley scholars have tended to neglect the sermons of Wesley's later years in favor of the fifty-three "standard sermons" that he himself identified as the foundation of his message. Their strong focus was on the doctrines of grace and the order of salvation. They had been published as *Sermons on Several Occasions* (I–IV) in 1746 when four decades of his ministry remained.

However, no consideration of Wesley's preaching message can be complete without taking account of the ninety-eight additional sermons. In fact, of all Wesley's writings, it is the whole body of Wesley's sermons that focus and expound Wesley's understanding of Christian existence most clearly.

During the decade from 1771 to 1781, Wesley published eight "new" sermons. It was not until 1771 that he began working on the only edition of his works he would prepare himself. This thirty-two volume edition, which was preceded by the fifty-three sermons published earlier, comprised sixteen volumes published in 1772, nine volumes published in 1773, and seven volumes published in 1774.

In the next decade (1781–1791), a surprising number of sermons appeared. More sermons appeared during this period than the number included in all of *Sermons on Several Occasions* (I–IV). Plus, the range of topics was far wider.

In these latter days, Wesley's own temperament had softened, and his ministry had taken on a less irregular cast. Even his taste in prayers and sermons seems to have reclaimed more traditional styles. In a letter to Mary Bishop in 1778, he wrote:

> I myself find more life in the Church prayers than in the formal extemporary prayers of Dissenters. Nay, and I find more profit in sermons on either good tempers or good works than in what are vulgarly called "gospel sermons." That term is now become a mere cant word. I wish none of our society would use it. It has no determinate meaning. Let but a pert, self-sufficient animal, that has neither sense nor grace, bawl out something about Christ, or his blood, or justification by faith, and his hearers cry out, "What a fine gospel sermon!" Surely the Methodists have not so learnt Christ. We know no gospel without salvation from sin.[29]

Clearly, what Wesley had in mind by "salvation from sin" was not simply the forgiveness of sin, as in justification or rebirth, but it was the expulsion of all sin as well, that is, sanctification or perfection.

Outler continues his evaluation of these later sermons:

> Despite their uneven quality, these later sermons exhibit Wesley's ripened Christian wisdom in a quite remarkable fashion, its broadened scope, its ample theological perspective, its quickened sensitivities to Christian social imperatives. They are, therefore, a remarkable achievement by a phenomenally busy old man, still leading a still burgeoning Revival. They give us a sight of the continued stretching of his mind toward a fuller understanding of his faith. Thus, they enlarge our resources for understanding that faith and his lifelong passion for an integrated vision of the Christian order of salvation.[30]

Early on, Wesley had said he had only one interest: how to get to heaven. Nevertheless, in his later years, he insisted Methodists were interested in one basic question only: Do you love and serve God? Therefore, he found it necessary to write new sermons, developing in more detail and with changing nuances the major themes of his early preaching.

For example, some sermons revisited old themes that needed refurbishing: "The Scripture Way of Salvation" (1765); "The Witness of the Spirit II" (1767); "On Predestination" (1773); "On Perfection" (1784); and "On Working Out Our Own Salvation" (1785).

"The Scripture Way of Salvation" was probably the best single summary of his doctrine of salvation. He had already preached from the same text (Ephesians 2:8) more than forty times. But, in these later years, new controversies with Calvinism and antinomianism[31] had arisen. This forced him to clarify—for himself as well as his people—what was at stake. In short, Calvinism insisted the sovereignty of God ruled out man's participation in his own salvation. Antinomianism taught that because we are saved by faith from life under the old Law, those laws no longer had a role to play.

His sermon called "On Working Out Our Own Salvation" was first published in the *Arminian* in 1783. It was important because it was his most thorough treatment of the idea of prevenient grace, the first of the gifts of grace. Even though he had preached from the same text he used for this sermon (Philippians 2:12–13) a few times in the early 1730s and had spoken of prevenient grace in some of his early sermons on original sin, it did not take its proper place in his scheme until late. Thus, it is included among the sermons that revisited and refurbished old themes during his later years.

In 1765, he wrote the sermon called "The Lord Our Righteousness" in which he dealt with a more recently raised issue concerning justification, that is, the difference and the relation between what were called "imputed righteousness" and "imparted righteousness."

In the same year, he wrote his second discourse on "The Witness of the Spirit." Again, he sought clarification on the distinction between the inward and outward witness, that is, the inward assurance known only to ourselves that God accepts us and the outward evidences visible to others.

Another discourse on repentance was a sequel to an earlier sermon "On Sin in Believers," which he had written in 1763. He felt it necessary to again deal with his unique definition of sin, that is, a voluntary, conscious act or attitude that breaks a known law of God.

In fact, these and other sermons and discourses written during the last two decades of his life were somewhat revisionist in spite of his denial that he had ever changed in his beliefs from his earlier days. Still, he did admit he had, many years before, abandoned the idea that assurance was essential to justifying faith.

There were sermons on such speculative theological matters as: "On the Trinity" (1775); "On Eternity" (1786); "On Divine Providence" (1786); "On the Omnipresence of God" (1788); "On Faith" (1788); and "The Unity of the Divine Being" (1789).

Among sermons on matters having to do with the reform of manners were: "The Use of Money" (1760); "National Sins and Miseries" (1775); "The Danger of Riches" (1781); "On the Education of Children" (1781); "On Redeeming the Time" (1782); "On Dress" (1786); "On Obedience to Parents" (1784); and "The Duty of Reproving One's Neighbor" (1787).

This unanticipated publishing task was deemed necessary because new circumstances and conflicts had arisen so that the people needed new guidance. But, for the most part, he still wrote plainly for plain people. Outler concludes:

> There is, however, no mistaking the fact that Wesley's homiletical style and theological substance had acquired fresh nuances over the years. Thus, in V–VIII, the reader may expect more ornamentation, more speculative formulations, more show of learning, more of an emphasis upon theology of culture. Salvation by faith alone is everywhere presupposed, but the stress is upon its outworkings in the new circumstances of the Methodist people (social, economic, cultural).[32]

The last time he ever preached was on January 17, 1791, just two months before his death. Henry Rack describes the scene:

> Propped in the pulpit by a friend on either side, he had delivered his last sermon in an almost inaudible voice; yet people still seemed to benefit from the sight of his venerable figure and long white hair.[33]

This sermon on faith was from Hebrews 11:1, a kind of valedictory to his whole preaching ministry. Richard P. Heitzenrater summarizes as follows:

> Though small in stature, Wesley had a presence that was commanding and a reputation for energy that was near legendary. The statistics of his industriousness became a matter of widespread fascination. He had published hundreds of books, preached tens of thousands of sermons, traveled hundreds of thousands of miles. His obituary in the Gentleman's Magazine is a telling tribute, even if discounted for polite hyperbole: "His personal influence was greater than, perhaps, that of any other private gentleman in any country...As the founder of the most numerous sect in the kingdom, as a man, and as a writer, he must be considered as one of the most extraordinary characters this or any

age ever produced." (EMW, 2:154–56)...Wesley was important for who he was as a person, as well as for what he thought and what he did. But he also bore that mark of genius that prevents observers from ever getting a complete grasp of just who he was or what he thought. His associations cut across normal party lines and his ideas bridged may polemical positions.[34]

John Wesley died on March 2, 1791. By that time, he was a venerable old man of eighty-eight years. He was much mellowed and gentled. At last, he was also highly respected and loved throughout the land.

To be sure, denominations spawned by the Wesleyan movement today vary in their interpretations of Wesley's message and in the degree of their adherence to his teachings. However, I have often returned to this man. His message is the beginning place in my search for a new vision of God for the twenty-first century and a spiritually compelling understanding of "salvation."

Wesley's Written Sermons

Though Wesley learned extemporary preaching while still at Oxford and used oral preaching throughout most of his life, he nevertheless counted on written sermons to extend his preaching ministry. The references to "oral" sermons seem to mean simply those preached without manuscripts, whether written out in preparation or not.

Richard Heitzenrater identifies two distinct purposes for the publication of the sermons. He says:

> Broadly speaking, his publication of sermons served two basic purposes and followed two basic methods. Awakening sermons for the general public were reproduced in many separate editions; the sermons and sermonic essays were also gathered into volumes of *SOSO (Sermons on Several Occasions)* to provide for the theological sustenance and growth of his lay preachers and members, as well as to define and defend his doctrinal tenets for skeptical scholars.[35]

Wesley was not only concerned with getting his sermons into the hands of contemporary readers. He was also interested in their accurate publication for future historians. In his personal library, he kept copies of the many editions. Not only did he include his sermons, he also kept his own handwritten corrections and revisions. Thus, he hoped to preserve his work accurately for the future.

So, we can see his written sermons were not usually manuscripts for use in the pulpit. Instead, they were written as preparation for oral preaching, distillates of extemporaneous sermons already preached, or sermonic essays written specifically for publication.[36] Not one of them is a transcript of an oral sermon.

It has been said Wesley preached approximately 20,000 sermons during the course of his ministry. Some doubt the number, but he did keep a register of his sermons throughout his ministry. (However, only the registers of sermons preached from 1747 to 1761 and 1787 to 1788 are extant.) He included the date and place of each. Many notations concerning sermons preached appear in his journals as well, even though the full record must be compiled from all sources, including the registers, journals, and diaries. The total cited above may have been extrapolated from these sources.

However, among the written sermons in the Wesley works are "some sermons ascribed to Wesley on inconclusive grounds, but deserving of notice."[37] According to Outler, there is also "a group of sermons that Wesley valued sufficiently to copy out from other authors and then preserve in his personal papers for more than half a century."[38]

The sermons published in his lifetime had a different purpose from his oral preaching. Outler claims Wesley believed the purpose of oral sermons was to proclaim and invite while the written sermons were chiefly for nurture and reflection. Thus, it is understandable that many of Wesley's favorite texts for oral preaching do not appear at all in the body of his written sermons and vice versa.[39]

Wesley's Own View of Preaching

Above all, Wesley saw himself as a preacher. In 1757, he wrote in his journal, "I do indeed live by preaching."[40]

Dr. Outler, a leading Wesley interpreter until his death a few years ago, wrote, "For Wesley, it was preaching that defined his vocation preeminently. This was the principal means of gathering converts into Christian fellowship and of nurturing them in it."[41]

Though our knowledge of his preaching content comes largely from his published sermons and they provided much of the nurturing of his people he believed was so important, it was his oral preaching that nurtured his own spiritual and intellectual life. The oral form also best connected the preacher with his hearers.

> He believed that oral preaching, to be effective, must be an interpersonal encounter between the preacher and his hearers. Hence he believed that oral preaching was the norm.[42]

The first occasion upon which Wesley is known to have preached extemporaneously was in the Castle at Oxford on November 10, 1734, not long before he left for Georgia. His earlier preaching seems to have depended upon having a manuscript before him or at least upon having written the sermon out ahead of time.

Wesley valued his preaching ministry highly and gave considerable thought to the whole preaching enterprise, as was made clear in his "Preface" to the first volumes of published sermons in 1746. He wrote:

> I now write (as I generally speak) *ad populum* to the bulk of mankind to those who neither relish nor understand the art of speaking, but who notwithstanding are competent judges of those truths that are necessary to present and future happiness. I design plain truth for plain people.[43]

Wesley was quite familiar with the literature on preaching of his time and of the previous century. Much of this literature sought to encourage the use of grandiose language. However, he also knew the Puritan literature on plain speaking, so he quite deliberately chose the latter and disdained the use of elaborate, flowery speech in his preaching. Of course, the choice was easier because that was also the style of his father's preaching. He had grown up with it.

This was in stark contrast to much of the most famous preaching of those centuries. Look at an exquisite example of the eloquence of John Donne (1573–1631):

> The church is catholic, universal, so are all her actions; all that she does belongs to all. When she baptizes a child, that action concerns me, for that child is thereby connected to that head that is my head too, and engrafted into that body whereof I am a member. And when she buries a man, that action concerns me. All mankind is of one author and is one volume; when one man dies, one chapter is not torn out of the book, but translated into a better language, and every chapter must be so translated…Any man's death diminishes me because I am involved in mankind; and therefore never send to know for whom the bell tolls; it tolls for thee.[44]

Even the less elaborate style of the *Prayer Book* and the *Authorized Version* (KJV) of the Bible was more ornate than Wesley liked, even though he knew that material well and could quote from it at will. His knowledge of the Bible was such that he could interweave the biblical language with his own so smoothly the seams rarely showed. He did this usually without references because he assumed his readers possessed a ready familiarity with Holy Scripture. As a result, his style was well-suited to the common man's ear. One observer even recalled hearing Wesley speak to a group of children. He never used more than two-syllable words.

The fact is that Wesley was indebted to the Puritans for many of his practices. That they influenced him in his adopted style of speech and led him to become a folk-theologian is just a bit ironic because he was at odds with the Puritans over their Calvinism. For example, Calvin denied humans had any part at all in their salvation, even though Wesley insisted they did. Nevertheless, the Puritans' radical insistence on the equality of all people before God was a part of their heritage he adopted when he went to the poor as his preferred audience.

In his "Preface" to his first four volumes of published sermons in 1746, he wrote:

> I have frequently spoken in public on every subject in the ensuing collection: and I am not conscious that there is any one point of doctrine on which I am accustomed to speak in public that is not here.[45]

That is, he had selected sermons from among those preached at least since 1733 and published them for his contemporary readers and for posterity. In 1746, he believed he had essentially completed the message he had to deliver. However, it turned out there was much more to say, including even a number of theological points still to be clarified. Most of the rest of his 151 published sermons were published in 1788 and during the next few years as *Sermons on Several Occasions* (volumes V–XI).

Before finishing his "Preface," he described his method of sermon preparation:

> I sit down alone; only God is here. In his presence I open, I read his Book; for this end, to find the way to heaven. Is there a doubt concerning the meaning of what I read? Does anything appear dark or intricate? I lift up my heart to the Father of lights...I then search after and consider parallel passages of Scripture...I meditate thereon, with all the attention and earnestness of which my mind is capable. If any doubt still remains, I consult those who are experienced in the things of God, and then the writings whereby, being dead, they yet speak. And what I thus learn, that I teach.[46]

These two sources, Scripture and Christian antiquity, were the first two parts of what has come to be known as the "Wesleyan Quadrilateral."

While Wesley felt he had resolved most of his outstanding questions at this point in his life, nevertheless, he was less certain than he became later. So he entered this invitation:

> But some may say I have mistaken the way myself, although I take upon me to teach it to others. It is probable many will think this; and it is very possible that I have. But I trust, wheresoever I have mistaken, my mind is open to conviction. I sincerely desire to be better informed. I say to God and man "What I know not, teach thou me."[47]

These written sermons usually follow the pattern described by Dr. Outler:

> The typical Wesley sermon begins with a brief *proemium*, followed by an expository "contract" between the preacher and the reader ("I am to show…" etc.). The reader is thus entitled to judge between the preacher's intention and his performance…And always it is the "application" on which the whole effort is focused; this makes most of the sermons intensely personal and practical. Wesley was content that others might be more exciting if he could be more nourishing.[48]

However, the fact of the matter is that Wesley frequently breached the contract by using the text as a pretext instead of as the material for a traditional expository sermon in which the passage was broken down into sentences, phrases, and even into words to be expounded.

Wesley was also intent upon improving the preaching of the preachers who entered the movement he had founded. Many were clergy of the Church of England, but many others were laypersons without professional training. At one point, he determined to teach them how to preach in plain language. So, he recommended an anonymous pamphlet called *The Art of Speaking* to them. Later, he abridged it under the title, *Directions Concerning Punctuation and Gesture*. They were to read and use it.

Wesley didn't lack for advice on such things as proper presentation either:

> In order to this, (to please all men for their good unto edification) especially in our public ministrations, would not one wish for a strong, clear, musical voice, and a good delivery, both with regard to pronunciation and action? I name these here, because they are far more acquirable than has been commonly imagined. A remarkably weak and untunable voice has by steady application become strong and agreeable. Those who stammered almost at every word, have learned to speak clearly and plainly. And many who were eminently

ungraceful in their pronunciation and awkward in their gesture, have in some time, by art and labour, not only corrected that awkwardness of action and ungracefulness of utterance, but have become excellent in both, and in these respects likewise the ornaments of their profession.[49]

Wesley kept his own "Minutes" of the annual meetings of his preachers. In his "Minutes" for June 18, 1747, in response to a question about preaching, he offered several suggestions:

1. Be sure to begin and end precisely at the time appointed. 2. Sing no hymns of your own composing. 3. Endeavor to be serious, weighty and solemn in your whole deportment before the congregation. 4. Choose the plainest texts you can. 5. Take care not to ramble from your text, but keep close to it, and make out what you undertake. 6. Always suit your subject to your audience. 7. Beware of allegorizing or spiritualizing too much. 8. Take care of anything awkward or affected, either in your gesture or pronunciation. 9. Tell each other, if you observe anything of this kind.[50]

In his "Letter on Preaching Christ," dated December 20, 1751, Wesley responded to another question about "preaching the gospel," an expression he did not much favor because it was so loosely used by many preachers. He wrote:

I think the right method of preaching is this: At our first beginning to preach at any place, after a general declaration of the love of God to sinners, and his willingness that they should be saved, to preach the law,[51] in the strongest, the closest, the most searching manner possible; only intermixing the gospel here and there, and showing it, as it were, afar off.

After more and more persons are convinced of sin, we may mix more and more of the gospel, in order to "beget faith," to raise into spiritual life those whom the law hath slain; but this is not to be done too hastily neither. Therefore, it is not expedient wholly to omit the law; but only because we may well suppose that many of our hearers are still unconvinced; but because otherwise there is danger that many who are convinced will heal their own wounds slightly; therefore, it is only in private converse with a thoroughly convinced sinner that we should preach nothing but the gospel.[52]

For Wesley, the "law" does not simply refer to the Old Testament commandments. It refers to all the commands and prohibitions that God has laid down anywhere. For him, the "gospel" refers to the good news that Christ has died for us, thus making God's love available to us for forgiveness and new life.

Nevertheless, says Outler, for Wesley, "...it was important that every sermon should proclaim the essential gospel as if for that one time only."[53]

How Others Viewed Him and His Preaching

John Wesley's public image was not always very favorable. In his early days, he was quite a popular preacher at Oxford University, where he regularly fulfilled his preaching responsibilities at St. Mary's Church as a fellow of Lincoln College. However, that popularity waned, and, after 1744, he was no longer invited.

He was also a frequent guest preacher at churches in the area, but he was soon banned from most of those pulpits until he was finally excluded entirely for preaching repentance of sins. Such language was offensive to the well-heeled parishioners who frequented those churches.

However, in his old age, many things had changed in the religious life of England, within the Wesleyan movement, and in Wesley himself. A time finally came when he was viewed with almost universal favor and his presence was thought to adorn the occasion.

How can we explain this change in his public image?

To begin with, of course, he was known for other things than his preaching. Samuel Babcock described him during his college days:

> (He was a) very sensible and acute collegian, baffling every man by the subtleties of logic, and laughing at them for being so easily routed, a young fellow of the finest classical taste, of the most liberal and manly sentiments.[54]

As a preacher, a large number of first-person witnesses have described him. They have characterized his preaching in a variety of ways. Heitzenrater says, "The tone of his voice was described variously as 'clear,' 'pleasant,' and 'conversational.'" He also mentions that "One listener, after commenting that Wesley's sermon was a 'combination of terror and tenderness,' noted that 'but for an occasional lifting of his right hand, he might have been a speaking statue.'"[55]

Dame Summerhill told Adam Clark fifty years later about her first encounter with Wesley when he came to Bristol to begin his field preaching. She said, after hearing him for the first time, she thought, "This is the truth." When she inquired where he was to preach next, she was told he would be in Plymouth, 125 miles away. She walked the distance just to hear him again, and walked back.[56]

As early as 1739, a stonemason named John Nelson described his experience hearing John Wesley preach:

> I was like a wandering bird, cast out of the nest, till Mr. John Wesley came to preach his first sermon in Moorsfields. Oh, that was a blessed morning to my soul! As soon as he got upon the stand he stroked back his hair and turned his face towards where I stood, and I thought fixed his eyes upon me. His countenance struck such an awful dread upon me, before I heard him speak, that it made my heart beat like the pendulum of a clock; and, when he did speak, I thought his whole discourse was aimed at me. When he had done, I said, "This man can tell the secrets of my heart; he hath not left me there; for he hath showed the remedy, even the blood of Jesus." Then was my soul filled with consolation, through hope that God for Christ's sake would save me.[57]

Of course, his enemies in the theological conflicts into which he entered with enthusiasm had rather different views of Wesley. For example, his Anglican critics saw him as a "confused" man. The Calvinists "had denounced him, not only as 'Arminian,' but also as a 'Papist,' a 'Presbyterian Papist,' 'a puny tadpole in divinity.'"[58]

Because his constant concern was with becoming and being a Christian, his views were characterized as "a medley of...Calvinism, Arminianism, Montanism, Quakerism, Quietism, all thrown together."[59] Other epithets directed against Wesley were often colorful and even amusing:

> "An Old Fox Tarred and Feathered"; "a designing wolf"; "a dealer in stolen words"; "as unprincipled as a rook and as silly as a jackdaw"; "a grey-headed enemy of all righteousness"; "a wretch"; guilty of "willful, gross and abominable untruth"; "a venal profligate"; "a wicked slanderer"; "an unfeeling reviler"; "a liar of the most gigantic magnitude"; "a Solomon in a cassock"; "Pope John"; "this living lump of inconsistencies," etc.[60]

Even his sister Emily complained he had reined in his feelings so tightly that he regarded "natural affection as a great weakness if not a sin."[61]

The middle years of Wesley's career saw many changes in English society and in the movement. Long-standing Methodists had new issues. The movement itself had grown exceedingly rapidly and had already begun to have a profound impact on the "manners" of English society. Wesley had aged and mellowed.

On October 15, 1769, upon hearing Wesley preach, Professor Johan Henrik Liden of Uppsala, Sweden, wrote:

Today I learned for the first time to know Mr. John Wesley, so well known here in England, and called the spiritual father of the so-called "Methodists"...He preached today at the forenoon service in the Methodist Chapel in Spitalsfields for an audience of more than 4,000 people. His text was Luke 1:68. The sermon was short but eminently evangelical. He has no great oratorical gifts, no outward appearance, but he speaks clear and pleasant...He is a small thin old man, with his own long and straight hair, and looks as the worst country curate in Sweden, but has learning as a bishop and zeal for the glory of God which is quite extraordinary. His talk is very agreeable...He is the personification of piety, and seems to me as a living representation of the loving Apostle John. The old man Wesley is already 66 years, but very lively and exceedingly industrious.[62]

An old man from Hull remembered Wesley as:

[A] bonny little man, with such a canny nice face, wearing knee breeches, black stockings, and buckles on his shoes, with his bonny white hair hanging on his black gown, and a clean white thing like two sark necks, hanging down on his breast.[63]

The impression Wesley made on George Osborn of Rochester was quite different. Mr. Wakeley reported:

He had heard much of Wesley, had read his writings and had an ardent desire to see him. About the year 1784 Mr. Wesley made a visit to Rochester...Mr. Osborn was captivated with the Founder of Methodism, and said the first impression made upon his mind by what he saw and heard from Mr. Wesley was "This man is a scholar." Others had represented Wesley to him in a different light, as fanatical and ignorant. Mr. Wesley's frequent references to recent publications, his natural and non-ostentatious manner of quoting the original Scriptures, his whole bearing and demeanour, even the manner of his handling the pulpit books, were all noticed as bearing on this point, and Mr. Osborn concluded that, so far as these indications might be relied on, there was no more fanaticism in the Founder of Methodism than in any of the more dignified and wealthy clergymen he had been accustomed to hear at the cathedral.[64]

In 1807, based on a large collection of eyewitness accounts of Wesley, Thomas Haweis, the evangelical historian, wrote:

John Wesley was of the inferior size [five feet three inches], his visage marked with intelligence, singularly neat and plain in his dress, a little cast in his eye observable upon particular occasions, upright, graceful, and remarkably active. His understanding, naturally excellent and acute, was highly stored with the attainments of literature, and he possessed a fund of anecdote and history that rendered his company as entertaining as instructive. His mode of address in public was chaste and solemn, though not illumined with those coruscations of eloquence which marked, if I may use that expression, the discourses of his rival, George Whitefield. There was a divine simplicity, a zeal, a venerableness in his manner which commanded attention and never forsook him in his latest years. When at four score he retained all the freshness of vigorous old age, his health was remarkably preserved amidst a scene of labor and perpetual exertions of mind and body to which few would have been equal.[65]

Henry Moore said, "John's preaching was all principles; Charles' was all aphorisms."[66] Alexander Knox, a close and discerning friend, said of Wesley, "He was, in truth, the most perfect specimen of *moral happiness* which I ever saw."[67]

As to the poor, Wesley wrote, "I love the poor…in many of them, I find pure, genuine grace, unmixed with paint, folly and affectation." Or again, "I bear the rich and love the poor; therefore, I spend almost all my time with them."[68]

To one of his more sophisticated friends, he wrote, "You have seen very little of the choicest part of the London society. I mean the poor. Go with me into their cellars and garrets, and then you will taste their [gracious] spirits."[69] The poor had to view Wesley from quite a different perspective than his enemies did. It was even different from that of his social equals and his colleagues.

However resentful many of polite society were of him and however critical and even cruel, theological opponents were—and however unhappy many of the ecclesiastical authorities were—the common people "heard him gladly and took him to their hearts."[70]

They were clearly drawn to him because he loved them. Perhaps that was the greatest secret of his preaching power. So he commended it to all his preachers in the strongest terms he could find:

> Ought not a "steward of the mysteries of God," a shepherd of the souls for whom Christ died, to be endued with an eminent measure of love to God, and love to all his brethren; a love the same in kind, but in degree far beyond that of ordinary Christians? Can he otherwise answer to the high character he bears, and the relation wherein he stands? Without this, how can he go through all the toil and difficulties which necessarily attend the faithful execution of his office? Would it be possible for a parent to go through the pain and fatigue of bearing and bringing up even one child, were it not for that vehement affection…which the Creator has given for that very end? How much less will it be possible for any Pastor, any spiritual parent, to go through the

pain and labour of "travailing in birth for" and bringing up, many children to the measure of the full stature of Christ, without a large measure of that inexpressible affection which "a stranger intermeddleth not with!"[71]

2

Deep Were the Roots

We are now looking for John Wesley's theological roots. Without understanding those roots, we are not in a very good position to understand his message. When I refer to his roots, I am thinking of the rich sources that fed his thought and were the grist for his theological mill as he sought to understand for himself and his people the possibilities of the Christian life.

Dr. Outler points out in his "Introduction" to the sermons in the new Bicentennial edition of Wesley's works that he "lived and worked in a plurality of cultural worlds." They were the Biblical world, the classical world, the world of early Christian history, the world of British Christianity, and the world of contemporary science and philosophy.[1] Each of these worlds shows up in his quotations and even more often in unidentified ideas and expressions. The task of tracing all his sources is formidable, though much progress is currently being made by the scholars. Outler further observes:

> ...the unexpected range and prolixity of his non-biblical sources, from Hesiod to Prior to Fontenelle. He quotes mostly from memory, altering his originals without hesitation.[2]

In 1756 Wesley prepared what he called "Address to the Clergy." By this time the Methodist movement had been underway for 27 years and his experience with a quite motley crew of preachers had forced him to give careful consideration to the "gifts and grace" that every preacher needed to possess or acquire. Unremarkably, the picture of a Methodist preacher which he drew in this rather lengthy document looks a lot like Wesley himself. In fact, his list of desirable acquisitions quite accurately represents the resources which he himself had acquired and used. They reflect his own roots:

> And as to acquired endowments, can he take one step aright, without first a competent share of knowledge? a knowledge, First, of his own office; of the

high trust in which he stands, the important work to which he is called? Is there any hope that a man should discharge his office well, if he knows not what it is? Secondly. No less necessary is a knowledge of the Scriptures, which teach us how to teach others; yea, a knowledge of all the Scriptures; seeing Scripture interprets Scripture; one part fixing the sense of another. So that, whether it be true or not, that every good textuary is a good Divine, it is certain none can be a good Divine who is not a good textuary...In order to do this accurately, ought he not to know the literal meaning of every word, verse, and chapter; without which there can be no firm foundation on which the spiritual meaning can be built?...Thirdly. But can he do this, in the most effectual manner, without a knowledge of the original tongues? Without this, will he not frequently be at a stand, even as to texts which regard practice only? But he will be under still greater difficulties, with respect to controverted Scriptures...Fourthly. Is not a knowledge of profane history, likewise, of ancient customs, of chronology and geography, though not absolutely necessary, yet highly expedient, for him that would thoroughly understand the Scriptures?...Fifthly. Some knowledge of the sciences also, is, to say the least, equally expedient. Nay, may we not say, that the knowledge of one, (whether art or science,) although now quite unfashionable, is even necessary next, and in order to, the knowledge of the Scripture itself? I mean logic. For what is this, if rightly understood, but the art of good sense?...Is not some acquaintance with what has been termed the second part of logic, (metaphysics,) if not so necessary as this, yet highly expedient? Should not a minister be acquainted too with at least the general grounds of natural philosophy? Is not this a great help to the accurate understanding several passages of Scripture? Assisted by this, he may himself comprehend, and on proper occasions explain to others, how the invisible things of God are seen from the creation of the world; how 'the heavens declare the glory of God, and the firmament showeth his handiwork;' till they cry out, 'O Lord, how manifold are thy works! In wisdom thou hast made them all.'...Sixthly. Can any who spend several years in those seats of learning, be excused, if they do not add to that of the languages and sciences, the knowledge of the Fathers? the most authentic commentators on Scripture, as being both nearest the fountain, and eminently endued with that Spirit by whom all Scripture was given. It will be easily perceived, I speak chiefly of those who wrote before the Council of Nice.[3]

The broad range of sources and tools that Wesley himself had already acquired were deemed more or less necessary for every preacher in his effort to understand the Scriptures, and might appropriately be considered to be part of Wesley's total method.

It is easily perceived that each one of the acquired endowments is to be used as a means of understanding and interpreting the Scriptures. Therefore, the center root was sunk most deeply into the Bible itself.

A Man of One Book

John Wesley claimed he aspired to be "a man of one book," referring specifically to the Old and New Testaments as well as the Apocrypha. This exaggeration required an explanation in view of the voluminous reading he calls for on the part of his preachers and in which he himself is known to have engaged:

> My design is in some sense to forget all that ever I have read in my life. I mean to speak, in the general, as if I had never read one author, ancient or modern (always excepting the inspired)...I shall come with fewer weights upon my mind, with less of prejudice and prepossession.[4]

He did not mean he intended to stop reading the early Church Fathers, secular literature, and his own Anglican literature. The fact he said he "designed in some sense to forget" suggests only that he intended his sermons should not be pockmarked with citations from other sources that most of his hearers could not fully appreciate. This makes sense because, in that same context, he claimed to be speaking in his sermons "plain truth for plain people." He did not intend to stop reading other sorts of books, but only planned to ignore them when he sat down to write his sermons.

Wesley's use of the Bible was constant and without apology, even though he sometimes felt free to ignore the context of texts on which he preached.[5] In that connection, it is of some interest that many persons tend to assume Wesley was what we now call a "fundamentalist." This is a false assumption on three counts.

First, the fundamentalist position that the Bible was literally inspired by God, that is, word-for-word, was not articulated as a belief "fundamental" to Christian faith until early in the last century.

Second, Wesley explicitly recognized that Christians interpret many things differently and have many different opinions on religious matters. Thus, he assumed interpretation was always necessary. In several places, he lists those things he believed are essential to Christian faith. In his sermon, "Catholic Spirit," his list identifies those things he took to be covered by the expression, "If thy heart is as my heart, give me thy hand." He does not refer to any theory about the inspiration of the Scriptures.

In the third place, he offers suggestions for interpreting problematic passages. Because there was no such thing as the modern discipline of biblical criticism in Wesley's time, he did not have its benefits for his own preaching and teaching. If such studies had been available, he would undoubtedly have been on top of all the latest developments. However, it is probably useless to speculate how that might have affected his message or his ministry.

He used such tools as were available. He knew Latin well enough so that he and his brother Charles privately conversed with one another in that language for sixty years. His knowledge of biblical Greek was thorough; his knowledge of classical Greek was good. He had a nominal knowledge of Hebrew. His favorite concordance was *Crudens*, but he had access to seventeen other New Testament concordances. However, Outler notes that, by midlife, he had become a walking concordance himself. He used the *Authorized Version* (KJV) of the Bible; however, when quoting from the Psalms, he preferred to quote from the *Book of Common Prayer*, based on Coverdale's *Great Bible*.[6]

Not only did Wesley work hard to find the meanings of words, phrases, and passages from the Bible, he also reveals his willingness to be quite selective in his choice of preaching texts. Outler reports his favorite sources for sermons were Matthew, Hebrews, John, Luke, and I Corinthians. Isaiah was his favorite Old Testament source, followed by the Psalms. He often cited the Apocrypha, especially the Wisdom of Solomon, even though he never took a preaching text from that source.[7]

He claimed that his whole purpose in searching the Scriptures was to learn about the means of salvation: preventing, justifying, and sanctifying grace. He recommended that search to his people as one of three primary means of grace, the others being prayer and the Eucharist.[8]

However, the Scriptures had to be approached in a proper manner, that is, with prayer for the guidance of the Holy Spirit:

> I do firmly believe (and what serious man does not) *omnis scriptura legi debet eo spiritu quo scripta est*: we need the same spirit to understand the Scripture that enabled the holy men of old to write it.[9]

In fact, Wesley did have his own plan for seeking the meaning of the biblical text. It is not compiled in one place, but Scott Jones has reconstructed it from separate places in his writings:

1. Speak as the oracles of God.

2. Use the literal sense unless it contradicts another Scripture or implies an absurdity.

3. Interpret the text with regard to its literary context.

4. Scripture interprets Scripture, according to the analogy of faith and by parallel passages.

5. Commandments are covered promises.

6. Interpret literary devices appropriately.

7. Seek the most original text and the best translation.[10]

Speaking the "oracles of God" simply means using the scriptural language itself without interpretation on the assumption that its language will always ring true and the basic nature of the human race will never be radically changed. The claim the Bible speaks to every generation assumes, at the very least, there is a universality of essential human needs running beneath all cultures.

The second rule speaks for itself, giving priority to the "literal sense" of any expression. But, the possibility of contradiction or patent absurdity is admitted. The appeal to the obvious, literal sense goes back to the Protestant Reformation protest against Roman Catholic interpretations of Scripture. This was common among the Puritans of the time. But, an absurdity could not be accepted, and some looser interpretation would have to suffice.

In respect to the third rule above, Wesley affirms the literal sense "taken in connection with the context." The context may be the surrounding verses, the book as a whole, or the entirety of the Scriptures.

In the first place, allowing "Scripture to interpret Scripture" means referring any question to what was known as the "analogy of faith," that is, the general tenor of the Scriptures as a whole. It also affirms that one may compare parallel passages and take the clearer one. That is, where two passages deal with the same subject, the clearer one is to be preferred.

"Covered promises" in the fifth rule refers to Wesley's way of treating commandments, not as laws, but as promises of the gospel. It enables him to hold on to the commandments while simultaneously rejecting obedience to the Law as the means of salvation. Grace will now enable him to observe the commandment, not as a law, but as a promise.

"Literary devices" in the sixth rule refers primarily to the legitimacy of moving from particulars to generalizations. For example, "whether ye eat or drink, do all to the glory of God" may be interpreted as "whatever ye do, do all to the glory of God."

The seventh rule concerns "most original text" and "best translation" and is an up-front recognition of the problems of translation and the uncertainty that attends even the Greek versions. Interestingly, Wesley admits his readiness, therefore, to take some liberties with the translations from which he is working.¹¹ His primary dependence on the literal sense of scriptural language reflects his assumption that, as sacred language, it should not need to be interpreted. However, his recognition of other factors, such as context, obscurity, and translation problems, makes it impossible to adhere to a strict literalism. It also implies the importation of the past into the present is always risky and requires great care in distinguishing what is universal from the historical particulars.

Probably the most important instance of importation on Wesley's part was his easy assumption that the ancient monotheism of the Old Testament Pentateuch, as modified in the New Testament period, was quite satisfactory for his own time and indefinitely into the future. The God of Moses was the giver of laws, the judge who pronounced sentence, and the provider of a legal means of Atonement for infractions. He was also arbitrary in his choice of a people to carry out his will. He was also masculine. Wesley took this image of God from the Bible and utilized it without serious examination because it still served the people's needs, especially the needs of the poor and poorly educated to whom he went in the eighteenth century. Nevertheless, we need to ask, "How long can it do so?" The hold of biblical presuppositions on the populace at large had already begun slackening, even though Wesley was scarcely aware of it.

Outler characterizes his approach to the Scriptures as follows:

> He had grown up with Scripture as a second language; even in his early sermons one sees the beginnings of his lifelong habit of interweaving Scripture with his own speech in a graceful texture. Later he would recall that it was not until 1729 that he began to be *homo unius libri*, but this could only mean a rearrangement of priorities, not a novelty…It was, instead, a matter of hermeneutical principle that Scripture would be his court of first and last resort in faith and morals.¹²

A "hermeneutical principle" is just a fancy way of identifying a principle of biblical interpretation. The quote affirms that Wesley's first source of authority for the development of his theology was the Bible.

However, he lived in other worlds as well as the world of the Bible. When his seven rules of biblical hermeneutics failed him, he looked to the Church Fathers for guidance as a means of interpreting the Scriptures.

Closest to the Fountain

Even though the ancient Church Fathers before Nicea (AD 325) are named last in his own list of recommended objects of knowledge, they were actually the very first outside source Wesley consulted in his study of the Bible. This is apparent in his description of his method:

> If any doubt still remains, I consult those who are experienced in the things of God, and then the writings whereby, being dead, they yet speak.[13]

Even when Wesley looked for models for the eighteenth-century church and contemporary spiritual life, quite naturally, he turned to the early or primitive church and the writings of the early Church Fathers.

Ted Campbell notes the Enlightenment thinkers saw history as swinging between the two poles of reason and the scientific view on the one hand and religion and superstition on the other. Therefore, in the age of the Enlightenment, its writers and thinkers, like Voltaire and Hume, saw themselves as men of reason and the scientific perspective, who were in company with the Greeks and Romans of ancient times. But, they saw the Dark Ages as times of religion and superstition, a perspective they, of course, rejected.

Wesley necessarily took a somewhat different view because his interest was in the church and its spiritual life rather than in secular society. Therefore, he looked to the primitive church and the early Church Fathers for his ideals instead of Greek and Roman culture.

Of course, this was not a search that Wesley originated. The ideal of English culture for the past two centuries had been to purify itself by reclaiming ancient models. English churchmen had engaged in the same search. They had debated the scope of the period of the primitive church, placing it variously at three to six centuries past canonical times.[14] Wesley himself settled on the Ante-Nicene period.[15] As a child of eighteenth-century Augustan England, whose intellectual culture was enamored of classical antiquity in architecture, literature, and the arts,[16] this was the direction he was bound to look.

Wesley was one of the best-read men of his time, according to Samuel Johnson, a favorite conversational partner of his who shared in this cultural vision. However, he sometimes confused the past reality of antiquity with his own present hope. He also had other sources to which he looked. This inevitably colored his perspective on antiquity and the models he believed he found there.[17] For example, he eventually accepted the *Book of Homilies* and the *Articles of Reli-*

gion of the Church of England as basic standards and tended to see antiquity filtered through them. Therefore, he felt free to adapt the Articles as the theological model for the church in America.

To trace all the sources of Wesley's vision is very difficult. It was further complicated because Wesley's understanding of the ancient church was distorted by his exaggerated view of its unity.[18] But, what Wesley thought he found there he called true or genuine Christianity, even though, before Nicea, the church was rife with controversy.

Even so, classical culture profoundly impacted the Church Fathers themselves. In fact, the Greeks and Romans also influenced Wesley sufficiently that he wrote both Greek and Latin grammars.

At the same time, Wesley kept abreast of contemporary scientific knowledge. Thus, he manifested a great interest in popular medicine and the phenomenon of earthquakes, about which both he and his brother Charles wrote. Wesley, even as a man of his own time, looked to the past for his ideals for the future, just as other churchmen and other Enlightenment thinkers did.

Outler notes Wesley was much more influenced by the Eastern Fathers and the developments in Eastern Orthodoxy than by the Latin West. His views of mysticism were shaped more by the Eastern doctrine of the Holy Spirit and its teaching about mysticism as "unitive" than by the "will-mysticism" of the Latin churches. Unitive mysticism emphasized the possibility of an actual merging or unity of the human spirit with the Spirit of God while will-mysticism focused on the act of conforming the human will to the will of God.

The Eastern doctrine of the Holy Spirit also influenced the development of Wesley's doctrine of prevenient grace (that is, the spiritual potential given to every human person) and of human freedom (that is, a gift of prevenient grace). The roots of these ideas he found in the Scriptures, but Eastern interpretations largely molded his own mature position.

At one point, Wesley was asked to describe the ideal Christian. His response was to write a piece called "The Character of a Methodist":

> What he had done, with no sense of incongruity, was to turn to the Seventh Book of the *Stromateis* of Clement of Alexandria (an Eastern Father), take its description of the "true Gnostic," and update it for the eighteenth century.[19]

He had also assiduously read the writings of the later mystics, thinking they could teach him how to find union with God. His mother, Susannah, was his constant companion in the study and discussion of those readings, especially during the time he served at Wroote as his father's curate:

> Most of my efforts were spent in sorting out my inner spiritual life. Much of this centered around my mother. We exchanged devotional tracts and read to each other from the mystical authors...I found myself becoming morbidly individualistic. The more I read, the more I wanted to pass my time solely in the company of the mystical authors.[20]

Later, he became highly critical of the mystical writers and rejected them until late in his life.

The idea of perfection, so characteristic of Wesley's whole ministry, was born through his reading of the Church Fathers, including Macarius the Egyptian, whom he read while living in Georgia. Of the Church Fathers, Outler says:

> Their concept of perfection as a process rather than a state gave Wesley a spiritual vision quite different from the static perfectionism envisaged in Roman spiritual theology of the period and the equally static quietism of those Protestants and Catholics whom he deplored as "the mystic writers"...Thus it was that the ancient and Eastern tradition of holiness as disciplined love became fused in Wesley's mind with his own Anglican tradition of holiness as aspiring love, and thereafter was developed in what he regarded to the end as his most distinctive doctrinal contribution.[21]

The Greek emphasis on divinization also attracted Wesley's attention with special force and highly influenced his interpretation of the Scriptures. The idea of divinization, as seen in some of the early Greek Fathers, for example, Origen, Clement, and Arius, was a major factor in Wesley's insistence on the possibility of a progressive perfection or holiness.

For example, Arius, following Plato and the Stoics, conceived of God as remote and unknowable. Therefore, salvation required a bridge between God and man, and Jesus was it. Arius, says Karen Armstrong:

> passionately believed that Christians had been saved and made divine, sharers in the nature of God. This was only possible because Jesus had blazed a trail for us...It was by contemplating Christ's life of perfectly obedient sonship that Christians would become divine themselves.[22]

Therefore, for Arius, Jesus was not God. Instead, he was on a lower level, intermediate between God and man.

Another major influence of the early Church Fathers was on Wesley's theory of spiritual knowledge. Plato, the Cappadocian Fathers, Basil, and the two Gregorys (AD 329–95) took the position that there were two kinds of truth:

- Rational truth that can be put into words and discussed, as is the case with philosophy.
- A level of truth that can only be expressed in myth and story, that is, religion.

This latter form of truth is deeper and can be perceived only through religious experience. It was not even to be written down and was only available to the initiated.

Basil called these two forms of knowledge "kerygma" and "dogma." Without a doubt, Wesley was indebted for his spiritual epistemology to this distinction in the writings of some of the Church Fathers. However, he did not espouse a doctrine of esoteric knowledge available only to a special class of initiates. Rather, the theory enabled him to accept certain doctrines without professing to understand them, such as the Trinity, the Incarnation, and the Atonement.

Thus, some charged Wesley with being an "enthusiast," partly because of the frequently emotional responses to his message made by his hearers, but also because of his emphasis on spiritual experience. He was insistent on the knowledge perceived by the "eye of faith." This is knowledge that could not be acquired through reason, even though, in Wesley's view, it could be explained up to a point.

In fact, he was an avid supporter of reason and logic as tools of discursive knowledge:

> Let reason do all that reason can: Employ it as far as it will go. But at the same time, acknowledge it is utterly incapable of giving either faith, or hope, or love; and consequently, of producing either real virtue, or substantial happiness. Expect them from a higher source, even from the Father of the spirits of all flesh. Seek and receive them, not on your own acquisition; but as the gift of God.[23]

Outler says of Wesley's indebtedness to the Eastern Fathers:

> In his early days he drank deep of this Byzantine tradition of spirituality at its source and assimilated its conception of devotion as the way and perfection as the goal of the Christian life…[24]

The Eastern Fathers may have had the edge over their Western rivals in direct influence, but the Latin West still had a great impact on Wesley, especially through the Council of Nicea and Wesley's own English Church. The original idea of the order of salvation as a process involving prevenient (universal), justifying (forgiving), and sanctifying (perfecting) grace came from St. Irenaeus, a Latin Father. Thus, salvation itself, like the perfection it embraced, was not a state to be achieved. It was a process to be undertaken. Central to all this was the activity of the Holy Spirit, which was understood to be the power that applied the saving grace all the way through the process.

When Constantine called a council of the church at Nicea in AD 325 to resolve some of the conflicts raging in the early church, both Arius and Athanasius, the successor to Irenaeus, had attracted significant numbers of supporters in anticipation of the confrontation. The issue between them was over who Jesus was and his relation to God. Arius saw him as a being midway between God and man. Therefore, his relation to God was that of perfect obedience to a God who had laid down the law. For Athanasius, Jesus was actually God in the flesh, incarnate. Thus, his relation to God was one of equality. The result was a great division occurred among the counselors. Athanasius wanted to say Father and Son were of the "same substance" like two bars of silver are of the same substance though distinguishable. The Greek word was *homoousion*. The alternate suggestion was to say they were *homoiousion*, that is, of similar substance. However, the compromise suggestion was finally rejected, and the doctrine of the Incarnation was adopted while the opponents of that doctrines were condemned as heretics.

So the Nicene Creed reads in English:

> We believe in one Lord, Jesus Christ, the only Son of God, eternally begotten of the Father, God from God, Light from Light, true God from true God, begotten, not made, of one Being with the Father...

That is how Jesus became God. When it was decided to include the following sentence in the creed, the Trinity was born:

> We believe in the Holy Spirit, the Lord, the giver of life, who proceeds from the Father and the Son, who with the Father and the Son is worshipped and glorified...[25]

The vote was not unanimous, and the debate continued for many years. However, to this day Athanasius' position represents orthodoxy.

Therefore, Wesley's heritage, via the Church of England, was on the side of Athanasius. The decisions of the Council of Nicea constituted a major part of his orthodoxy. That included his acceptance of the doctrines of Incarnation and the Trinity.

The Nicene version of the Trinity also prepared the way for the doctrine of justification through the Atonement. That is, it claimed God was incarnate in Jesus (in other words, Jesus was God). Thus, Jesus was of sufficient value to the Father that his death could pay for the sins of the rest of humanity and thereby satisfy the Father's own demand for justice. As a result, he atoned for others' sins and made God's grace available for the justification of those who believed it.

The decisions of the Council of Nicea in respect to the Trinity, the Incarnation, and, later, the Atonement represent the influence of the Latin West on Wesley, even though these were precisely the speculative doctrines he accepted but did not pretend to understand.

However, because Wesley was influenced by Arius and other Eastern Fathers in respect to what became his doctrine of sanctification by grace, he had the problem of incorporating both sanctification by grace and justification by grace within his doctrine of salvation by grace through faith. That is, he had to put his Eastern influence in touch with the influence of the Western church. So, in order to hold both things together, not only did he make justification dependent on the grace of the Atonement, but sanctification (divinization) was made dependent on the Atonement. That merger turned out to be crucial to his whole preaching message.

Thus, we may see the convergence of several emphases from the time of the Ante-Nicene Fathers.

An English Churchman

Although Wesley drew much from his knowledge of the early Church Fathers, the resolution of his theological searching did not come from the "fountain." Instead, it came from the immediate context of his ecclesiastical existence, that is, from the church of which he was a priest.

Following his experiences with the Moravians, he finally returned home to his own communion. There he found the theological position that would serve him as the basic structure for all subsequent developments in his thought. The merger of justification and sanctification under the umbrella of the Atonement occurred because the issue of justification was finally made clear to him when he began in mid-November of 1738:

> [T]o more narrowly inquire what the doctrine of the Church of England is concerning the much controverted point of justification by faith; and the sum of what I found in "The Homilies" I extracted and printed for the use of others.[26]

The theological context of this incorporation was his rejection of mysticism in favor of faith. He had studied the mystical writers in order to find peace with God through the disciplines of mysticism. Not only did mysticism promise him peace through union with God, but he expected divinization or sanctification as well. When he instead chose to seek peace through justifying faith in the Atonement of Jesus, it left him still in need of sanctification. After all, holy living had been his desire from the start. Through the Homilies, he found both could be expected in sequence under two separate gifts of grace guaranteed by the Atonement. They were both parts of the same process. He could then combine both justification and sanctification under the grace that only the Atonement of Jesus made available. Wesley had already been preaching salvation by faith for a number of years, but the incorporation enabled him to see each of the gifts of grace in its relation to the others.

His sermon on "The Circumcision of the Heart" in 1733 had described the holiness he sought through faith, but his efforts to find an assurance that God actually accepted him was still in vain.

However, fifteen years after the 1733 sermon, he finally inserted the new paragraph in which he affirmed that reconciliation and forgiveness by the unmerited grace of God made possible by the Atonement had to precede the process of divinization, or sanctification, which he also attributed to the grace of God won by the Atonement.

Wesley developed this doctrine of salvation as an ellipse. Outler explains this metaphor:

> Its double foci were the doctrines of justification and sanctification in a special correlation, two aspects of a single gracious intention, but separated along a continuum of both time and experience.[27]

What this produced was an "organic continuum." For Wesley, the process of gradual sanctification, however, would have to be disciplined by use of the means of grace: prayer, searching the Bible, the Eucharist, fasting, and so forth. For Arius, the contemplation of the obedience of Christ was expected to issue in divinization.

The debate about justification had dealt with the question of the causes of justification (that is, the grace that pardons), whether Christ's death was the formal or meritorious cause of it. The Calvinists came down on the side of the formal cause because no real change was involved, only a change in the legal relationship. That is, by grace, God imputed righteousness to the one who believed in the Atonement and thus changed her or his relationship to God to one of acceptance. Wesley finally came down on both sides. He affirmed the formal cause, which produced a change in the legal relationship of the believer to God. He also affirmed the meritorious cause, which produced a real change. Thus, some degree of righteousness was already imparted to the believer. How Christ's death accomplished either remained a mystery for Wesley. To this day, it remains an enigma for most.

Wesley's view was that the first role of grace, applied by the Holy Spirit and called prevenient or preventing grace, gave each human being the power to participate in his own salvation as a response to God's initiative. Justification, as the first focus of the ellipse, goes beyond the imputation of righteousness, the change in standing before God, and begins the process of real change. For Wesley, the debate over imputed or imparted righteousness was based on a false distinction. As was his wont, he opted for both/and. Justification was the beginning of ongoing change.

Wesley found this view of justification, sanctification, Holy Spirit, and grace already incorporated in essence in the *Book of Homilies*.

Reason as a Tool

The role of reason in Wesley's repertoire of theological tools often occupied his thoughts. In fact, it was included prominently in his description of the qualities needed to be a good minister. However, he was anxious to carefully spell out both its uses and its limitations. From William Law, he had learned to be suspicious. He wrote to him, reminding him he had said:

> "Religion is the most plain, simple thing in the world. It is only, we love him because he first loved us. So far as you add philosophy to religion, just so far you spoil it." This remark I have never forgotten since; and I trust in God I never shall.[28]

However, the accusations that he was an "enthusiast," as well as his struggles to articulate his message, forced him to defend his use of reason on several occasions. In a sermon called "The Case of Reason Impartially Considered," he touted reason as a defense against the absurdities of "enthusiasm." He wrote:

> Among those that despise and vilify reason you may always expect to find those enthusiasts who suppose the dreams of their own imagination to be revelations from God. We cannot expect that men of this turn will pay much regard to reason.[29]

Scarcely a breath later, he warns against overvaluing reason:

> How natural it is for those who observe this extreme to run into the contrary! While they are strongly impressed with the absurdity of undervaluing reason, how apt are they to overvalue it! So much easier it is to run from east to west than to stop at the middle point! Accordingly we are surrounded with those we find on every side who lay it down as an undoubted principle that reason is the highest gift of God…They are wont to describe it as very near, if not quite infallible. They look on it as the all-sufficient director of all the children of men, able by its native light to guide them into all truth, and lead them into all virtue.[30]

He himself possessed a remarkable memory and a keen mind. He valued these natural endowments and hoped to find them in his preachers. However, in "An Address to the Clergy," he recognized such gifts were from "nature" and had not been given to everyone:

> To begin with gifts; and, (1) with those that are from nature. Ought not a Minister to have, first, a good understanding, a clear apprehension, a sound judgment, and a capacity of reasoning with some closeness? Otherwise, how will he be able to understand the various states of those under his care; or to steer them through a thousand difficulties and dangers, to the haven where they would be?…Secondly. Is it not highly expedient that a guide of souls should have likewise some liveliness and readiness of thought? Or how will he be able, when need requires, to "answer a fool according to his folly?"…Thirdly. To a sound understanding and a lively turn of thought, should be joined a good memory; if it may be, ready, that you may make whatever occurs in reading or conversation your own; but however retentive, lest we be "ever learning, and never able to come to the knowledge of the truth"…[31]

The mind was the means by which the truth could be tested and explained, even though certain direct spiritual perceptions did not submit to reason, as he had learned from the Church Fathers.

Passing then to "acquired endowments," he begins to turn down the screws. The mind is made responsible for a very broad range of practical knowledge:

> Seventhly. There is yet another branch of knowledge highly necessary for a Clergyman, and that is, knowledge of the world; a knowledge of men, of their maxims, tempers and manners, such as they occur in real life Without this he will be liable to receive much hurt, and capable of doing little good…Eighthly. Can he be without an eminent share of prudence? that most uncommon thing which is usually called common sense? But how shall we define it?…an habitual consideration of all the circumstances of a thing…Ninthly. Next to prudence or common sense, (if it be not included therein,) a Clergyman ought certainly to have some degree of good breeding; I mean address, easiness and propriety of behaviour, wherever his lot is cast: Perhaps one might add, he should have (though not the stateliness; for he is "the servant of all," yet) all the courtesy of a gentleman, joined with the correctness of a scholar.[32]

In these statements, he implies the mind is both the receptacle of knowledge and the practitioner of logic, that is, a reasoner. Unlike Scripture, the witness of the Church Fathers, or the "eye of faith," reason is not a source of knowledge. It cannot produce spiritual truth or justifying faith. It cannot create hope, love, or righteousness. But it can manipulate ideas. Like a careful philosopher, Wesley analyzes the uses of the term "reason." First, reason can mean having reasons or motives for doing or believing something. Second, reason sometimes refers to relations between things. But relations, he notes, cannot exist apart from the things related. Thirdly, reason means understanding as a faculty "of the soul." The last is Wesley's meaning. It performs three related functions:

- It apprehends or conceives of something in the mind.
- It judges or determines the thing in relation to other things, that is, distinguishes one thing from another.
- It discourses or moves "from one judgment to another."[33]

In this definition of reason, Wesley includes knowledge under the first two functions and the use of logic under the third function, which he calls "discourse" here. Therefore, reason's role was to test hypotheses, discover errors, reveal absurdities, and compare parallels in the Scriptures. It was not so much a source as a tool. Moreover, it belongs clearly to any methodology.

He affirms anyone will admit this use of reason in everyday practical matters. However, his question is: "It may do much in the affairs of men. But what can it do in the things of God?"[34] He then answers himself:

> The foundation of true religion stands upon the oracles of God (the affirmations of Scripture)...Is it not reason (assisted by the Holy Ghost) which enables us to understand what the Holy Scriptures declare concerning the being and attributes of God? Concerning his eternity and immensity, his power, wisdom, and holiness? It is by reason that God enables us in some measure to comprehend his method of dealing with the children of men...what is that faith whereby we are saved; what is the nature and the condition of justification...what is the mind that was in Christ, and what it is to walk as Christ walked.[35]

Reason, as distinguished from Scripture and Christian antiquity, is not a source of knowledge. Instead, it is an instrument for understanding and discoursing about spiritual matters. Given the manipulation of ideas in which he engaged in developing his theology and the explanations he used in his sermons to teach his followers, it is no wonder he vigorously defended his constant use of reason.

The Problem of Experience

Thirty years ago, Dr. Outler presented us with what he called the "Wesleyan Quadrilateral." He described it as a "theological method."

It did not pretend to provide a rigid methodology, but it did provide useful clues for our investigation of Wesley's theological roots. In addition to his roots in his own church, we have seen how Wesley used the first three sources in the Quadrilateral. However, the fourth, Experience, is highly problematic.

This method was intended to be a distillation of the major steps Wesley took as he utilized his sources in the development of his theology. He identified the four steps as Holy Scriptures, Tradition, Reason, and Experience. That is, Scripture is the primary source of doctrinal truth. Tradition or Christian antiquity is the secondary source and interprets the meaning of Scripture. Reason is a tool to assist the understanding of Scripture and Tradition. Experience is the final test.

In his advice to his preachers, Wesley produced a long list of gifts—natural and acquired—as instruments for the better interpretation of the Scriptures. They were clearly drawn from the sources that fed Wesley's own theological journey. They also included the first three items from the Quadrilateral. The only item missing from Wesley's own list is Experience. This may be because his appeal to Experience was a part of his method only in certain kinds of cases, that is, only in those cases involving some kind of inner, private experience in the life of the believer.

Wesley's emotional experience of assurance at Aldersgate is often assumed to be what is meant by experience. Is this what Wesley meant by the "witness of the spirit"? Here is how he talks about that:

> How does it appear that we do love God and our neighbor, and that we keep his commandments? Observe that the meaning of this question is: How does it appear to us and not to others? I would ask him, then, that proposes this question, How does it appear to you, that you are alive, and that you are now in ease, and not in pain? Are you not immediately conscious of it? By the same immediate consciousness, you will know if your soul is alive to God; if you are saved from the pain of proud wrath, and have the ease of a meek and quiet spirit. By the same means you cannot but perceive if you love, rejoice, and delight in God.[36]

This inward testimony is contrasted with the testimony of outward evidence. Therefore, it can only verify truths referring to a spiritual reality about which there exists a theological proposition that comes from some other source. In fact, in Wesley's discussion above of the "witness of the Spirit with our spirits," the examples he cites suggest such a spiritual experience may be taken to be a certain kind of faith. They are a kind of spiritual perception, but they are not an emotion, like assurance.

This is not the same thing, therefore, as the assurance of grace Wesley experienced at Aldersgate. The "warm heart" was an essentially emotional experience. At first, Wesley took it to be a necessary experience in order to be justified, forgiven, and reconciled to God. In other words, he initially took the emotional experience of assurance to be the faith that justifies. In that case, the experience of assurance itself could confirm the truth of the doctrine of justification, a doctrine he had already accepted and preached to others.

Such an understanding of the "witness of the Spirit with his spirit that he was a child of God" accepted and received by him may have been one reason for the charge he was an enthusiast. That is, he appeared to be depending on emotion instead of reason for his beliefs. In fact, Wesleyanism has often been called the "religion of the warm heart," implying the right kind of emotional experience is the criterion for the presence of saving faith. In fact, Wesley's experience of assurance soon faded from his consciousness and was no longer seen as identical with justifying faith, that is, faith that one is actually forgiven and reconciled to God. The warm heart is not essential to the faith that justifies. Rather, an emotional accompaniment of faith is optional.

Many other doctrines are clearly not subject to corroboration by experience in the same manner in which Wesley first held assurance or the "experience of grace" to confirm that the truth of the doctrine applied to him. Included among them are the speculative doctrines of theism, Trinity, Incarnation, and Atonement, that constitute Wesley's theological presuppositions.

My question, therefore, is still whether experience belongs to Wesley's theological method in any case at all. It is the one element Outler included in the Quadrilateral that had not already been identified in the literature with which Wesley was familiar. What can experience, as a source or tool of theological method, mean if assurance is not identical with faith (as the Moravians had persuaded him it was)?

So, if an emotion is not itself faith, what about the spiritual experience of seeing with "the eye of faith"? Perhaps seeing the invisible and so forth, as an analogy with Wesley's examples of experiencing pleasure or pain, may still prove useful.

Spiritual Experience as an Option

"Spiritual experience" is a different kind of experience from the "experience of grace" or assurance. Basil and the Cappadocians were a source of Wesley's theory of spiritual knowledge. That is, they contributed the idea that there is a kind of direct experience of spiritual truth that is not discursive but can be communicated only through myth, story, drama, poetry, and so forth. Wesley sometimes spoke of this kind of experience as the essence of faith. The "eye of faith" perceives spiritual truths. But, for Wesley, these revealed truths may, at least in some cases, be manipulated by reason, discussed, compared, explained, and, up to a point, understood. For example, such truths as the Trinity, Incarnation, and Atonement may be subjected in some measure to discussion. He was bold enough late in his career to attempt to do so in some of his sermons.

This makes Wesley an empiricist in the philosophical sense that all knowledge comes through experience, even though the organ for some of that knowledge is the "eye of faith" instead of the five natural senses. So, how can this understanding of "spiritual experience" be a confirmation of the "oracles of God" and thus comprise one element in the Wesleyan Quadrilateral?

In the first place, one may simply claim that only the authors of the Scriptures received the truths to which they witnessed through direct spiritual experience. In that case, the idea of spiritual experience could only serve as an explanation of the source of the oracles of God, but it could not be expected to serve as part of a method of testing or understanding them because it would not be available to anyone except the original writers.

In the second place, spiritual experience might function as the direct apprehension by a contemporary individual of new spiritual realities. In that case, it may still occur apart from the witness of Scripture or other discursive explanations of doctrine. Thus, the door would be wide open for continuing revelations of new or even different theological truths. I believe Wesley might not deny that possibility, but he would need to take care lest it expose him anew to the charge of enthusiasm. Nevertheless, it may have actually given him some of his freedom for the reformulation of the Christian message in which he was constantly engaged. Of course, in the Quadrilateral, experience is treated as the fourth step in the method of interpreting Scripture, not as a source of spiritual truth.

However, there may be occasions when some scriptural doctrine could be confirmed by a direct "spiritual experience" of any individual, that is, by their "eye of faith" just as long as it was never used for new revelations of truth not set forth in the Scriptures. Such an individual experience could confirm the doctrine of justification by faith in the blood of the cross as a general truth.

Therefore, a spiritual experience of the biblical truth that we are justified by faith might contribute to the confirmation of the truth of the doctrine. In that case, experience would have to mean seeing with what Wesley called "the eye of faith," but it still could not refer to assurance.

Thus, we are left with Wesley's definition of faith as "spiritual experience." Wesley, in his discussion of faith, sees spiritual experience as susceptible to the application of reason in a way similar to the way reason is used to understand or interpret the testimony of Scripture and tradition.

However, Basil and others treated such spiritual experience as esoteric and not subject to reason's manipulations, but they did not yet have the problem of confirmation of scriptural truth because the canon of New Testament Scripture had not yet been established in their time. Their discussion simply concerned the source of spiritual knowledge.

Because Wesley already recognized the role of reason in theological construction, we could perhaps separate direct spiritual experience (revelation?) from Wesley's understanding of faith, which includes belief in propositions, and place it ahead of reason in the following reformulation of the Quadrilateral: Scripture,

Tradition, Experience, and Reason. Faith, in Wesley's full sense of the term, (including both *fiducia* [trust] and *fides* [assent to proposition]), then becomes the result of the method. The emotional accompaniments are then rendered optional. Of course, this is possible, but I do not believe it is the sense usually applied to the term "experience" either by Outler or most other commentators.

More Roots

Of course, there are roots we have not examined that would provide a more comprehensive theological method.

There is our knowledge of the natural world through which the Scriptures say and Wesley recognized that God has revealed his power and glory. The German scholars, Klaiber and Marquardt, have asserted that knowledge of God—both his goodness and his judgment—is extra-biblical and may be had independently of the oracles of God. According to them, Wesley's explanation of the Bible's failure to inform was due to usurpation of the credit by false gods and idols.[37] Therefore, such knowledge might be used as corroboration of biblical testimony concerning God's character and activities.

Professor D. A. Reily, a Brazilian Methodist historian, has suggested further that the natural phenomena of birth and growth may have provided Wesley with a kind of model or paradigm. Thereby, nature may have served him in his interpretation of the scriptural doctrine of salvation as a process that moves from being dead in sin through birth to growth and final perfection. Thus, knowledge of the natural world may become a resource for biblical understanding by means of analogy.

In fact, in his "Address to the Clergy," Wesley included a broad spectrum of worldly knowledge as useful for understanding the Scriptures, even though he made no explicit reference to the biological paradigm as helping to shape his doctrine of progressive salvation.

Besides these sources, there were the testimonies of those who were part of the movement he brought into being and nurtured through fifty years of ministry. Unquestionably, his opponents were also valuable aids in the process of sharpening both his understanding of the issues and his articulation of his positions. It could be said each of these resources provided reasonable further steps in his theological search and learning.

Therefore, I suppose we could speak of Scripture, Tradition, Reason, Nature, Denomination, Spiritual Friends, and Theological Opponents as constituting a Wesleyan methodology for the development of theological knowledge. I do not mean to be facetious, but I am only suggesting the Quadrilateral is quite arbitrarily limited. Clearly, none of these qualifies as Experience in Wesley's or Outler's usage.

Perhaps the greatest value of the Quadrilateral is that it helps us to focus on the critical importance of the multiplicity and diversity of the sources that go into the development of any new theological vision.

Wesley's widespread dependence on so many sources meant he faced an immense task as he worked through the many apparently incompatible emphases that fed into the process. We may be grateful for the freedom and ingenuity with which he employed them for the sake of his people.

3

Saved by Grace

In the "Preface" to the first edition of his sermons, Wesley expressed his consuming passion to discover how to get to heaven:

> I am a spirit come from God, and returning to God: just hovering over the great gulf; till, a few moments hence, I am no more seen; I drop into an unchangeable eternity! I want to know one thing—the way to heaven; how to land safe on that happy shore.[1]

However, he gradually discovered that salvation was neither the arrival in heaven nor some moment in one's life when one's arrival was assured. Rather, it included the process of getting there. The hope of arrival was a great motivating force for launching and keeping him on the journey. But salvation was the whole package.

However, his message of salvation required certain theological presuppositions. There are four of them that I am calling speculative because Wesley treated their manner of being as unknowable mysteries. Still, he called upon them as he formulated his teaching about salvation.

They were:

- His image of God (a version of theism)
- The doctrine of the Trinity
- The doctrine of the Incarnation (God in the flesh of Jesus)
- The doctrine of substituionary Atonement.

The last three were all derived from the basic image of God, and Wesley inherited them all from the Latin church through his own Church of England.

The Speculative Doctrines

In spite of the radical nature of his salvation message, Wesley remained faithful to his inherited speculative orthodoxy. In his writings, there are a number of summaries of his theological position, usually with a distinction drawn between essential doctrines and opinions, but he never treated any of these summaries as a litmus test for salvation. Among his longer statements is his abridgment of the *Book of Homilies* and *A Plain Account of Genuine Christianity*. The following is a shorter and quite succinct statement from the conclusion to his *Compendium of Natural Philosophy*. In fact, it names the doctrines I have just called speculative:

> Let him firmly believe there is but one God, the object of any Divine worship whatever; and think and speak of him under that plain, scriptural distinctivity of Father, Son and Holy Ghost; leaving the incomprehensible nature of that union and distinction, to the great author of our faith himself. Let him believe Christ to be the only begotten Son of God, in the obvious import of these words, and leave the manner of that inconceivable nature and distinction to the veracity of God. Let him believe, that Christ did as truly make an Atonement to God for us, as one man atones for another to a third person; and leave the unintelligible part of that Divine operation for the subject of future praise and contemplation. Let men, I say, believe as far as they then clearly understand without perplexing themselves or others with what is incomprehensible, and then they fulfill the whole purpose of God in all his revelations.[2]

In this passage, he affirms a monotheistic view of God. This concept suggests God is at least transcendent if not also discrete. "Transcendent" implies that at least a part of God is outside or beyond his creation. "Discrete" implies God is totally separate, denying any part of the reality of God can be found as a part of something else, even though he may still have an impact on his creation. He also names the doctrines of the Trinity, the Incarnation, and substitutionary Atonement as necessary even while they remain incomprehensible.

However, other listings include other items. Colin Williams writes:

> A review of Wesley's writings indicates that the essential doctrines on which he insisted included original sin, the deity of Christ, the Atonement, justification by faith alone, the work of the Holy Spirit and the Trinity. It is important to notice, however, that Wesley refuses to list a definite number of "fundamental" articles.[3]

In William's summary listing, he adds three items to Wesley's list cited above: original sin, justification by faith, and the work of the Holy Spirit. Each is a part of Wesley's doctrine of salvation. They are all distinguished from the speculative doctrines by virtue of their reference to certain conditions or changes in the spiritual life of believers. Speculative doctrines are not available for that kind of testing unless one can trust the "eye of faith."

The following are Wesley's presuppositions. In fact, they are the old wineskin that needs to be replaced with a new vision of God in order to hold the new wine, that is, a revised understanding of salvation.

1. Western Theism

The theism inherited by Wesley begins with his description of God quoted above: God is one. This is based on the Hebrew tradition about Yahweh, whose uniqueness was distinguished from the polytheism of the Canaanites. This is the monotheism that appears in the three great religions of the Western world: Judaism, Christianity, and Islam. The Western world has been re-creating that image ever since its rise with the early Hebrews. Both Christianity and Islam have been such spin-offs. Each has added its own emphases and made its own adjustments.

For the Hebrews, God was a discrete being able to interfere at will with the workings of his creation. Moreover, he was male, the lawgiver, the judge, the prosecutor, and the executioner. He also set up a system whereby the people could make blood sacrifices to cover their disobedience to his laws.

This early image of God very quickly began undergoing modifications. Some prophets said they really did not like blood sacrifices very much, but preferred justice and righteousness instead. In the Christian version, Jesus came along and ran afoul of the religious authorities because he challenged their image of God. He even declared God's kingdom, or rule, was in them. He refused to blame God for natural disasters such as the falling of the Tower of Siloam and observed that the rain falls on the just and the unjust alike.

The early church entered into strenuous controversies when the leaders of the churches disagreed on the content of their belief about Jesus. For instance, some of them affirmed God was in everyone in the same way and with the same potential that he was in Jesus.[4]

By the end of the fourth century AD, the early theistic image of God had undergone further changes. Most of the earlier characteristics of God remained; for example, he was still male and remained the lawgiver and judge. Now, however, he provided an advocate for sinners, "Jesus Christ the righteous." Jesus was declared to be "of the same substance" as the Father, so the doctrine of the Incarnation came into being. Moreover, the groundwork for the substitutionary theory of the Atonement by the blood of Jesus was laid. That is, because the Son had been declared equal with the Father, he was sufficiently precious to the Father so that he could serve as the only necessary sacrifice for the sins of the whole world, thus rendering the sacrificial system of the Jews obsolete. The Holy Spirit further modified the transcendence of God. He entered into the creation as God's presence and power. He was also declared to be of the same substance as the Father, thus completing, along with Father and Son, the doctrine of the Trinity.

Wesley also ventured late in his career to write more speculative sermons about the nature of God. In a sermon called "The Omnipresence of God" written in 1788, just three years before his death, he wrote:

> In a word there is no point of space, whether within or without the bounds of creation, where God is not. Indeed this subject is far too vast to be comprehended by the narrow limits of human understanding.[5]

As one of the traditional attributes of God, it is also incomprehensible, particularly when one considers he is also said to be a discrete entity. How can he be in every point in space and still not be, in some sense, part of the natural world?

In another late sermon, written in 1789, he wrote of "The Unity of the Divine Being":

> But who can search out this God to perfection? None of the creatures that he has made. Only some of his attributes he has been pleased to reveal to us in his Word. Hence we learn that God is an eternal being...Nearly allied to the eternity of God is his omnipresence...This one, eternal, omnipresent Being is likewise all-perfect. He has from eternity to eternity all the perfections, and infinitely more than it ever did or ever can enter into the heart of man to conceive; yea, infinitely more than the angels in heaven can conceive. These perfections we usually term the attributes of God...And he is omnipotent as well as omnipresent...The omniscience of God is a clear and necessary consequence of his omnipresence.[6]

These are not only the orthodox attributes of the image of God inherited by Wesley. He affirms they are also incomprehensible.

This is John Wesley's basic image of God, orthodox theism.

2. The Trinity

The doctrine of the Trinity was an addendum to the ancient theism. It was also a part of Wesley's theological inheritance. While God as Father is named in the Scriptures as well as Jesus as the Son of God and the Spirit variously as the Spirit of God, the Spirit of Jesus, and the Holy Spirit, there is only one indirect reference to the Trinity. That reference is found at the end of the Gospel of St. Mark in which the disciples are commanded to go into all the world to baptize in the name of the Father, the Son, and the Holy Spirit. That formulation, our scholars tell us, was inserted in Mark later, after the doctrine of the Trinity had been formulated and officialized by the church in AD 325. Until then, there was no Trinity.

Wesley's speculative sermon called "On the Trinity" was finally written in 1775. In it, he wrote quite specifically concerning his stance toward this strange entity:

> There are three that bear record in heaven: And these three are one. I believe this fact also (if I may use the expression)—that God is three in One. But the manner how I do not comprehend; and I do not believe it. Now in this, in the manner, lies the mystery; and so it may; I have no concern with it: it is no object of my faith.[7]

His use of the Trinity was negligible, but it influenced his doctrine of salvation in two ways. It included the doctrine of the Incarnation and, by extension, the Atonement. Second, it included the Holy Spirit by whose power grace was applied throughout the process of salvation.

3. The Incarnation

Of course, the issue of the Incarnation was involved in the Trinity because it dealt with the relation between the Father and the Son. While Wesley put little stock in the Trinity as a useful (though essential) item of belief, the incarnation was important to him because of its facilitation of the doctrine of the Atonement. At the same time, the definition of that relationship offered by the Council of Nicea was as incomprehensible to Wesley, as it is to many of the rest of us. It also remained controversial for many years. Most of the bishops of the church went on after Nicea teaching their former views. Even Athanasius, who had won the contest at Nicea, was later exiled at least five times. Armstrong describes the ensuing confusion:

The show of agreement pleased Constantine, who had no understanding of the theological issues, but in fact there was no unanimity at Nicea…It was very difficult to make his (Athanasius') creed stick…Further, Athanasius' creed begged many important questions. It stated that Jesus was divine but did not explain how the Logos could be "of the same stuff" as the Father without being a second God.[8]

Therefore, we can read the history of the debate between the Arians and the Athanasians and understand its nature. But the result remains irrational. It does nothing to explain how the Son can also be God, even if he is of the same substance.

4. Substitutionary Atonement

Most of Wesley's writing about the Atonement involved an explanation of its benefits, not its nature.

However, in his sermon "Justification by Faith," he rejects certain theories of the Atonement. Wesley says justification, that is, trust in the forgiveness made possible by the death of Christ, contrary to what the ransom theory of the Atonement claims, does not "clear us from accusation by Satan."[9] That doctrine would require that Jesus be God's payment to Satan in exchange for the claim that Satan had on human beings. Now God could have mercy on them.

He then rejects the theory that affirms the Atonement "clears us from accusation by the Law."[10] The forensic (legal) theory of the Puritans, he says somewhat incorrectly, affirms the Atonement deceives God into treating us as if we had been acquitted because we were not actually guilty.[11] On the other hand, the Puritan notion was that, because of Jesus' death, his righteousness is imputed to us. That is, we share vicariously in the righteousness of Jesus' obedience in going to the cross. Wesley's belief in a substitutionary atonement, however, also seems to free us from "accusation by the law" because Jesus' sacrifice is a substitute for the sacrifices or merits that sinners owe for their sins against the law.

His real difference with the Puritans was over their insistence on imputed righteousness (in which Jesus' righteousness is credited to our account) and Wesley's claim that Jesus' righteousness was not only imputed but was also actually imparted to the believer. (By legal relationships, I mean those based on trade-offs like the *quid pro quo* of salvation by good works or credits to our moral bank accounts in the doctrine of the "imputation of righteousness.") Wesley refuses to make the distinction and claims that both things occur in justification.

However, he ends this discussion by saying the "plain Scriptural notion is that justification is pardon, the forgiveness of sins."[12] In other words, we are pardoned for the sake of Jesus' sacrifice. As important to Wesley's whole doctrine of salvation as the Atonement is, in the end, he refused to try to explain how it works:

> Justifying faith implies, not only a divine evidence or conviction that "God was in Christ reconciling the world unto himself," but a sure trust and confidence that Christ died for my sins, that he loved me and gave himself for me.[13]

That is it. He just does not understand how Jesus' death accomplishes that. Therefore, he writes of it:

> It is true that I can no more comprehend it than his lordship Lord Huntingdon; perhaps I might say than the angels of God, than the highest created understanding. Our reason is here quickly bewildered. If we attempt to expatiate in this field, we find no end, in wandering mazes lost.[14]

It was enough to believe Jesus had to die as a substitute for all the world's sinners in order to satisfy God's demand for justice and assure his ability to forgive. Because that satisfaction had been made, salvation was available to any and all who came to trust, not so much in God, but in the efficacy of the Atonement of Christ.

Therefore, its benefits were massive. No Atonement—no grace—period. For Wesley, the effects of the Atonement were retroactive. Without the Atonement, there was not even the prevenient grace that gave each person the ability to believe and choose. If there is no Atonement, there is no escape from the original sin in which all are born. Without it, there is no salvation because it was the means by which grace was made available to human beings.

Focus on Salvation

Theologically speaking, what mattered to Wesley was the doctrine of salvation or what Albert Outler has identified as the *ordo salutis,* the order of salvation. Most of his preaching and teaching was based on this doctrine. However, his discussions of his theistic view of God, the divinity of Christ, and the Atonement served as context for his doctrine of salvation, even though most of his writing on those subjects came relatively late in his career. However, even then, they were for the edification of those who were already on their spiritual journey because they had been largely presupposed during the time of his focus on salvation.

Their importance for his doctrine of salvation rests on the way in which they served together to make grace appear available from a God they understood to be one who first demanded justice. Only the Son who was also God had enough merits to pay for the sin of the rest of the world.

Perhaps an analogy will at least suggest the role the speculative doctrines play in Wesley's theology. Suppose we want to play a game of tennis. We know the game involves moving a ball back and forth between two players, but we do not know much more about it until we have the equipment. We therefore ask what we need in order to learn to play the game. We are told we need a court of a certain size with a certain kind of surface. We will then need a net that crosses the court at a certain height. Next, each player will need at least one racket and a pocket full of balls of a certain size and quality. He is then ready to learn the game—and the game is the thing.

In order for Wesley to develop his doctrine of salvation, he needs appropriate equipment. The speculative doctrines are his equipment. Just as the game of tennis depends on the kind of equipment and its size and quality, the doctrine of salvation depends significantly on the speculative doctrines, the doctrinal presuppositions. For example, if the court is triangular instead of rectangular, the game immediately changes in nature. The rules will even have to be rewritten. Or, if the surface is clay instead of grass, the game is played differently. If God is not a lawgiver with the need for a means of Atonement, then the definition of salvation itself is radically modified.

Wesley could teach that salvation is not a *quid pro quo* because of his theological equipment. He used the Atonement, which was dependent both on the Incarnation and on a God who is the judge, to allow a person to gain access to God's grace by faith without paying for it by his own efforts. It is then not a transaction between a person and God in which God promises something if we meet his conditions. His presuppositions make this possible.

Even to this day, popular discussion tends to identify salvation with an event of some kind, usually emotional and focused on life after death. What Wesley describes as justification by faith, many people identify as the whole of salvation. Wesley had come to see salvation as including both justification by grace through faith and the ongoing process of sanctification or holiness of life by grace through faith.

In Sam Keen's cover comment on Thomas Moore's book *Care of the Soul*, he says:

> This book may just help you give up the futile quest for salvation and get down to the possible task of taking care of your soul. A modest, and therefore marvelous, book about the life of the spirit.[15]

The assumption on the part of Keen seems to be that salvation and the life of the spirit are two separate things. One (a guarantee of heaven) is impossible; the other (nurture of the spiritual life) is possible.

For Wesley, the impossibility of the project is not the issue. Rather, the issue is the necessity of the struggle toward a goal. When Ozzie Smith, the St. Louis Cardinal's flashy shortstop, was inducted into the Baseball Hall of Fame, he said in his acceptance speech, that nothing is good enough if it can be made better. In Wesley's thought, salvation was not an impossible state. It was a process of moving in hope toward the goal of a perfect union with God. Our connection with God can always be made better.

The focus of Wesley's preaching, especially in the earliest decades of his ministry, was this doctrine of salvation. A very helpful glimpse at that message may be gained from the striking set of fused disjunctions Albert Outler describes in his "Preface" to *John Wesley*, a carefully organized anthology of Wesley's writings:

> He managed to transcend the stark doctrinal disjunctions which had spilled so much ink and blood since Augsburg and Trent. In their stead, he proceeded to develop a theological fusion of faith and good works, Scripture and tradition, revelation and reason, God's sovereignty and human freedom, universal redemption and conditional election, Christian liberty and an ordered polity, the assurance of pardon and the risk of "falling from grace," original sin and Christian perfection. In each of these disjunctions, as he insisted almost tediously, the initiative is with God, the response with man.[16]

The disjunctions arose out of his readings in the early Church Fathers and other writers of antiquity as well as from his contacts with contemporary movements represented by the Church of England, the Moravians, the Puritans, and the Calvinists. The result of his efforts to resolve the disjunctions (as listed in Outler's quote above) was a quite remarkable doctrine of salvation.

Salvation was no longer focused on heaven in the same way because one of Wesley's transcended disjunctions was the uniting of the two things, the life of the spirit and the hope of heaven. This kind of effort required theological liberty.

Theology, no matter how correct it might be, could not produce salvation or holiness. It could not procure the favor of God or teach us the things of God. His interest in theology was only as a kind of road map on this journey of salvation, the journey of hope he preached. What touched the lives of his hearers was his announcement of the grace of God alongside his demand for accountability—another disjunction overcome.

Wesley did not come to this position except by a painful, circuitous route. With his mother, he read the mystics. At the university and in Georgia, he immersed himself in Christian antiquity. Back at the university, he labored relentlessly with his student friends to do all the necessary good works that would gain him the peace he sought and assure him of his entry into heaven at last. Still, nothing worked, not even his mission to the Indians in Georgia, which lasted about a year and a half. He still had no assurance he was in the good graces of God. Even his experience at Aldersgate failed him.

Finally, Wesley discovered the *Book of Homilies*, which taught him to see that salvation included both justification by grace through faith and the ongoing process of sanctification or holiness of life by grace through faith.

Of course, the general idea of salvation by grace through faith was a view common to Paul, Luther, Calvin, and the Moravians. However, its form as a process was found in the official position of the Church of England of which Wesley was a priest. It was not only outlined in the homilies, but it was implied in the *Articles of Religion* which Wesley eventually edited for use in the American colonies. However, it was a doctrine familiar neither to most English churchmen nor the unchurched poor.

Shortly after his discovery of the homilies, George Whitefield invited him to take up the work in Bristol, which he was leaving to return to America. The revival then began, and the fruits of his preaching exploded across the land for the next fifty years and beyond. The focal message of his preaching was his doctrine of salvation, which was also his doctrine of grace. Thus, he was prepared for the future theological conflicts in which he found himself engaged, especially those with the Calvinists. Through these controversies, which erupted sporadically, his doctrine of salvation was clarified and honed.

Because Calvin began with his doctrine of the sovereignty of God and Wesley began with the question how to get into heaven, they treated the doctrine of salvation by grace through faith differently. Calvin's interest was primarily theological; Wesley's interest was primarily practical and existential.

The logical consequence of the Calvinists' key notion of the sovereignty of God, buttressed by certain passages of Scripture, was that human beings were predestined by God to be saved or not, leaving humans with no say of their own. Wesley's concern with the spiritual life of the Christian meant he needed to give hope to people by respecting their capacity to control their own future. Therefore, the Calvinists charged Wesley with being an enthusiast because his position on human freedom appeared to fly in the face of the logical consequence of the doctrine of the sovereignty of God. Wesley believed the Calvinists' logic led them to ignore the spiritual needs of the people.

Wesley then found it necessary to justify his dual focus by using the doctrine of prevenient grace, that is, the free gift of spiritual existence given to every human being, to make human freedom a gift from God and thereby allow God to remain sovereign. He also thought he was protecting grace as unconditional.

Whether his doctrine of grace is or is not rationally coherent, it nevertheless enabled him to proclaim grace and demand accountability within the framework of the *ordo salutis*, the "order of salvation." That was the message that spoke powerfully to the needs of his lower-class hearers and served his concern with living the Christian life in hope. So, the function of Wesley's message differed somewhat from that of the Calvinists, who, in England, counted the Puritans and dissenters, who tended to be members of the middle and upper classes, among their supporters. They were more likely to be concerned with maintaining logical coherence than finding hope for impoverished, powerless lives.

Nevertheless, there are interesting parallels between Wesley and the Calvinists. The simple, but classic, summary of Calvinism was formulated at the Synod of Dort in the Netherlands in 1619. It used the acronym TULIP and was intended to represent the logical consequences of the basic idea of the "sovereignty of God."

From the idea of God's sovereignty, there is thought to follow the consequence that the human being is totally depraved and there can be no good in him. Otherwise, he could save himself by his own efforts. God would then no longer be sovereign and in complete control. Thus, the "T" in TULIP stands for "Total Depravity." God alone chooses or elects who will be saved. "U" stands for "Unconditional Election." God's election is not conditional upon anything that any person can do. That is where the Calvinist insistence that faith is passive comes in.

That being the case, the death of Christ can atone only for those who have been elected. "L" then represents "Limited Atonement." From all this, it follows that God's grace is irresistible. Those saved by God's gracious choosing can do nothing to influence what God decides. Hence, "I" means "Irresistible Grace." Finally, because faith is passive and man can do nothing about it, there is no chance for him to fall from grace, that is, to change what God has decided. That then gives us "P" for "Perseverance of the Saints." Once saved, one is always saved.

These Calvinistic relationships between man and God appear to be logical or even mechanical instead of personal or spiritual. Wesley was looking for a spiritual way of understanding the relationships of salvation. He could not accept that humans are robots, but he insisted faith is active and they could exercise freedom and self-discipline. However, his problem came when he tried to keep God's unmerited and unconditional love or grace at the same time that he assigned freedom of choice to the human being.

In order to do that, Wesley had recourse to the notion of the gifts of prevenient grace, one of which was the capacity for faith. A person could use this capacity or not. Because prevenient grace had to be unmerited in order to be grace at all, he had to pull in the idea of the retroactive Atonement made by Jesus' death so that God could still take all the credit for the spiritual aspect of all human beings even before Jesus' death.

The context of these debates was Wesley's preaching scheme: saving grace has four stages or phases in each of which a unique, but yet related, gift of grace is bestowed. Following "prevenient grace," there are "justifying grace," "sanctifying grace," and "glorifying grace." This grace, in its whole breadth and with all its four gifts, is the source of Wesleyan salvation and the meat of his preaching message. Wesley makes this point in what was probably the most often preached of his sermons and the clearest statement of the doctrine of salvation, "The Scripture Way of Salvation":

> What is salvation? The salvation which is here spoken of is not what is frequently understood by that word, the going to heaven, eternal happiness...It is not a blessing which lies on the other side death, or (as we usually speak) in the other world...It is a present thing, a blessing which, through the free mercy of God, ye are now in possession of...So that the salvation which is here spoken of might be extended to the entire work of God, from the first dawning of grace in the soul till it is consummated in glory.[17]

He then narrows his subject for the sermon to the two central parts of it: justification and sanctification. However, the first and last parts, prevenient and glorifying grace, are essential parts, like bookends holding things together. The heart is in the middle.

I believe we can import this framework into the twenty-first century as a model for our new understanding of the spiritual life. It is an understanding made possible by our new vision of who God is.

The Four Gifts of Grace

1. Grace Gives Us Freedom and the Power to Believe

The first gift of grace in this scheme is called prevenient. That is, it comes before the special gifts of grace and is given to each human being. Without it, the human is nothing except a beast. With it, he becomes a spiritual being with the freedom to make decisions and other attributes unique to the human species.

Wesley's doctrine of prevenient grace did not receive a thorough treatment until he published a sermon called "On Working Out Our Own Salvation" in the *Arminian Magazine* in 1783. The following is how he describes this first gift of grace:

> If we know and feel that the very first motion of good is from above, as well as the power which conducts it to the end; if it is God that not only infuses every good desire, but that accompanies it and follows it, else it vanishes away, then it evidently follows, that "he who glorieth" must "glory in the Lord."...For allowing that all the souls of men are dead by nature this excuses none, seeing there is no man that is in a state of mere nature; there is no man, unless he has quenched the Spirit that is wholly void of the grace of God. No man living is entirely destitute of what is vulgarly called natural conscience. But this is not natural; it is more properly termed, preventing grace.[18]

In other words, prevenient grace is the gift from God by which each person alive is spiritual and therefore has various spiritual capacities such as good desires, a sense of something transcendent, a conscience, freedom to decide, and a capacity for faith.

Even though he had preached from the same text he used for the sermon cited above (Philippians 2:12–13) a few times in the early 1730s and had spoken of it in some of his early sermons on original sin, it did not take its proper place in his scheme until late. As a result, it is included among the sermons that revisited and refurbished old themes during his later years.

What precisely is this grace that not only provides a spiritual life to every human but also saves through faith? It is the unmerited, unconditional love of God for all his children. For Wesley, these spiritual gifts were given to the very first human beings because the Atonement was retroactive. It was secured for all when God gave his son to the cross as a substitute for all the sinners who merited his condemnation.

However, all other gifts of grace are received by faith, the possibility of which is afforded by the first gift of grace. Wesley explains faith on analogy with natural vision:

> All things are possible to him that thus "believeth." "The eye of his understanding, being enlightened," he sees what is his calling.[19]

That is, it involves a spiritual sense by which the human being can perceive spiritual things. Assent to propositions is also involved in faith, but it is secondary to the spiritual experience that already allows any person to see the mighty works of God in the world of nature, according to both St. Paul and Wesley. St. Paul says:

> Ever since the creation of the world his eternal power and divine nature, invisible though they are, have been understood and seen through the things he has made.[20]

Wesley also allows for other rudimentary forms of faith, such as a longing for the transcendent that all people experience because of prevenient grace. This universal experience of spiritual things is the beginning of faith that may develop on a continuum to its fullest manifestation.

Outler claims "the insistent correlation between the genesis of faith and its fullness marks off Wesley's most original contribution to Protestant theology."[21]

Wesley continues:

> Everyone has some measure of that light, some faint glimmering ray, which sooner or later, more or less, enlightens every man that cometh into the world. And every one, unless he be one of the small number whose conscience is seared as with a hot iron, feels more or less uneasy when he acts contrary to the light of his own conscience. So that no man sins because he has no grace but because he does not use the grace which he hath.[22]

Thus, the Atonement becomes retroactive by endowing all who came before with their spiritual reality. No one can claim credit for his faith, even for its weakest manifestation.

Ironically though, according to this system of thought, grace was not really unmerited because it was the merit of Jesus (that is, his obedience) that earned God's grace for everyone else. There was still a trade-off. The gift of prevenient grace was made available to us by that trade-off. So, it is not really unmerited, and, in that sense, it is not even grace. But, this is Wesley's effort to synthesize grace and responsibility. It is an heroic effort, but it is abortive all the same. It reveals one of the contradictions into which his theism cast him.

2. Grace Gives Us a New Start

Each person not only begins life as a spiritual individual because of prevenient grace, but he is also an original sinner. That is why justification by faith (that is, pardon) is necessary. By utilizing the myth of Adam's fall in the Garden of Eden, Wesley teaches that the image of God in which human beings were created was broken and in need of restoration. This broken image of God in each person can only be restored by a special gift of God's grace, one that can be received only by faith. It is called justifying grace.

Justification by grace through faith is often taken to be the whole meaning of salvation. For Wesley, it is only the start of the process. It includes a small package of parts. They are:

- The act of repentance for sin
- The act of trusting (faith) in the Atonement for forgiveness
- The experience of feeling accepted by God or assurance (optional)
- The beginning of a new life.

All these things are possible only because of the grace of God made available by the Atonement and actually applied by the Holy Spirit.

The following is what is involved in justification by grace through faith, according to one of Wesley's most systematic treatments of the subject. It starts with original righteousness:

> In the image of God was man made; holy as he that created him is holy, merciful as the author of all is merciful, perfect as his Father in heaven is perfect. As God is love, so man dwelling in love dwelt in God and God in him.[23]

That original righteousness, which even the most avid defender of the doctrine of original sin will affirm, is also the ideal for the future that Wesley and many others have pursued. However, this scheme affirms all individual persons, after Adam and Eve, also start out with the broken image of God in them that produces all kinds of sinful actions. Wesley writes:

> To the entire law of love written in his heart…it seemed good to the sovereign wisdom of God to superadd one positive law. "Thou shalt not eat of the fruit of the tree that groweth in the midst of the garden"; annexing that penalty thereto, "In the day thou eatest thereof, thou shalt surely die."…Man did disobey God;…And in that day he was condemned by the righteous judgment of God.[24]

Therefore, sin is also the basis of this picture. Wesley defined sin as "a voluntary transgression of a known law of God." But then he asks:

> [I]s "a voluntary transgression of a known law" a proper definition of sin? I think it is of all such sin as is imputed to our condemnation. And it is a definition which has passed uncensured in the Church for at least fifteen hundred years…The thing is plain. All in the body are liable to mistakes, practical as well as speculative. Shall we call them sins or no? I answer again and again, Call them just what you please.[25]

In order to return to that original righteousness, sinners must repent of their sins:

> Then only, when they feel the burden, will they groan for deliverance from it. Then, and not till then, will they cry out, in the agony of their soul "Break off the yoke of inbred sin, And fully set my spirit free! I cannot rest till pure within, Till I am wholly lost in Thee."[26]

Bernard Holland, in his book called *A Species of Madness* (Wesley's own phrase), looked into the phenomena that so often accompanied repentance of sin in the early years of the revival. Holland asked why John Wesley's preaching produced the groaning, the crying out, the agony of soul, and the falling into faints while Charles Wesley's and George Whitefield's preaching did not. His conclusion was, when the people began to groan while Charles or George was preaching, the preacher began to relax his pressing for repentance, assuming the groaning was a sufficient sign they were being justified. John Wesley did not make that assumption and pressed on with his descriptions of their sinfulness and its consequences in the expectation that justification did not happen until, beyond repentance, they had actually received the faith that they were forgiven by God's grace. Thus, these were the manifestations usually associated with the experience of justification.

When he was charged with depending on emotion rather than on reason, Wesley explained in "A Farther Appeal to Men of Religion and Reason":

> It is my endeavor to drive all I can into what you may term another species of "madness" which I term "repentance" or "conviction," as preparatory to the gift of faith.[27]

Later, he rejected this earlier method. After 1744, the ecstatic manifestations diminished. He finally came around to say, "It is high time for us to return...to the plain word 'He that feareth God and worketh righteousness is accepted with him.'"[28] When sinners come to believe they are forgiven (that is, justified or acquitted by God's grace gained by the death of Christ), they begin a new life. That new beginning is called "rebirth," "regeneration," or being "born again."

This package of events Wesley calls, after Paul's language, justification by grace through faith.

A helpful analogy for the way this and the remaining gifts of grace work in Wesley's scheme might be that of the water that cannot flow down a dammed stream. When a spillway is built to allow the water to pass through the dam in measured amounts, the pressure of the water itself causes it to flow. Similarly, once prevenient grace has given spiritual reality to the individual, the remaining gifts of grace flow only when—by repentance and faith in the Atonement—the blockage is removed and grace can do what a merciful God, who also demands justice, has always been trying to do. He can give the gift of justifying faith by which his forgiveness is received. A new start on life is then undertaken.

We may even want to think of the Atonement as the spillway in the dam, prepared and ready for use. Repentance is the switch that opens the spillway. Forgiving grace flows like water and brings reconciliation with God. It moves down the streambed, irrigating the soil as it goes. New life begins and sanctification or holiness begins sprouting.

A number of issues raised by this description of justification have produced continuing discussion. The first is the distinction between justification and sanctification.

Theologically speaking, the new life, which justification includes, is called "regeneration." Popularly, following the Nicodemus story, it is called being "born again." Sometimes, this new start is accompanied by a surge of feelings: love, peace, joy, and renewed hope. This may be a signal that the new life has begun, that is, the growth of holiness has begun.

However, the issue had once been whether sanctification (holiness) had to precede justification, or vice versa. The great reversal Wesley made earlier was from the precedence of sanctification to the precedence of justification.

In order to focus on justification as antecedent to sanctification, Wesley employs the following argument:

> It is our "unrighteousness" to which the pardoning God is "merciful"; it is our iniquity which he "remembreth no more." This seems not to be at all considered by those who so vehemently contend that man must be sanctified, that is, holy, before he can be justified; especially by such of them as affirm that universal holiness or obedience must precede justification...For it is not a saint but a sinner that is forgiven.[29]

Thus, he affirms faith is the necessary condition of justification and the only necessary condition. That faith is in the grace purchased, effected, or otherwise secured by the Atonement of Jesus. That, of course, still leaves the issue whether faith in the Atonement must be prior to or simultaneous with one's trust in pardoning grace. But in either case, the merits secured by the Atonement are required for God's grace to be available, thus vitiating the nature of grace as unmerited.

Wesley finally asks:

> What is justification?...It is evident from what has been already observed that it is not the being made actually just and righteous. This is sanctification; which is in some degree the "immediate fruit" of justification, but nevertheless is a distinct gift of God and of a totally different nature. The one implies what God does for us through his Son; the other what he works in us by his Spirit.[30]

Another closely related issue is whether salvation is by faith, reason, or good works. Wesley's affirmation that faith was the means of salvation put him at loggerheads with the current preaching in the parish churches of England. For the most part, the church in his time taught that persons could count on reason and good works for their good standing with God.

Wesley explains that neither the imitation of Christ, good works, nor reason was sufficient to gain peace with God:

> Reason, however cultivated and improved, cannot produce the love of God; which is plain from hence: It cannot produce either faith or hope; from which alone this love can flow. It is then only, when we "behold by faith what manner of love the Father hath bestowed upon us," in giving his only Son that we might not perish, but have everlasting life, that "the love of God is shed abroad in our heart by the Holy Ghost which is given unto us."[31]

For Wesley, only when the works are done out of love are they done as God has commanded. This implies the love he commands is possible only when the individual has given up all claims to any credit or any righteousness of his own. When that has happened to a person, his love can be unconditional, just like the grace of God that has justified him or her. For human beings, such total unconditional love is impossible without this new birth, that is, this new life given to them through their justifying faith. The love demanded of the believer is possible only when the believer, like God, makes no demands of merit on the part of those for whom he performs acts of mercy.

However, there is still a problem with this argument. The Atonement has already paid for the sins of those one is called on to love. Therefore we cannot lay down conditions for loving them even if we want to. Our loving them is at least facilitated by the Atonement. But since God's grace was not really unconditional, our loving is somehow tainted as well. The Atonement has again failed to fulfill its promise.

One other controverted piece of Wesley's doctrine of justification by faith, closely related to the above, arises when he says:

> If it be objected, "Nay, but a man before he is justified may feed the hungry or clothe the naked, and these are good works," the answer is easy. These are in one sense good works; they are "good and profitable to men." But it does not follow that they are, strictly speaking, good in themselves or good in the sight of God. All truly good works...follow after justification, and they are therefore "good and acceptable to God in Christ" because they "spring out of a true and living faith."[32]

For Wesley, saving faith—whether for justification or sanctification—is active. It is something the individual does with the freedom grace has given him. This is one of the arguments Wesley had with the Calvinists, who insisted that faith is passive and does not involve any kind of positive action on the part of the believer. The importance of this distinction can be seen when we consider that Calvinism insisted those who believed were predestined to do so by God's action alone. Nothing good or evil they did thereafter could change that.

Finally, even if the feeling or emotion of assurance is received, that is a bonus. Though Wesley once believed it was necessary for salvation, he later relegated assurance to a less exalted status and, therefore, made nothing of his Aldersgate experience after the first few weeks. He came to see it as one of assurance instead of conversion or justification. It was the Moravians who had made such a large thing of it. In his introduction to Wesley's sermon on "Justification by Faith," Outler notes:

> [H]is preoccupation with "holy living" and "the means of grace" before 1738 had obscured the priority of justifying faith as antecedent to, and the ground of "the faith that works by love."[33]

This did not mean he abandoned his hope for sanctification, but he wanted it clearly distinguished from justification. He even made it dependent upon prior justification.

I have always loved the line from "Rock of Ages" by Augustus Toplady, a Calvinist rather than a Wesleyan, which says, "Be of sin the double cure, save from wrath and make me pure."[34] What is that but sanctification preceded by justification?

3. Grace Gives Us the Mind of Christ

Justification is not a lot more than a new start, even though that is not a small thing either. Now the real journey begins. This is the gift of sanctification. Our analogy of the river and the dam also suggests the flowing river below the dam not only starts a new life. It continues to nourish it and produce blossoms and fruit as long as the water is allowed to flow through the spillway. Faith and continued repentance for reappearing sins are necessary, lest the spillway be stopped and the water cease to flow. Therefore, attention must be paid to the maintenance of the spillway, the routing of the water flow, the planting of seed, the spread of fertilizer, and the horticulture of holiness if life is to flourish and produce. At last, it can make us perfect when the final blockage, that is, death, has been removed, if not before:

> From the moment we are justified, there may be a gradual sanctification, a growing in grace, a daily advance in the knowledge and love of God. And if sin cease before death, there must, in the nature of the thing, be an instantaneous change; there must be a last moment wherein it does exist, and a first moment wherein it does not.[35]

This process lasts as long as the individual uses the "means of grace," that is, receives the sacrament, prays, fasts, studies the Scriptures, engages in spiritual conversation, and so forth. In Wesley's view, these are the ways by which one nourishes the faith that keeps the spillway open. Perhaps Wesley would want to say the Holy Spirit is the weight that applies the grace, just as it is the pressure of the water that forces it through the gate.

Along with the spiritual disciplines, there needs to be an expectation that, as grace continues to pour in, there will be a gradual growth in grace day-by-day and year-by-year. Wesley thought he could observe among his followers that the more earnestly they expected growth, the more quickly and steadily they grew.

As the process continues over time, one moves closer and closer to that point at which one passes from a state in which sin, as the "voluntary transgression of known laws," is present to the state in which it is not. This is the moment Wesley calls "instantaneous sanctification." This is the goal of the process of sanctification. As such, it is part of the process.

Wesley had also been much taken with William Law's description of holy living. That, along with the early Church Fathers' discussions of divinization, the mystical writers' search for union with God, and the *Book of Homilies'* acknowledgment of aspiring holiness, had encouraged Wesley in his preoccupation with holy living. Outler believes that preoccupation, early on, had tended to distract him from justification. This explains why his great sermon on "Circumcision of the Heart" had focused entirely on sanctification with justification inserted some fifteen years later. This is what he says of circumcision:

> [T]hat "circumcision is that of the heart, in the spirit, and not in the letter," that the distinguishing mark of a true follower of Christ, of one who is in a state of acceptance with God, is not either outward circumcision or baptism, or any other outward form, but a right state of soul, mind and spirit renewed after the image of him that created it is one of those important truths that can only be "spiritually discerned."[36]

This circumcision of the heart, he says, requires humility (that is, repentance) that removes from us those "high conceits of our own perfection" and thus entirely "cuts off that vain thought, 'I am rich, and wise and have need of nothing.'" It also requires faith, hope, and love. The following is one of Wesley's descriptions of the goal:

> In every thought of our hearts, in every word of our tongues, in every work of our hands, to show forth His praise who hath called us out of darkness into His marvelous light! O that both we, and all who seek the Lord Jesus in sincerity, may thus be made perfect in One![37]

Wesley quotes Jesus' prayer before his crucifixion to back up his claim that such entire union is possible:

> I ask not only on behalf of these, but also on behalf of those who will believe in me through their word that they may all be one. As you, Father, are in me and I am in you, may they also be in us, so that the world may believe that you sent me.[38]

His use of this Scripture implies that perfection was that oneness or union with God he had sought from his earliest conversion to religion in 1725. When asked further what he meant by perfection, he writes:

> We mean one in whom is the mind which was in Christ, and who so walketh as [Christ] walked; a man that hath clean hands and a pure heart; or that is cleansed from all filthiness of flesh and spirit; one in whom there is no occasion of stumbling, and who, accordingly, doth not commit sin.[39]

That requires still further explanation:

> No one then is so perfect in this life, as to be free from ignorance. Nor secondly from mistake; which indeed is almost an unavoidable consequence of it; seeing those who "know but in part" are ever liable to err touching the things which they know not.[40]

However, he also writes:

> This much is certain: they that love God with all their heart and all men as themselves are scripturally perfect.[41]

And also:

> Let the same mind be in you which was in Christ Jesus.[42]

In "A Plain Account of Christian Perfection," he writes:

> It is "perfect love" (I John iv:18). This is the essence of it; its properties, or inseparable fruits, are, rejoicing evermore, praying without ceasing, and in everything giving thanks (I Thess. v:16 etc.).[43]

In "Circumcision of the Heart," he summarizes it all:

> If thou wilt be perfect, add to all these, charity: add love, and thou hast the "circumcision of the heart." "Love is the fulfilling of the Law," "the end of the commandments."[44]

Therefore, he specifically does not mean by "perfection" that we come to either possess perfect wisdom or make no errors in judgment. Wesley says perfection is "not absolute." He then explains how that can be so:

> I believe there is no such perfection in this life as excludes these involuntary transgressions which I apprehend to be naturally consequent on the ignorance and mistakes inseparable from mortality…I believe a person filled with the love of God is still liable to these involuntary transgressions.[45]

Clearly, Wesley says here that perfection is the condition in which one has a perfectly clear conscience. Who does not want a perfectly clear conscience anyway?

One may want to ask, however: might not one have a perfectly clear conscience and yet not be filled with the love of God or the mind of Christ? His definition of sin, arising from his concept of God, is rife with such puzzles.

In any case, perfection is the goal of sanctification, which, he says repeatedly, is a "gradual" process. Entire sanctification or perfection is the ideal end of that process. Wesley never separates "perfection" from the process of sanctification. They are parts of one another. Moreover, those sermons dealing with the means of grace, style-of-life issues, and other matters of proper conduct (and there were many of them) can be seen as taking their place mostly under the rubric of sanctifying grace and serving as guidance for living a loving, useful, and happy life.

There remains one more little fly in this ointment of Wesleyan perfection. There were many—and there are yet many—who are troubled by what some called the "melancholy" of Wesley's message about sanctification. They charged him with being without humor, fun, or enjoyment. He was anxious to dispel this misapprehension. He had always believed holiness and happiness went together. So, he writes the following in a kind of footnote to his description of holiness:

> Not yet does it forbid us (as some have strangely imagined) to take pleasure in anything but God. To suppose this is to suppose the foundation of holiness is directly the author of sin, since he has inseparably annexed pleasure to the use of those creatures which are necessary to sustain this life he has given us.[46]

Because he does not specify, I assume those "creatures" to which he refers must include friends, food, and sex because they are necessary to sustain the life he has given us. God has attached pleasure to such activities so they can make their proper contribution to sustain life. Life is necessary if we are to love God. Such loves and pleasures are therefore quite proper and within the scope of perfect love.

Of course, we want to go on to perfection. Even a preacher must desire such a result.

4. Grace Gives Us Heaven

The fourth gift of grace is what Wesley thought of as heaven and called "glorifying grace." Heaven is far from being the whole of salvation, as Wesley learned. Yet, life beyond death in full union with God served as the ultimate object of Wesley's hope.

He did believe in a final tribunal before which all must come, thus reclaiming his theistic vision of God as lawgiver and judge. In a sermon especially prepared and delivered before the court meeting in Bedford in 1758, he writes:

> But will their evil deeds too—since if we take in his whole life "there is not a man on earth that liveth and sinneth not—will these be remembered in that day, and mentioned in the great congregation?"…How is it consistent with the promise which God has made to all who accept the gospel covenant, "I will forgive their iniquities, and remember their sin no more?"…It may be answered, it is apparently and absolutely necessary, for the full display of the glory of God, for the perfect and clear manifestation of his wisdom, justice, power and mercy toward the heirs of salvation, that all the circumstances of their life should be placed in open view, together with all their tempers and all the desires, thoughts, and intents of their hearts. Otherwise, how would it appear out of what a depth of sin and misery the grace of God had delivered them?[47]

However, the greatest incentive was the hope for that perfect union with God that surely awaited him as the fulfillment of his journey of faith. So, we are back with that same passion with which he started when, with the mystical authors in hand, he sought in the rectory at Epworth with his mother to find union with God.

In spite of his blind spots and puzzles, John Wesley provides us with a pretty solid piece of ground to stand on as we turn to the task of seeking a new vision of

God and a new way of filling out the framework of salvation he offers us. How shall we proceed responsibly with this task? That is the question now.

4

In Search of a New Vision

The orthodox Christian theism of Wesley's speculative presuppositions does not offer a credible message for the twenty-first century. Neither does any form of theism because they all share the posit of a discrete God of judicial stature. Our need in these times is for a new vision of God and, with it, a new understanding of salvation. By that, I mean a new vision of the incredible possibilities that reside in each human spirit and a practical plan for their realization.

The doomsayers are quick to announce the impending death of the church and the disappearance of the Christian faith. I also believe the church, as we have known it, is dying. I am convinced the faith, as we have known it, is ebbing away. But the AA member knows the darkest hour is the hour in which hope is born. Death is the time of resurrection. Therefore, this is the time for the rebirth of Christian faith. Only thus can the church be reborn. This is the time for hope.

The search for a new image of God is being forced upon us by a growing dissatisfaction with the theistic image of God and the other doctrines it has spawned. They have become impotent for an increasing number of people because the modern mind demands at least two things that orthodox belief does not adequately provide: rational consistency and a connection with concrete experience. There is a growing dependence on making sense. Blind faith is increasingly suspect. Only that which we can experience is credible. Only if we can somehow sense, feel, or know it as self-evident can we believe in it.

There are at least three additional reasons the church and the ancient faith are in trouble. First, the old God is not delivering as we have long deluded ourselves into thinking he is or should be. The inexorable progress of science and technology and the opening up of new fields of scientific investigation are filling the gaps in our knowledge and our ability to meet our physical and psychological needs. No longer do we have to count on God, as we have understood him, to fill all those gaps. Second, our culture in the West is rejecting the moralism of much of Christianity, a moralism that has grown in the soil of our old vision of God as a lawmaker and judge. Moral relativism is rendering our moral absolutism obsolete. Third, a creeping individualism is making conformity to a lifestyle or the mores of our class society unacceptable. Thus, it threatens the community life the churches have usually attempted to promote on the basis of cultural homogeneity.

Those who are in a state of reaction against these signs of the times are those who are still looking for authoritative statements on belief. They tend to migrate either to fundamentalist or confessional congregations because they want to be told what to believe. Even those who are willing to wrestle with doctrinal or spiritual issues in their own search for understanding often become entangled with inherited images and definitions or end up grasping at every wind of doctrine that blows by and every faddish promise of renewal that shows up on the horizon. Only a comprehensive revisioning can avoid becoming just another fad.

Therefore, an adequate revisioning requires a rationally consistent system of thought and a firm foundation in personal experience. It needs also to be able to meet human needs, which are not simply gaps in present scientific knowledge or technology. Among such needs, for example, is a form of moral guidance that is not constituted of rules and laws. Another is the need for human connections not based on cultural, national, or racial homogeneity.

So, the question to which I am turning my attention in these next chapters is: How can we find that new message for the twenty-first century? The short answer is that we can do that if we are able to find a message that works for those impacted by the cultural changes we have just identified. It can work:

- If we make clear the inadequacy of our inherited theism, including that of John Wesley

- If we can replace that inherited theism with a new image and concept of who God is based on some firm and universal human experience

- If we can incorporate the implications of that new vision of God into the framework of Wesley's message on grace

- If we are able to address the universal human needs persisting beneath all cultural differences, including those needs that existed both in Wesley's time and ours.

Upon fulfillment of these conditions, I suggest we will have found the essential message he was delivering to the people he addressed in the eighteenth century. This is the challenge of the twenty-first century.

Wesley and Theism

Because Wesley assumed there was a continuity of human needs linking all periods of history, he was willing to import old ideas and ideals from the past. It was also the basis of his confidence in the lasting utility of the "oracles of God" that he found in the Scriptures and the view of God he had inherited.

However, when it came to distinguishing between the universal and the particular, Wesley was not as discriminating as we might wish. The fact that human beings have universal basic needs in all periods of history does not imply that ancient ideas, doctrines, or models are also universal. Cultural shifts leave the needs intact, but the means of meeting those needs may be culturally dependent. He was inclined to assume the particular ideas or models he found in his studies of antiquity were as universal as the needs of the people those ideas or models were intended to serve. For example, he assumed the practice of ritual Atonement was as universally meaningful as the need for reconciliation was universal. It is not necessarily so, and his theism is not the answer to the universal needs of human beings in the twenty-first century either.

Therefore, the importation of ideas and models from the past requires great care in distinguishing between what is universal and what must be carefully evaluated for its cultural appropriateness before importing it into a new era. We are setting ourselves to this task right now.

The secret of Wesley's preaching power was the content of his message. That is where we must look for the essential Wesley, that is, the spiritual message underneath the distracting accoutrements of his theistic presuppositions.

When he preached, something he said struck at the heart and consciousness of his hearers. There was also something in the self-awareness, not only of the poor in the fields and at the mine pits, but even of many who were among the elite of eighteenth-century English society, whom he occasionally addressed, that enabled them to respond to his message. Albert Outler notes:

> It was Wesley's message that struck home. People were not excited by his eloquence but were moved by his vision of the Christian life and his gospel of universal redemption...Hope in this world as well as the world to come delivered to people without hope.[1]

That message was his doctrine of grace, not the speculative doctrines. However, the speculative doctrines of theism supported his understanding of grace and salvation. Our critique must begin with theism because his theism was his problem. By excising his speculative doctrines and providing an alternative vision of God, we will be enabled to uncover the preaching message independent of his theistic image of God and its corollaries. In turn, that will make it possible to deal with many of those theological tangles troubling increasing numbers in these times.

In spite of the doctrines of the Incarnation and the Trinity, Wesley's image of God is clearly still theism, though somewhat muddied. The Incarnation seems to modify God's discreteness by picturing him as occupying the same space as the human Jesus while his omnipresence would not allow that limitation on the space he occupies. At the very same time, the Holy Spirit, who, as a part of the Trinity, is also God, is like the wind. He comes and goes, and no one knows whence or whither. Because he apparently moves around, he is distinct from creation, along with the rest of the Trinity, and remains an independent, discrete reality even though God is said to be omnipresent.

Furthermore, Wesley's God is still the lawgiver, judge, prosecutor, and executioner. He is still an arbitrary intervener in natural affairs and a player in power politics, that is, he bestows favored nation status, is one who punishes nations for "taking Jesus out of the schools," and so forth. Because he is free to act according to his own whims, he is someone who is subject to manipulation, bribes, and the persuasions of an almost magical use of prayer.

Even so, there is much about Wesley I like. I like it that Wesley was more interested in living the Christian life than having the correct views. I like it that he worked much harder at developing a preaching and teaching message than at filling out a full-blown system. I like it that, for him, salvation was a process, not an event. I also like the fact he rooted his teaching in a long, honorable theological heritage and he used a great deal of theological liberty in formulating a new version of the message of salvation. To the degree I am able, I intend to emulate him in respect to my concern with the Christian life, my search for a preaching message, my devotion to salvation as a process, my use of my own heritage, and my freedom to think, as they say, outside the box.

The continuities between Wesley and my proposed reconstruction are the framework of his doctrine of salvation and the universal human needs common to all times and places. The discontinuities are his theistic assumptions and traditional language on one hand and the alternative view of God and a new vocabulary with new symbolic imagery on the other.

In effect, the rejection of his theism is the rejection of all theism because the essential elements of theism remain the same in its various versions.

The Rejection of Theism

Fortunately, theism has not been the only way that Christian theologians have thought of God, however orthodox it has become. Nevertheless, the inherent irrationality of theism needs to be addressed and revealed to justify our rejection of it and our subsequent substitution of a new vision of God.

1. Other Rejections

Long before Nicea, Origen, an influential theologian from Alexandria in Egypt, struggled with the way the world had come into being and concluded it had "emanated" from God's mind. The idea of creation *ex nihilo*, which suggests the world is something totally distinct and different from God was, therefore, not a real option for him. Even the so-called creation stories in Genesis did not clearly affirm creation out of nothing but may be taken to imply an ordering of the chaos instead. However, as an emanation from God, the universe shared in God's reality in some fashion. A variety of forms of emanationism have arisen in the West, always in rejection of the idea of creation by a theistic God.

In the nineteenth century, a German philosopher named Kraus developed a theory he called pan-en-theism, a variation on pantheism, which is a theory stating all that exists is God, or, vice versa, God is all that is. Kraus' pan-en-theism, on the other hand, affirmed the notion that God included the whole of creation in himself, but, in some way, he was also transcendent to it.[2]

Some years ago, Charles Hartshorne proposed a largely philosophical alternative to theism based on Alfred North Whitehead's process philosophy. Hartshorne also called his vision "pan-en-theism." His was an interesting, sophisticated effort driven by philosophical motives. He argued for a transcendent aspect to the God who is also all that is.

In recent years, Bishop John Shelby Spong has launched a long-term attack on theism from a psychological perspective. He finds that theism in the church produces a spiritual dependency that destroys individual self-reliance. In a recent book, he writes:

> The religious promise to provide the security that enables one to cope with life's intransigence has become for me nothing more than a delusion designed to keep human beings dependent and childlike.[3]

He then proposes an alternative to theism, derived in part from Bonhoeffer's suggestion that what we need is a Christianity without religion. By this, Spong means a denial of what he calls the supernatural. His other argument against theism is that modern science has increasingly reduced the space once thought to be occupied by the activities of the theistic God. In other words, he claims theistic explanations are being replaced by scientific explanations.

We must now take our own critical look at theism and detail its deficiencies. To critique theism requires that we first understand the nature of theological images.

2. Images

Almost invariably, our ideas about who God is involve certain sensory images. I prefer image to metaphor or simile in this context because it implies a sensory experience rather than a grammatical function. However, images, including similes, metaphors, and analogies, are all risky because they can imply unintended features or aspects of the reality. For example, when one refers to the Lord as "my Shepherd," the image can suggest he cares for the sheep so they can be sheared, butchered, or otherwise used for the shepherd's own purposes. However, that was not the intention of Psalm 23.

Alternatively, take the analogy that treated justification by grace as a river with its dam and its spillway. Someone might ask, "Does this mean, if the human race does not succeed in releasing enough grace into our lives fast enough, the pressure of grace will rise until it breaks through and destroys us all?" Well, that is a part of the analogy that was not intended to apply to the way grace works. Metaphors, analogies, and other images are like that. They are risky and incomplete. They prove nothing, but they may illuminate.

Nevertheless, images, as I am referring to them, are imagined objects of the senses. Spiritual entities usually have images of some sort associated with them in a person's mind as a way of thinking about them. Christian orthodoxy's version of theism is a perfect example of the way in which spiritual entities are often experienced as sensory images.

Not only does Christian theism have its visual image of God as a male person, it has come to utilize a whole series of additional sensory images, some of which are visual. They could also be auditory. For example, in Morris West's novel *The Navigator*, the author speaks of "the voice of God—the rumbling at the deep foundation of things."[4]

The images of spiritual realities may even be olfactory, for example, "Jesus...like the fragrance after the rain." They might be gustatory, for example, "the foretaste of glory."

One might also suggest the image of the discrete God of theism is "spatial" because he is a person occupying one space while his creation occupies another space. When Wesley wrote about the omnipresence of God, he used a somewhat different spatial image. The idea of incarnation suggests space again because two realities, Father and Son, are represented as occupying the same space because both are God. There is a legal image, too, because God is a lawgiver and judge. Quite apart from the biblical images, the Trinity causes one to think of numbers, a kind of numerical image. The Atonement conjures the picture of God making a deal with himself in which he trades Jesus for the rest of humanity. A transactional image?

The fact that images are usually associated with spiritual entities is a phenomenon regularly observed when persons are asked to say something about God. The images are not always those the biblical stories give us. Many people have not been aware of the images they use, but they find themselves creating images when they must talk about God. For example, one gentleman, who was asked to say something about the providence of God, pondered a few moments and said, "I think of providence as a tapestry and God as the weaver."

When the images are only imagined, the reality of the spiritual entities represented tends to disappear because there is no way to verify their reality. That is one of the problems with the theistic images we have inherited. Contemporary people tend to require experienced realities instead of imagined images in order to believe. Therefore, a viable new image of God is going to require something better than an imagined sensory image such as Wesley's male judge (Genesis) who is three in one (Trinity), sitting on a heavenly throne (discrete or at least transcendent), making trades on the internet (Atonement), and rising up long enough from time to time to answer someone's request (prayer). As you can see, imaginary images can run away with themselves and thus become even more unbelievable.

Late in his career, in his sermon "The Unity of the Divine Being," Wesley identified the attributes of God as eternal, omnipresent, all-perfect, omnipotent, omniscient, holy, and spiritual.[5] These attributes are not totally imaginary sensory images because they are rooted in our experience of ourselves as humans. They are obviously drawn from those attributes we recognize as present in embryonic form in our own lives. In each case, the human attribute is simply raised to the nth degree and assigned to the person of God.

Temporally limited becomes eternal. Spatially limited becomes omnipresent. Defective becomes all-perfect. Limited in power to act becomes omnipotent. Limited in knowledge becomes omniscient. Sinful becomes holy. Limited by natural law becomes spiritual. At least we experience in ourselves these attributes in limited degrees. Only in the nth degree do they become imaginary and quite unbelievable, especially when applied to the same entity.

Because atheists reject some idea of who God is, along with the images they associate with that idea, it is highly likely the basic idea and image they reject is that of the theistic God as a discrete, arbitrary operator. In any case, they always reject some idea or image of God, but they say nothing about other possible ideas or images. Consequently, they may be among the best candidates for a new vision of God if it involves something actually experienced.

I do not mean to suggest everyone in the Christian community today strictly adheres to this description of the theistic God. Many persons have made their own adjustments. They have often conjured their own images, whether compatible with orthodoxy or not. I believe, however, only rare systematic theologians have attempted to produce a comprehensive or coherent alternative definition.

3. Attributes

The picture of God as characterized by a whole set of perfect attributes drawn from the imperfect attributes of human beings has been called "anthropomorphic," meaning "in the form of a human being." The problem is not with its anthropomorphism. It is with the distortion of the human attributes assigned to God. That is, when all the attributes are asserted to be perfect, they often end up contradicting one another when one attempts to explain what happens in his world.

The classic example is the question: How can a God who is simultaneously holy (perfectly good) and all-powerful allow suffering in the world? This is not a childish question; it is a very reasonable one. It arises because the theistic description of God is irrational. He cannot be both absolutely good and absolutely powerful and still allow suffering without a serious denigration either of the concept of the good or of the concept of power.

Of course, popular religion also struggles with the implications of traditional Christian theism. Confusion arises when the clear expectations, which the theistic image raises, do not materialize and we are forced to develop far-fetched justifications for that failure. Take a variation on the question asked above: Why does God allow bad things to happen to good people? The implication of the question is that God, who is both all-good and all-powerful, has nevertheless decided to allow something bad to happen. The explanation of that puzzling action often states he has secret reasons that outweigh the obvious claim (obvious as long as the theistic image of God as lawmaker and judge remains) that good persons should be exempt from suffering. That is, with a God of judgment, only those who sin should suffer punishment.

Of course, the logical consequence of this argument is the bad thing that happens is not really bad at all. Instead, it is good because God is both good and, as also omniscient, he knows best. To ask such questions about the theistic God turns us into intellectual contortionists when we seek to find answers. We become spin masters for the sake of religious politics.

On the other hand, take the glib answer I received to my childish question: "Why didn't God answer my prayer for a jackknife for Christmas?" The answer: "He did answer your prayer. He just said 'no.'" Actually, that was not a childish question either. It was an obvious question asked about the behavior of a theistic God. But, as a friend said to me, the answer was a cop-out. It was a cop-out only because a better answer was available. One might have explained that God knew such a knife was too dangerous for a small boy to play with, so he intervened with Santa Claus to prevent the appearance of the knife. So God, being all-powerful and all-wise, intervened in my case. So where is the catch in that? Well, my little friend down the street got a knife. Where was God for him?

Jesus himself, as the Gospels present him, often tried to spiritualize the disciples' understanding of God, thereby placing their relationship with God on a completely different basis. For example, the friends of Lazarus asked, "Could not he who opened the eyes of the blind have kept this man from dying?" Jesus' response was to simply turn the question away as irrelevant, implying God just does not work that way. Instead, he asked, "Did I not tell you that if you believed, you would see the glory of God?" Why didn't he give them a direct answer? He was more interested in blowing them away with the magnificence and wonder of God than explaining anything in terms of a God who was showing himself to be a fickle operator.[6]

Alternatively, consider the time, as reported in the book of Luke, when he spoke of the eighteen who were killed when the Tower of Siloam fell on them. He asked:

> Do you think that they were worse offenders than all the others living in Jerusalem? No, I tell you; but unless you repent you will all perish just as they did.

Why did he refuse to answer the question he himself posed to them? It must have been because the question presupposed a kind of God he did not want them to believe in. Instead, he turned their attention to the need for a change of focus in their lives.[7]

An especially vicious manifestation of theism appears when we combine the image of God as a lawmaker with his omnipotence. He who makes the laws and executes judgment has power over all who believe in his reality. Moreover, all who represent him are the brokers of power on behalf of that image. Not only do they control the conduct of the believers, they endow the faithful with the authority that God claims to exercise. They themselves become the judges, the prosecutors, and the executioners, wallowing in their power and flaunting their self-righteousness.

Fiction? No, fact. I know just such a congregation. The main concern of the pastor and most of the members has become weeding out those they have decided are possessed by Satan from their membership. Homes are cursed, and innocent people are shunned. The consequence has been unbelievable suffering and even lawsuits.

The history of the church is stained with the cruel exercise of power from the Crusades to the Inquisition to the Salem witch-hunts, all in the name of a theistic God who demands correct belief in order to merit salvation. In modern times, the idea of the lawgiver God continues to appeal to those seeking power. Moreover, in the Western world, political power is almost systematically wielded in the name of this image of God.

Obviously, the all-powerful theistic God has been used to explain many phenomena that science now claims to make clear. However, much remains to be understood that science can never illuminate. There are questions needing to be answered that science does not even ask, and there are existential concerns to be dealt with that psychological treatments can only cover with a veil of pretense. Therefore, Spong's rational reason for rejection of the theistic image of God is not wrong. It is merely inadequate.

Rather, the theistic image of God creates so much intellectual confusion that modern persons find it and other images associated with it both mystifying and useless. This kind of problem is found in all the three great Western religions.

4. Trinity

In addition to the previous observations about the implicit conflicts among the perfect attributes assigned to the theistic God, there are problems with the doctrine of the Trinity that render it inadequate for these times.

First, there is the claim that God is one but also three in one. The Trinity (Father, Son, and Holy Spirit) is a contradiction of God's oneness, and it has spawned some of the most tortuous intellectual manipulations in the history of the West.

Wesley's refusal to deal with the issues surrounding the doctrine of the Trinity was not due to his ignorance of the debates in the early church that resulted in the Nicene Creed. Rather, he was very well-read in those debates. However, the questions that had given rise to the big debate were also being asked all over the Christian world in those years, not only by the clerics but also by the man in the street.[8] Many of those questions are still among those that traditional Trinitarianism poses for modern persons.

As a numerical image (three in one), the Trinity has sometimes been expressed in this awkward construction: "The Father is God; the Son is God; and the Holy Spirit is God." When its traditional formulation is used, as in baptism or other rites, we get, "In the name of the Father, the Son and the Holy Ghost." That also sounds like three deities, doesn't it? As often as I have tried to explain it to parishioners or friends or make sense of it to myself, I am never satisfied. I can readily understand why John Wesley, as well informed as he was, decided to leave it alone as a "divine mystery," which seems to be another term for unintelligible conundrum.

Even if we treat "three in one" as an analogy rather than a metaphor, we encounter the problem that all analogies pose. Certain features or characteristics are comparable, while others simply do not apply and can easily mislead the casual user. In this case, for example, Father, Son, and Spirit all refer to God. So, are they all just different names for the same thing, the one theistic entity who is God? If so, then there is no "three in one" at all. The names are just that—names. Alternatively, they may refer to certain differing features or functions of God, for example, "Father" refers to his creativity, "Son" refers to his self-revealing activity in Jesus, and "Spirit" refers to the active energy of God. Neither of these matches either the classic Nicene formulation or the three in one image.

When we call God omnipotent, we treat him as a kind of puppeteer. That is, he intervenes from time to time in the world and manipulates things, either according to his mysterious will or in response to petitions and intercessions from his human subjects.

The frequent insistence that he is also immanent, that is, present within us and throughout the natural world in some form other than as an interventionist, seems to be an almost desperate reach in response to the need for relationship. In any case, it is incompatible with the theistic image of God as a completely discrete being who is capable of discretionary intervention. Or, if we treat immanence as the presence of the Holy Spirit, that also fails. It fails because the Spirit, as part of the Trinity, must remain discrete and separate. Furthermore, if the Holy Spirit is seen as the immanence of God in the world, it cannot be seen as a presence that is both given and taken away. It cannot come and go like the wind without destroying God's omnipresence and his omniscience.

Tradition has insisted that each part of the Trinity is a person. Again, can one entity be both the Father of the Son and the Son of the same Father? We have tried very hard historically through the ecumenical councils of the church to explain this strange entity, usually using Aristotelian categories in an effort to draw a coherent picture. What stymied Wesley about the Trinity was just this incomprehensibility of the "divine mystery." No less does it put off thoughtful persons in these times.

Of course, the image of the theistic Trinity may have once been awe-inspiring just because of the mysteriousness of its incomprehensibility. Treating God as a discrete entity, as theism does, thrusts us into an intellectual maelstrom, one spin of which is the Christian doctrine of the Trinity.

5. Incarnation

The incarnation of a theistic God in the human Jesus is a strange claim and invites multiple theories. The problem with the Incarnation was already suggested in previous comments about the Trinity. What do we have in Jesus? A split personality with two identities? Traditionally, we have insisted that is not what we want to say when we speak of Jesus as the God-Man. What do we want to say? God is one entity, and Jesus is another? The author of the letter to the Philippians tried to resolve this puzzle long before it hit the fan at Nicea. He says of Jesus:

> [W]ho though he was in the form of God, did not regard equality with God as something to be exploited, but emptied himself, taking the form of a slave, being born in human likeness. And being found in human form he humbled himself and became obedient to the point of death even death on a cross.[9]

The language used here seems to imply, in order to avoid having two divine selves attached to one body, that Jesus started out as some kind of divine being in a divine form or body that occupied equal status with God but was not the same as God. He then put off that divine body and put on a human body. Because his preexistent divine self was now attached to a human body, he could become obedient to whom? To a different divine being (the Father) who asked him to go to the cross? Then, Jesus and God are not one. They are two divine beings, even if they are of the "same substance" as the Nicene Creed asserted much later. Two diamonds are of the same substance, but they are not the same thing. The unity of God is destroyed, no matter how you cut it.

Stories of the virgin birth of Jesus are missing from two of the four Gospels. Mark and John, the earliest and latest of the gospels, were not interested in making a case for Jesus' divinity by affirming his miraculous conception. <u>What was important was the spiritual relationship between God and Jesus</u>. No amount of Aristotelian philosophy can describe that relationship as one of identity.

6. Atonement

The doctrine of theistic Atonement suffers a somewhat different kind of problem. The image here is transactional. That is, according to the ransom theory of the Atonement, two spiritual entities, God and Satan, have struck a deal. By giving his son, God pays Satan a ransom for the souls of sinners. In exchange, God has a claim on sinners for their salvation.

On the other hand, if one adopts what is called the <u>"substitutionary theory"</u> of <u>the Atonement (the one Wesley used)</u>, one sees God engaging in an internal transaction. In this deal, the demand of his justice that sinners pay a penalty for their sins is satisfied by sending Jesus to the cross as a substitute for all the sinners of the world. That way, God frees himself to have mercy upon the sinners who repent and plead the "merits of Christ" or trust in the "power of his blood." <u>Without first satisfying his demand for justice</u>, <u>God cannot exercise grace</u>.

We can understand how this interpretation of Jesus' death came about. The Jewish religion, with its lawmaker God, depended upon the Atonement made for the sins of all the people when each year, on the Day of Atonement, a scapegoat was driven into the desert to die, bearing the people's sins upon his head.

As a small child, I saw in my church one night a stereopticon slide of the scapegoat being driven into the dunes. I cried all night. My father raised goats for their milk and meat, and I loved them because I often had to care for them. I understood when they were butchered for meat, but I could not understand the cruelty of driving them to die of hunger and thirst in the desert, especially when they had not done anything wrong. That was not justice! It did nothing for my understanding of God as the provider of forgiveness. Nor does it now help my understanding of God as my lover when I think of him sending Jesus to the cross to pay for my sins. That strikes me still as more like cruelty than justice. However, the reason for the cruelty of it all is because it depends on God being a judge, a maker of deals, a trader, or even a bookkeeper. After all, the only reason Jesus was valuable enough to God to serve as payment for the sins of the whole world was because he was his own favorite Son. Thus, the image of Trinitarian theism makes this kind of legalism seem quite rational.

Of course, Paul, who often had recourse to his own Jewish heritage of theism, wrote about Jesus' death in terms of the old notion of Atonement: "Now that we have been justified by his blood, we will be saved through him from the wrath of God."[10]

Nevertheless, he quoted their poets when he spoke to the Greeks in Athens of the God "in whom we live, move, and have our being."[11] Thus, even Paul suggested, according to this particular passage, a highly spiritual relationship with God. It seems to reflect a more relational perspective than the idea of Atonement does as the basis of our relationship with God. At least in that one episode, the Jewish idea of a discrete theism was rejected.

At the same time, the evangelical theme in Paul's writing that "we are saved by grace through faith and that not of our own doing"[12] is an explicit rejection of salvation as a *quid pro quo* in which we exchange our good deeds, our decency, our honesty, or whatever other quality we want to put on the table for the assurance of salvation. Rather, in the verse quoted above, salvation is the gift of a new relationship with God.

As long as we leave it there, we are not committed to a theistic image of God. Instead, we trust our salvation to rest on God's sheer grace. However, the moment we turn around and make his grace depend on a bargain he has made between his own demand for justice and his desire to grant grace, we are in trouble again. We have reverted to a deal-making God.

Paul's outspoken rejection of salvation through the Law appears to be very much a spiritualization of the relationship between God and his children. Nevertheless, his reliance on the Atonement as a trade-off sucks the spirit right out of it and is a result of his old Jewish theism in which disobedience to the Law had to be paid for. That is, Wesley had God making one deal (the Atonement) so he would not have to make another (salvation by merit).

Of course, Wesley could not disagree any more categorically with the previous critique of Atonement than when he wrote to Mary Bishop in 1778:

> Nothing in the Christian system is of greater consequence than the doctrine of Atonement. It is properly the distinguishing point between Deism and Christianity. "The scriptural scheme of morality," said Lord Huntingdon, "is what everyone must admire; but the doctrine of Atonement I cannot comprehend." Here, then, we divide. Give up the Atonement and the Deists are agreed with us.[13]

Mr. Wesley was wrong about the result of giving up the doctrine of the Atonement. As we shall soon see, it does not necessarily result in the adoption of deism. Instead, it allows us to see God in a far more intimate view than the cold, distant light projected by deism or even original theism.

By depending on the Atonement for justification Wesley accepted a legal relationship appropriate to a theistic image of God. That is, he did not reject the "imputation of righteousness," but he kept the "impartation of righteousness" as the beginning of sanctification. In his teaching about sanctification or holiness, he also strove to affirm a personal faith relationship between the individual and God rather than a trade-off between the two. However, that was also a trick because the grace necessary for sanctification also depended, for Wesley, on the Atonement. His theistic image of God makes such inconsistencies possible, maybe even inevitable.

Wesley's problem was that he was trying to synthesize the two rival traditions of evangelical faith and holy living.[14] He wanted to say both justification (pardon) and sanctification (holiness) are by God's grace, but he also wanted to say the human subject was free and responsible for trusting the Atonement of Christ and for using the means of grace. A transactional view tended to remove the responsibility because it depended upon an external relationship (the legal relationship of the Atonement) rather than an internal relationship between the human spirit and God. This problem led to Wesley's polemic with the Calvinists concerning the doctrines of "irresistible grace" and "perseverance of the saints."

The Calvinists said the limited Atonement (for the elect only) wrought through Jesus' death was a deal struck and therefore irresistible (irresistible grace). Thus, the new relationship between the believer and God, dependent on the Atonement, was irreversible and legally binding (perseverance of the saints). Spiritual relationships were not involved. They were only transactions between legal entities.

Wesley accepted the universal Atonement made by Jesus, which he also viewed as a done deal. God's grace could now be offered to everyone, but it was not irresistible. For him, the ongoing relationship between the believer and God was dependent on the believer freely continuing to believe in the Atonement and freely choosing to use the means of grace. But, Wesley made that human freedom itself dependent upon the retroactive effects of the Atonement. Thus, the theistic God, as a discrete individual, tends to make even that relationship external instead of intimate. So, in spite of Wesley's efforts to maintain the relationship between persons and God as an internal, spiritual relationship, his theism keeps externalizing these relationships, that is, legalizing them. Wesley's instincts were right, but his theistic heritage created problems for him and continues to make it very difficult to appropriate him for our own time.

Other theories of the Atonement, such as the moral influence theory, appear to be efforts to avoid the embarrassments of a deal-making God, but they may retain other problems that theism poses, such as the possibility that God could still be relied upon to do things that one should take responsibility for himself (Spong's concern).

7. Grace Itself

Finally, the way Wesley dealt with the concept of grace is self-contradictory because it depends on his image of God. The problem manifests itself in the debate between Wesley and the Calvinists.

Wesley tried to keep both grace and responsibility by deriving responsibility from the gift of prevenient grace. The Calvinists could not buy that maneuver because they had the idea the Atonement was limited to those elected by the sovereign God. But prevenient grace, also bought by the Atonement, was universally available rendering all persons free to believe. Thus the conflict.

In the end, Calvinism itself fails the test of reason because it also depends on the Atonement purchased by Jesus' death. Therefore, both are finally left without grace because, for both, grace is conditioned on the death of Christ, and conditional grace is self-contradictory.

The basic problem for both Wesley and Calvin is their theism, that is, their view of the kind of God they are dealing with. As long as he is the judge, his first demand is justice. Grace must be somehow manufactured. They just went about manufacturing it in different ways.

Of course, the counterargument to the previous statement is, because it was the Father who freely gave his Son, the only condition involved was one God himself met out of his own love. But that renders the Atonement unnecessary because it requires God's grace to be available as well as effective before the Atonement. It also requires that Jesus become a pawn in the sovereign God's hand without any human freedom to decide as a free individual for himself. Therefore, his obedience does not even come into play, and no merit can be attributed to him. Consequently, there is no righteousness to be either imputed or imparted to sinners.

Furthermore, it runs again into the Trinitarian tangle. That is, the Father demands obedience from the Son so that obedience may be credited to the account of the sinners of the world who owe God for their own disobedience. But the Son is also God. So he is apparently paying himself in the act of obeying himself, a very strange kind of transaction that effectively destroys the unity of the Trinity.

We can see how Wesley himself sometimes strayed in the synthesizing process from a strict adherence to the theistic image in his efforts to maintain the relationships between man and God personal and spiritual rather than legal and logical. But he always came back to it. He moves back and forth between the need to spiritualize salvation and the transactional or legal nature of his theistic foundation. This produced some of the inconsistencies and confusions that his enemies often complained about.

When trying to answer questions either for parishioners or for ourselves, this is also very much the problem we struggle with. Often, we ignore the implications of our theistic assumptions in order to provide answers of a more relational nature. Traditional theism characteristically implies legal relationships, even though the prophets and Jesus, as portrayed sometimes in the Gospel of John and very significantly in the noncanonical Gospel of Thomas,[15] have resisted those implications. We ourselves often resist the legalisms without consciously recognizing their source in the theistic image of God.

Both Calvinism and Wesley tried finding different ways of affirming "salvation by grace through faith." Neither was entirely successful. Wesley failed from a rational point of view; Calvinism failed from both a spiritual and, finally, a rational perspective as well.

Jesus and the early church struggled to reject the theistic image of God, but it kept creeping back in. I believe Christianity, almost without realizing it, was a rebellion against the theism of Judaism and the legalized relationships it entailed. From Jesus forward, the Christian faith has been an effort to spiritualize the faith and all its relations. It is an effort that has yet to produce appropriate results. The decisions at Nicea and later councils set the Christian movement back by centuries.

Neither Wesley's version of theism nor any other theism will be capable of meeting the challenge of the twenty-first century. When we understand differently the idea of God and the way we think of the Incarnation and of Jesus' death, then a revised understanding of grace, faith, and salvation in its several forms or stages will begin making their response to the existential needs we all have, including our need for understanding.

All of this will enable us to focus directly on spiritual, emotive, and will-based relationships rather than logical or legal relationships among ourselves, God, and other persons as well. Then we can also get rid of the supermarket concept of prayer (that is where the products we want are there for those who please God, that is, can pay) and the lottery concept of miracles (that is where we put in our nickel and hope for the best).

We can then find common spiritual ground with the whole human race. This is our theological task.

How Does Theology Work?

Perhaps the best way to think of this somewhat formidable term "theology" is simply to say that "theology is God-talk." What else, in fact, is preaching? Furthermore, there is nothing more critical to our teaching, counseling, and worship than clarity on what we mean when we say "God." Any explication of Christian faith must always begin with some theory about what or who God is, even though the history of a faith is based on the experience or the awareness of some mystery. Karen Armstrong, in *A History of God*, says:

> Throughout history men and women have experienced a dimension of the spirit that seems to transcend the mundane world...However we choose to interpret it, this human experience of transcendence has been a fact of life.[16]

Early on in the human saga, it was enough to give a name or names to those mysteries. At some point, they acquired images by which they were identified. That theology usually makes use of images is even illustrated in modern philosophical theology, for example, Tillich's geological image of God as the "ground of being."

Humans then began seeking ways to deal with them, to communicate with them, to placate them, to ask questions about them, and to seek to explain them. When questions about the mystery and what the images implied began appearing, the effort to describe and define them gave rise to a whole system for dealing with them. Thus, a religion began evolving. In essence, that is how religions with their theologies, rituals, symbols, and stories came into being.

However, each preacher and many who are not and never will be preachers have been, in some measure, forging their own theological understanding out of the teachings of their religious inheritance, their own dissatisfactions, the alternatives they have encountered, and their own life's experience. In fact, this is exactly what Wesley himself did. It is also what humans have always done when old notions of God—or the gods—have begun to fail. Armstrong has made a compelling historical case for this claim. She formulates her conclusion as follows:

When one conception of God has ceased to have meaning or relevance, it has been quietly discarded and replaced by a new theology.[17]

She explains the reason that is possible is that "it is far more important for a particular idea of God to work than for it to be logically or scientifically sound."[18]

This fact explains why Wesley's less than coherent message nevertheless worked for those who did not demand coherence, but responded to the imagery of his message of salvation. It was less successful with those who did insist on reason and were therefore leery of anything that smacked of emotion.

However, orthodox theism is failing to meet the universal human needs in the present time, in large part just because it is logically unsound. Increasingly, the modern mind will not accept an internally illogical understanding of God. That is why the rather striking historical phenomenon reported by Armstrong is repeating itself in our time.

The effort to find a substitute image of God clearly requires a significant degree of theological liberty in these times and is, therefore, in line with historic precedent. Wesley's own theological project also involved both an eclectic approach and a liberal dose of theological liberty for its accomplishment. In that sense, I am securely settled in the Wesleyan tradition.

Finding the right formulations for addressing the universal human needs in Wesley's own time also required that he adapt and refocus the classical or orthodox language of the early church and his own Church of England tradition on the universal needs of the people he addressed. For him, those needs were dressed in the garb of the poor and the hopeless. They were not looking for logical coherence. They were looking for hope.

Moreover, it meant picking and choosing special foci for his preaching. He simply accepted the mysteries of the great doctrines of the Trinity, the Incarnation, and the Atonement as presuppositions. But, for his description of the Christian life, he focused on the doctrine of salvation as a lifelong process, that is, he focused on the game. Though he wanted to know "how to get to heaven,"[19] his teaching about salvation was only incidentally about heaven. It was primarily about living in communion with God or, to say it differently, about "taking the journey of faith."

Thus, in Wesley, I find a great deal of theological liberty even while finding a willingness to draw heavily on the past, especially on the period prior to the Council of Nicea in AD 325 when the doctrine of the Trinity was formulated and the groundwork laid for the doctrine of substitutionary Atonement. In a similar way, our theological vision will draw upon Wesley's teaching and still be freely reformulated.

This project will require the exercise both of imagination and reason. Of course, most theologians have recognized that no explanation or description of God is ever adequate. Even so, Wesley affirms the universal need for understanding:

> The desire of knowledge is a universal principle in man, fixed in his inmost nature. It is not variable, but constant in every rational creature, unless while it is suspended by some stronger desire...It is planted in every soul for excellent purposes...But although our desire of knowledge has no bounds, yet our knowledge itself has. It is, indeed, confined within very narrow bounds; abundantly narrower than common people imagine, or men of learning are willing to acknowledge.[20]

Though he did not recognize the inherent irrationality of the theism he had inherited and, therefore, failed to question it, he vigorously defends the use of reason in a letter to Dr. Rutherford:

> You go on, "It is a fundamental principle in the Methodist school that all who come into it must renounce their reason." Sir, are you awake? Unless you are talking in your sleep, how can you utter so gross an untruth? It is a fundamental principle with us that to renounce reason is to renounce religion, that religion and reason go hand in hand, and that all irrational religion is false religion.[21]

The universal need to understand, when confronted with the unknown, cannot be obliterated from the human psyche. Without concepts produced by human thought, we are unable to function in terms of ideals, goals, and actions. Therefore, some concept of God, however imperfect, is essential to our spiritual life. I am taking this stance when I discuss the new concept of God required by the effort to formulate a new vision for these new times. This position does not claim that reason can discover the whole truth. However, without conceptualizing, we are left at sea, disoriented and ineffectual.

Most theology is an intellectualization of some image of God, along with a set of associated images. It utilizes images, pictures, and stories that paint a larger picture of reality. For example, the biblical story from Genesis to the Revelation is such a construction composed by many different people during many years under a variety of historical circumstances. The final test of a theological construction cannot be the certainty of its absolute truth. Rather, the bottom line is its ability to meet the universal needs of human beings. But, when the concept itself begins to show its incoherence, it becomes unbelievable and ceases to work.

A new vision can afford to be neither incoherent nor based on an imaginary image. It must be based on some experience of reality.

A New Focal Image

Currently, there is a very broad groundswell of interest in things spiritual. Spirituality rather than religion suggests the promise of an exciting future.

Of course, the appeal of science remains strong. The products of science and technology and their promises for the future, especially in the world of computer technology and genetic engineering, will continue to occupy our attention. Moreover, science will continue to answer many questions about how things work in the natural world.

Is it possible that scientism and its claims to solve the problems and answer the significant questions will dominate this new century and finally destroy the burgeoning interest in spirituality? I see no chance of that. The suggestion that science or any kind of cultural change will ever obliterate the sense of awe inspired by the numinous or the mysteries and therefore remove the need to name them or seek some kind of understanding by which to cope with them seems ill-founded to me.

This is especially certain in view of the inherent inability of language and the formulations of science to reduce even natural realities to definitions and theories. If this last claim sounds excessive, remember all language, even scientific language, is comprised of abstractions like stars, germination, atoms, stem cells, and so forth. Such terms denote no single thing, only sets of things. Even descriptions of illustrative examples utilize the generalizations of language.

Mystery remains and will remain. Science will continue to fail when it attempts to explain the world of spirit or respond to the underlying, universal needs of human beings. Therefore, I believe the twenty-first century will see a declining degree of trust in the ability of science and technology to deal adequately with those universal human needs that will always be present.

Some of the contemporary interest in the spiritual dimension of life takes occult forms, for example, the fetishes of the Caribbean and the popular Candomblé (of African origin) as well as the more philosophical spiritualism of Kardecism found in Brazil. Some of it also draws on Eastern religious traditions such as Zen and Transcendental Meditation. Certain features of intergalactic space fiction and film, such as "the Force" and "grocking" make a strong appeal. Even television angels and psychics seem to have struck a chord of longing. There is a growing interest in ESP, clairvoyance, and other paranormal phenomena, and spiritual or faith healing.

Even the phenomena associated with the charismatic movements, which have had another renaissance in the churches during the last thirty years or so, may be seen as manifestations of the current fascination with spiritual matters. The media may remain essentially skeptical (or even cynical), but I believe noninstitutional spirituality is in. It may well be a manifestation of the primitive awareness of something that, to use Armstrong's phrase, "transcends the mundane."

I was fascinated recently when I visited a farmer's market in Vermont to see a large display of "Garden Spirit Sticks." These were attractive sticks from two feet to six feet in length, carved with figures and often in the form of Celtic crosses. They are thrust into the ground to a depth of eight inches perhaps. Their use is whimsically described on attached cards as follows:

> It's been said invisible elf-like creatures called Elementals inhabit the forest and woodlands. Their energies balance and harmonize their surroundings to help dispel negativity. Garden Spirit sticks are created to attract these spirits to your yard or garden. Earth, metal, wood, water and fire come into play in the making of these sticks. These five energetic forces of nature blend to enhance their ability to attract these beings. Elementals will dance in your garden to help bring fruitful harvests.

The fact people are paying good money for the spirit sticks only proves they have extra money to spend. However, even such myths and their popularity say something about our fascination with the idea of spirits. Their association with nature tells me the idea of spirit does not rule out the natural world as antithetical to the spiritual, but it suggests it is intimately engaged with the spirit.

I do not mean, by citing these spirit phenomena, to affirm the validity of any of them. I am only pointing to the currency of the idea of spirit.

The problem with much of the interest in things spiritual is that it is a patchwork of ideas and practices with little or no coherence. There is no rational context for the pieces, no framework or integrated point of view, and no comprehensive vision.

At the same time, it appears to me the idea of spirit is capturing the imagination of youth as well as many older, disillusioned (but thoughtful) adherents of our religious institutions. Therefore, I believe what we need right now is a theological vision that can provide a context, a framework, and a point of view for this growing interest. I believe the focal image required is that of the *primary reality of spirit.* We need to respond to the current fascination with spirit and engage the universal existential exigencies of human beings by putting forth a new focal spirit image of God based on a universal human experience with all the possibilities this image suggests.

We will systematically resolve most of the problems identified by substituting this fresh vision of God and creating a spiritual theology. We will then have an understanding for our preaching, our teaching, and, most importantly, our living. Such a vision can speak powerfully to these new times. To articulate such a message is our task in these next three chapters.

5

Spirit Is God

If we are going to substitute a new vision of God for Wesley's theism and the other speculative doctrines of Trinity, Incarnation, and Atonement, we need an image to work from that avoids the insubstantiality of imaginary images and starts from something that is real in our human experience. Such an image will illustrate the possibility that more than one theological vision might be able to serve the same universal needs of human beings, depending on the time and intellectual context. To grasp this point is to move significantly toward the discovery that Wesley's preaching can be used in our time without accepting all his theological presuppositions.

The vision I propose neither purports to be a fully developed system nor takes into account the various versions of spirit suggested by religious, psychological, or philosophical thinkers. Instead, it uses what appears to be a very commonsense meaning of spirit that eschews the more esoteric and slippery uses of the term that Outler discusses in his article, "Spirit and Spirituality in John Wesley."[1]

The following, based on the simple notion that spirit is the primary reality, is my cryptic definition of a spiritual theology: God is all spirit, and all spirit is God.

Versions of such a vision of God have appeared throughout the history of religions. Hints of it have peeked through the testimonies of the Christian Gospels and the cogitations of the early Fathers of the Christian church.

A perusal of some of the noncanonical materials reveals that many of the issues that arose in our critique of the speculative doctrines were already the subject of controversy long before the canon of the Scriptures was established. This was also true prior to the Trinitarian and Atonement debates, which were not resolved until the Council of Nicea or later. For example, Jesus, according to the *Gospel of Thomas*, was not the exclusive source of salvation for the world. But, as Elaine Pagels has argued, all persons were treated there as embodying the same spiritual possibilities as did Jesus.[2]

In this respect, Thomas disputed the Gospel of John, which affirmed Jesus' exclusive role in the familiar verse:

> God so loved the world that he gave his only son, so that everyone who believes in him may not perish but may have eternal life.[3]

In disputing the book of John, Thomas also rejects the Christological basis for most Atonement theories. Because the choice of John over Thomas for the New Testament canon had not yet been made and the orthodox speculative doctrines were not yet promulgated, this issue was still open during the first centuries after Jesus' death. In this sense, the present chapter is a continuation of some very early debates within Christian history.

My purpose here is to elaborate a focal image of God as spirit without the encumbrances of theistic residue. Unfortunately, most challenges to orthodoxy have had legal and forensic tag ends fluttering like banners in their wake. It is not an easy task, and I may well have let slip telltale signs of my own struggles to shed the God of laws, judgments, and sacrifices for whom grace is a secondary attribute conjured up out of the primary attributes assigned to God. Grace as unconditional love cannot be derived from the attributes of lawmaker, judge, and the sacrificial system. Therefore, if we are to use grace in our revisioning, we must protect it from any surreptitious condition that we might allow to cling to it.

The image of God as exclusively spirit will meet one of our basic requirements because it is a reality all humans experience in that we experience ourselves as spirits. Thus, we know what we are talking about. It does not posit an entity whose reality is purely speculative and whose works and deeds are taken to provide dots we can connect in order to come up with the existence of a divine entity. This is what at least one of the traditional philosophical arguments for the existence of God attempted to do. Of that entity, we can know nothing nor can we discover the connections between the entity and the works and deeds we do experience.

The focal image of God as spirit will also enable us to both accept responsibility for our own healing and offer us the immediate gifts of God for our spiritual growth. It will do this without forcing us to contend with the theistic conflict between freedom and grace. Therefore, it promises salvation through spiritual growth without turning our own efforts into salvation by merit, thus dispensing with grace.

Our relationship with God is understood as intimately spiritual rather than legal, but it still reflects the fundamental shape of Wesley's doctrine of salvation. It also retains Paul's own evangelical formulation:

> For by grace you have been saved through faith, and this is not your own doing; it is the gift of God, not the result of works, so that no one may boast.[4]

It should be noted, however, this quote is taken from the Atonement context that Paul provided earlier in the same chapter.

In a similar manner to that in which the speculative doctrines provided the presuppositions for Wesley's doctrine of salvation, our vision of God will provide the foundation for our doctrine of salvation as a theological treatment of growth and wholeness. Even Wesley felt comfortable using a therapeutic metaphor to describe the process when he wrote:

> "But can Christ be in the same heart where sin is?" Undoubtedly he can; otherwise it never could be saved therefrom. Where the sickness is, there is the physician.[5]

The new vision of God for the twenty-first century will enable us to preach, teach, and live the essential Wesley.

The Nature of Spirit

My starting point is our knowledge of the self-aware human spirit. Wesley himself found this knowledge to be as sure as any knowledge we can have, even though many questions still remain. He asks:

> Well, but if we know nothing else, do not we know ourselves? Our bodies and our souls? What is our soul? It is a spirit, we know. But what is a spirit?...How is the soul united to the body? A spirit to a clod? What is the secret, imperceptible chain that couples them together?[6]

It has been encouraging to discover that Ralph Waldo Emerson, the New England transcendentalist, believed the human spirit was the touchstone for all human understanding. Not only was this true for our knowledge of the soul, it was true for our knowledge of nature as well. Of preaching, he wrote in his "Divinity School Address" in 1838:

> But with whatever exception, it is still true that tradition characterizes the preaching of this country; that it comes out of the memory and not out of the soul; that it aims at what is usual, and not at what is necessary and eternal; that thus historical Christianity destroys the power of preaching, by withdrawing it from the exploration of the moral nature of man; where the sublime is, where are the resources of astonishment and power.⁷

Is our knowledge of the human spirit any clearer in the twenty-first century than what it was in the eighteenth century of John Wesley? Surely not very much. Yet, we know it from inside, as Emerson was aware. We know what spirit is almost without having to describe it. Nevertheless, the image of spirit bears some inspection. It requires us to make an effort to understand, at least to the limit of our imperfect powers to know. There is certainly no surer starting place than this.

Clearly spirit, as we experience it in ourselves, is not an amorphous something out there, like a specter or a ghost. It is not simply a feeling or emotion like the "spirit of Christmas." Psychologists, philosophers, and religionists all have their own ways of analyzing and dividing the human personality. We are accustomed to hearing of the psyche with its psychological features and pathology. We speak of the soul, which is usually one kind of thing for religion and something a little different for nonreligious thinkers. On the other hand, we suppose spirit to be some set of qualities—perhaps mysterious and hidden—of the human personality.

When I treat spirit as my focal image, I am specifically not using it as a metaphor or a simile. Image, in the sense in which I am using it now, is not a sensory image. It is, instead, an unmediated experience of a reality. It is like being able to see without the use of an eye. In other words, I gain this knowledge of spirit from inside it because, as a self-aware human spirit myself, I experience it with immediacy. Therefore, its reality is not speculative. We all immediately know its nature. It includes whatever we otherwise characterize as mind, soul, psyche, or spirit.

The reality that defines spirit is self-awareness. It is whatever experiences itself. Self-awareness is not one of the qualities that belong to spirit. Instead, it constitutes its essence as spirit. It is the center around which the spiritual realities are collected that it recognizes as being parts of itself. Therefore, spirit is understood only by reference to what we call "the human spirit." In fact, on the level of the human species, the spirit is also aware of its own self-awareness. It therefore has the power of self-examination.

Spirit is aware of the other powers it derives from its self-awareness and exercises. I cannot produce a catalogue of all the spiritual powers. Moreover, everyone will have a different way of naming them. However, the following are eight powers that seem immediately apparent. First, spirit thinks. It reasons. That is, it analyzes, synthesizes, relates, classifies, deduces, induces, and, in a word, understands. Second, spirit imagines. It foresees what might become real. Because it is also intelligent, it can distinguish between possibilities and impossibilities. Third, spirit evaluates things and actions, that is, it assigns values. Values are degrees of importance we attach to things in relation to taste or utility or to actions in relation to their results. Fourth, spirit decides. Using imagination, intelligence, and evaluation, it makes choices among alternative possibilities. Fifth, spirit acts. It follows its decisions with action, employing the body and/or the various powers of the spirit to achieve results.

Sixth, the combination of the powers to decide and act can be called the power of self-control or free will. Seventh, with these powers in combination, spirit becomes creative. It makes or manufactures things that have not existed before. Eighth is the power of communication. There are, in our experience of our own spirits, the phenomena of extrasensory perception and thought transference. These are somewhat controversial, but careful attention will usually persuade most people they are experiences that occur almost daily. They are so common an occurrence that we seldom notice them.

There are destructive, divisive powers of the spirit as well, such as the powers of alienation, resentment, hatred, jealousy, exclusivity, and so forth. Each power of spirit exists in tandem with its negative, that is, its absence. The absence of any power of the spirit may also exert an influence. That is, it may become a power in itself. For instance, spirit includes the power of survival, that is, the drive to live. The negative of the power of survival is the absence of that drive, a power that may come into play in the act of suicide. Spirit, as I am using the term, is active through its many powers, positive and negative as well as good and bad, to produce effects.

Other powers of our own spirits may be seen as combinations of those mentioned previously. All these spiritual powers are elaborations of the central reality of self-awareness. Therefore, it is apparent that spirit is power. It is alive and active. Thus, our knowledge of spirit is derived from the reality and nature of our own spirits.

The World of Spirit

The above characterization of spirit forms the basis for my assertion that there is a "spirit world." However, by that, I do not simply mean there are many human beings running around the world and each is a discrete spiritual being, resulting in a world full of as many spirits as human beings. It is true we speak of human beings as spiritual beings, but they are not discrete and independent beings. As atoms are interconnected and interactive in the natural world, human spirits are interconnected like atoms in the spirit world. The power of spiritual communication binds the spirit world together inseparably because it belongs in varied degrees to all self-aware spirits. It is the glue of the spirit world.

Perhaps we can think of ourselves as fish in the ocean of spirit. The ocean is so close to the fish and so much a part of them that they do not see it. It is their life, and it flows through them as they move through it. So, the world of spirit is the ocean in which we live, move, and have our being. Mostly, we do not see it and do not know it is there, just because it is spirit like we are.

Take an analogy from St. Paul. He writes of the church as the body of Christ:

> For as in one body we have many members, and all the members do not have the same function, so we, though many, are one body in Christ, and individually members one of another.[8]

Similarly, I want to suggest each human spirit and any other self-aware spirits inhabiting the animal (or even the plant) world are members of the one all-inclusive spiritual body that is the spirit world. Each is different in its combination of spiritual powers. Some are healing and creative; some are divisive and destructive. As the members of a body may be diseased and require healing, the individual spirits constituting the spirit world are often defective and dysfunctional and require healing and completion. As the head of the body is ultimately in control, we may posit a self-aware head of the spirit world whose purpose is to heal itself by making its parts whole.

Thus, all spirit minds are part of the world of spirit on analogy with the physical organs that are parts of the physical body. The head of the physical body knows and wants what is right and good even while some of its organs are diseased and dysfunctional. Just so, the self-aware head of the world of spirit is whole in itself and wants wholeness for its parts because they are often defective and in need of healing. The communication holding all spirits together in one spiritual body, or world, occurs at some level all the time. However, our awareness of it is still spasmodic and episodic. It remains to be more fully developed, as do the rest of the healing powers.

Of course, spirit is not necessarily limited to human beings. What I am trying to get my mind around here is the idea that much—if not all—of the natural world is inhabited by spirit. That spirit world functions by what we may call "spiritual regularities." They bind the whole spirit world together in one magnificent reality through communication. They are also in constant interaction with the natural world. Thus, we can think of each individual self-aware center—whether human, animal, or even plant—as a property or member of the whole spirit world. In the self-aware head of that spirit world, the unifying, healing powers dominate the destructive, unhealthy powers. But, in its members, the unhealthy, divisive powers are still functional.

We can affirm a self-aware Head of the spirit world because we ourselves experience self-awareness as the unifying center of our own spirit life as well as the control center of most of the body's functions. It is self-evident that no spiritual powers can exist without the experience of self-awareness. For the phenomenon of self-awareness, no natural explanation exists. Thus, all human spirits—as well as lower levels of spirit life—are part of the world of spirit.

One may object that the hypothesis that there exists a self-aware Head of the spirit world cannot be proved in any scientific way. Without a doubt, that is correct. Nevertheless, it is at least as conceivable as the theistic hypothesis and is far more coherent and productive.

In this manner, the focal image of God as spirit has become our definition: All spirit is God, and God is all spirit.

The World of Spirit and the World of Nature

We are now entering an area that will likely seem especially problematic for our discussion. Nevertheless, these questions demand some kind of serious response.

The interaction between the spirit world and the natural world is a phenomenon often observed under the rubric of body/mind relationship. Spirit, as self-aware, is thus distinguished from body or nature as essentially unaware of itself. Wesley himself marveled at this thought, "I am now an immortal spirit, strangely connected with a little portion of earth."[9]

This distinction between spirit and nature may meet resistance from those who are excessively disturbed by the threat of dualism. However, the distinction must be recognized because all distinctions that language expresses require acknowledgment. The interdependent relationship between the two, as described subsequently, may help to alleviate any qualms.

To that end, let us switch for a moment to the great biblical stories of creation where some of the spiritual powers mentioned previously appear. In the first Genesis story, chaos and the "formless void" already exist so that creation is actually the imposition of order, law, and system by the Spirit of God upon that raw material. According to that story of creation, spirit is the power to create something new out of whatever it has at hand. However, we can understand and believe that, not because of the story of creation, but because we do that ourselves all the time.

In the biblical story, the Spirit of God is said to have brought order out of chaos, thus suggesting spirit is intelligent and nature depends on spirit for its form and law-abiding ways. Philosophically, the question is whether the natural world already has a structure the mind discovers or if the mind imposes order on the raw material of nature according to the requirements of the mind itself. However, I want to claim all order in the natural world is both originated and understood by the spirit's powers of creativity and intelligence. I cannot prove this affirmation, but I have made it because even the order we appear to discover in nature is not known or knowable except by mind. In other words, the only place where I experience order immediately is in my own mind. My knowledge of order in nature is mediated rather than immediate, and it is mediated through my mind.

In the story, not only did the Spirit that moved over the chaos and the formless void in the act of ordering possess the power of intelligence, it also had the power of imagination. Intelligence, or the power to order, requires some kind of guidance. The power of imagination is absolutely critical if the spirit is to exercise creativity. The architect needs to see the final product of his planning before he can draw up the specifications. The power of imagination is a major part of such creativity. Thus, positive powers often work interdependently with one another.

Neither story of Creation in Genesis, however, says anything about creation *ex nihilo*, that is, out of nothing. That idea does not clearly appear until the fourth century AD.[10] Neither can we find any such power within our own experience of the human spirit.

The relationship between spirit and nature may, however, be further conceived through the substitution of emanation for the concept of creation *ex nihilo*. In fact, this was Origen's theory long before the notion of creation *ex nihilo* appeared. Is it not at least conceivable that spirit can create something quite new out of itself as emanation suggests?

After all, some scientists have suggested self-consciousness is an emanation from a certain configuration of cells in the brain and the nervous system of the body so that the body itself is self-aware. However, the reverse seems even more readily possible because we know directly that spirit includes the powers of thought, order, imagination, and creativity. We do not know that about neutrons or electrical impulses. So, at this point, I think we must recognize the possibility that spirit can originate something quite new out of itself. In this case, the natural world may be thought of as an emanation from primordial Spirit. Such a world would be law abiding and potentially transformable into spirit again if the natural world at some point should no longer be necessary.

Furthermore, the origin of human and other centers of self-awareness may be thought of like the phenomenon of self-reproduction in the natural world. What a fertile image this suggests! The spirit world gives birth out of herself to new spirits. Perhaps a better analogy is that, as a body constantly produces new cells that remain a part of itself, the spirit world produces new spirits that remain a part of itself. These new spirits are then attached to the bodies she also has emanated.

The network of spiritual powers/values is probably as complex as the laws of the natural world, if not more so. But, when I speak of spiritual laws or of a spiritual power producing or causing something, I am using the analogy of nature. So, my discussion of the spiritual powers and the values we assign to them does not propose to describe this network adequately or provide anything like a textbook for the exercise of spiritual power. It merely suggests the kind of process with which we are dealing when we speak of spirit.

The spirit world is a realm whose own laws not only govern communication within the spirit world, but it also interacts with the laws of the natural world as well. This relationship may be suggested by the analogy of the distinct, but interdependent, relationship between the realms of physics and chemistry or between the body and the mind in the human being. Each has its own laws that limit and cooperate with the laws of the other.

Take physics and chemistry. The laws governing the movements of the pistons in our automobiles are affected by the laws governing the chemical composition of those pistons. Chemical laws cooperate with the mechanics of the pistons' action when they keep the pistons hard, and they limit their action if their chemical composition renders them too soft or too flexible. Similarly, the role of the mind in the healing process impacts the body while the pathology of the body may render the mind defective. Doctors can sometimes treat ailments of the spiritual powers with drugs. Gene therapists and psychotherapists also may try to manipulate them. Therefore, we may readily conceive of a world of spiritual laws both limiting and cooperating with the laws of the natural world.

May we not take this body of spiritual laws to be the referent of the "Word" or "Logos" of which John speaks in his magnificent prologue?

> In the beginning was the Word, and the Word was with God, and the Word was God. He was in the beginning with God. All things came into being

through him, and without him not one thing came into being. What has come into being in him was life, and the life was the light of all people. The light shines in the darkness, and the darkness did not overcome it.[11]

John's view seems to be that spirit is law-abiding, but it is also successfully engaged in the struggle between light and darkness. That spirit should involve laws at all may seem like a contradiction. Still, we are aware spirit works according to its own unique regularities we only vaguely understand. In fact, we attempt to use them whenever we pray, engage in other spiritual exercises, or make self-controlling decisions.

I have been calling the various properties or qualities of spirit by the term "powers" or "power/values" because spirit is not a passive object. It is a living, moving, energetic reality. It is constantly changing, affecting the world around it and being affected by its environment.

At this point, you may wonder what has happened to the traditional idea of soul. Frankly, I want to avoid this concept that has been variously defined by both theologians and psychologists. For example, it was traditional in earlier times to locate the soul in a realm somewhere between the subconscious and the understanding. Thomas Moore, in *Care of the Soul*, says:

> We live in a time of deep division, in which mind is separated from body and spirituality is at odds with materialism. But how do we get out of this split? We can't just "think" our way through it, because thinking itself is part of the problem. What we need is a way out of dualistic attitudes. We need a third possibility, and that third is soul.

So now he has a tripartite view of the human person instead of a dualism. It is helpful—neither for my purposes nor his resistance to dualism—to complicate things further. I believe the image of spirit can both avoid an unnecessary complication and bridge the split about which Moore is properly concerned.[12]

The following is an example of what I have in mind. When a healing of the body takes place, it often happens apart from any conscious effort on the part of the mind or spirit of the individual. An antiseptic or a medication is applied, or perhaps a diseased part is surgically removed. Then the wound or illness heals. It heals because the things that block its healing have been removed. It may even heal without treatment. Is the healing power simply a natural process of the body? Clearly, natural laws come into play when physical healing occurs, but the removal of the impediment may often be the effect of an interaction between spiritual and natural laws. The power of the self-aware spirit is often brought to bear through prayer and other spiritual disciplines. It then works to remove both the natural and spiritual barriers to healing, thus allowing the healing process to go forward. The healing power of the spirit is another way to think of the power of unity, the power seeking oneness and peace in place of disunity and dysfunction.

The natural laws and spiritual laws constantly interact with one another. They conflict with one another. They influence one another. They limit one another. They assist one another. I suggest the area of their most intimate meshing is the subconscious layers of the spirit, variously identified and described by psychologists.

Consequently, we may suppose the body exercises influence on the subconscious levels just as it does on the conscious levels. Of course, the subconscious also affects the body's functioning. Therefore, this shadowy area between conscious self-awareness and the body is the area in which body and spirit are most thoroughly in constant interaction. It is the interface between spirit and body where the laws of both realms mesh, but it cannot exist apart from its relationship with some self-aware center and its conscious powers.

In fact, the phenomenon of hypnosis suggests some self-aware powers can disappear into the subconscious but continue to influence the body. For example, one may be driving along while working on a sermon in one's conscious mind or perhaps carrying on an imaginary conversation and be totally unaware of the requirements of safe driving. Nevertheless, all the rules of the road are observed, stop signs and red lights are obeyed, and the car makes all the right turns necessary to arrive at home. Then, thinking back, one cannot remember stopping at a single light or making a single turn. When one's attention is so intently fixed upon one function, others may disappear from the conscious mind but continue to function in relation to the body. Similarly, one may deliberately bring forward into self-awareness certain powers or functions that have been temporarily buried.

For all these reasons, one must assume the subconscious is continuous with self-awareness and does not exist apart from it.

Thus, the interface between spirit and body takes place through the interaction of spiritual and physical laws operating both consciously and unconsciously. No separate postulate of soul is needed. Again, Ockham's Razor, that is, the simplest explanation is always preferable to the more complicated, seems to apply here.

Is it any wonder we are often in a state of confusion about ourselves? All of this is why I often think of myself as a mystery living in the midst of the Mystery. It also explains the epitaph I have asked to be inscribed on my gravestone: "He gloried in the Mystery."

So, we still have left—far and away—enough of mystery about the life of God and what we've called the "spiritual laws" by which he operates that we can appreciate and even respond emotionally to the following contemporary spiritual:

> I fell on my knees and cried holy! Holy, holy, holy! I clapped my hands and sang glory! There was glory, oh glory! Glory! I clapped my hands and sang glory! I clapped my hands and sang glory! I sang glory, glory to the Son of God! I sang glory to the son of God![13]

As I write this, I have begun to wonder if there can ever be any other imagery with the power of the traditional images of certain parts of the biblical story. My response to my own question is: Of course, we can use some of the great images, even in the twenty-first century. When we do, they must be pegged to the new understanding. Furthermore, new images, new poetry, and new music will arise out of the creativity of human spirits touched by a new vision of the Great Spirit.

The Purpose of the Spirit Who Is God

Powers/values of the spirit provide the raw material from which decisions are made. In the previous discussion, I assumed the ideal result is unity, harmony, and peace. I believe this to be the goal toward which God, that is, the spirit world, is working.

The power of unity can be conceived to be the power that seeks such things as connection, union, love, understanding, reconciliation, and wholeness in relationships as well as healing and peace. It is the power that seeks to overcome its opposite, alienation or dysfunction.

The destructive or divisive powers/values sometimes seem to achieve ascendancy. But, in the grand sweep of human history, the movement appears to be toward harmony and peace. Another observer may draw a different conclusion. However, the testimony of our own experience is more persuasive than history. To me, it seems self-evident that, not only are harmony and unity more desirable than alienation and disease, they are, for that very reason, more powerful.

If it does not seem self-evident to you, think of it this way. As a human spirit, I have certain needs that are also essential for every spirit, including the Spirit who is God. Primarily, these include the need for connection and unity as well as for wholeness and peace. Because this must also be what God most needs and desires, it will be more powerful than its negative. Already in his own self-awareness, he is holding the negatives in subjection and seeking throughout the spirit world to subdue the negatives in all his parts.

The power of unity heals the body, mends the tensions between body and spirit by subduing and robbing the divisive spiritual powers of their energy, integrates the mind and outward behavior, and seeks to create what we often call "peace of mind." It seeks the removal of enmity and distrust among persons and groups of persons. Unity and peace are the touchstone, not only for our understanding of the purpose of God, but for all our decision making as well.

St. Paul lists what he calls "gifts of the Spirit." He says these vary from person to person, but they are "activated by one and the same Spirit, who allots to each one individually just as the Spirit chooses."[13] Paul also writes about what he calls the "fruits of the Spirit."[14] He says they are always signs of the Holy Spirit's presence. We can see that Paul's lists of fruits and gifts of the Spirit are suggestive, but they are far from being adequate to the task of identifying all the spiritual powers. Nevertheless, both the fruits and the gifts identified by Paul would seem to function as spiritual powers/values in our context.

For example, Paul says healing is a gift that a person is either given or not as the Holy Spirit chooses. Of course, there are persons who seem always to produce alienation and dis-ease wherever they go. However, I believe this is very rarely seen. Rather, there is usually some balance between the two, and nearly every person exercises some power of healing in certain circumstances, even without knowing it.

Emotions and attitudes are also active, energetic powers that always exist attached to some center of self-awareness. What may sometimes seem to be free, floating spirits, for example, when the mob spirit appears to take possession of a crowd of people, are actually the power of spiritual communication or, perhaps better, the power of thought transference at work. This is the power that, according to spiritual laws or regularities, also enables such phenomena as ESP and clairvoyance to occur. Attitudes or moods, as well as ideas, are often communicated nonverbally and apart from body language. Furthermore, I suspect what we often speak of as "charismatic presence" is an aspect of this power and is very common in our human experience. So, just think about this power of spiritual communication, and pay close attention to see how often it might occur in your experience in the course of a single day.

Self-awareness thus becomes the source of our freedom to choose. Not surprisingly, Paul includes self-control among the fruits of the Spirit. What is that except the power to decide and act? The absence of this freedom to choose would be submission to impulse, habit, or conditioned responses. I do not mean to suggest all impulses, habits, and conditioned responses are bad. Instead, self-control implies the power to make willed changes in them rather than submitting to them without examination. They may be judged to be undesirable in some circumstances but desirable in others. That judgment is often necessary because such habits and impulses do produce results (exercise power), and it may be those results will determine if they are desirable or not. The greater the self-awareness, the greater the freedom or self-control.

It is necessary to remember that many—if not all—powers can be used either for destruction or peace. Even the value/power of patience may produce negative results. What if Jesus had been patient that day in the temple when his anger boiled over and he, no doubt with a certain degree of calculation, overturned the money tables of those who were exploiting the people? Is anger not then sometimes also desirable, as might impatience be when its absence is apathy? However, anger and impatience are desirable only if they are controlled anger or impatience, that is, designed to achieve a positive end.

Anger that seeks only to destroy is certainly undesirable when tested against the goal of unity or peace. I know it gets complicated, but we have always known that making decisions is a risky business at best.

Another power/value suggested by Paul that comes into play in the process of making decisions is generosity. Its opposite is greed. Generosity is the ability to give without expectation of recompense. It is at least one way of defining what we mean by grace or unconditional love. That is, love may also be called "unconditional giving." Separately, Paul lists love and calls it "a more excellent way" and designates it as "the greatest of these."[14]

Love implies giving those things that enable the object loved to become what it is meant to be. My analogy for this kind of generosity or love is the act of caring for or nurturing. For example, one does specific things when caring for a rose bush so it will produce the best possible roses. However, these measures are somewhat different from the specific ways in which one nurtures a tomato plant in order to produce the best possible tomatoes. Unconditional generosity does not seek to make an oak tree out of a carrot seed. Love seeks the fulfillment of the potentialities of the object loved, not what the object loved can do for the lover. The Great Spirit's purpose for every human spirit is that it become fully human. This is an appropriate way to think of unconditional love or grace.

Paul often mentions joy as a spiritual value/power, but joy is a very special power that is given as the individual becomes increasingly aware of his own freedom and commits himself in hope to participate in the life of the spirit world. He experiences joy in the very struggle to subdue the destructive powers and bring about the harmony or unity that the Spirit who is God seeks to establish throughout the creation. In other words, one rejoices in one's own struggle because one trusts the victory set before him or her. One resents neither the struggle nor the pain often accompanying it. I think of it as the joy of hope.

It is important to distinguish joy from the traditional sense of happiness. Usually, we think of happiness as the pleasure or contentment produced when we achieve or receive something we have strongly desired and which we may or may not have worked for. Happiness focuses on a pleasurable outcome while joy focuses on the exhilaration of the struggle.

All these spiritual powers, in their relations to one another, are found intertwined and interdependent in individual spirits. They interact according to their own laws or ways that are exceedingly complex, but they are present everywhere in the life of the spirit world.

My experience of life reveals to me that spiritual powers, like unity and hope or alienation and despair, are always being communicated by extrasensory means among the individual spirits in the spirit world. However, the Spirit who is God encompasses all these centers of self-awareness—along with their constituting powers—and constantly seeks to guide and empower those individuals in the use of their powers. By his own powers of communication, he seeks to enhance all the powers that contribute to unity and peace so that division and disease are finally subdued.

As with many perceptions, there are several ways in which one may see an object, usually depending on the purpose of one's investigation. The preceding analysis of the human spirit in terms of spiritual powers/values serves well our concern with the complex freedom of the human spirit to exercise self-control and cooperate with the purposes of the Great Spirit.

The freedom to find options, evaluate them, calculate their results, and act, which comes with self-awareness, is most fully available to the Spirit who is God himself and only secondarily to human spirits. Obviously, destructive spiritual powers, such as despair, divisiveness, alienation, and so forth, make their opposites both conceivable and desirable. Nevertheless, they are doomed at last because the goal of the Great Spirit is harmony, unity, and peace.

The consuming purpose of the Spirit who is God cannot be fully realized until God, guiding and enhancing our own efforts, has made all spiritual life perfect, that is, has subdued all divisive powers by the greater powers of unity, love, and peace.

Degrees of Self-Awareness within the Spirit Who Is God

I have previously implied and now want to affirm that there are variations of self-awareness among human beings and other species of natural beings in which spirit may be found.

In one of his lectures, T. S. Eliot observed that, the higher the level of self-awareness, the greater the suffering. At the same time, those whose level of self-awareness was lower suffered less from the same conditions.[15]

In any case, the more aware we are of self, the more acutely we are aware of our isolation and the more deeply we sense the need for connection. We may begin to see ourselves as discrete entities and the rest of the world as "the other" or even as the enemy. A sense of alienation and loss can become acute.

There appears to be a strange about-face involved in the process of becoming increasingly self-aware. Finally, the irony is that, as one becomes increasingly isolated and alienated by his growing self-awareness, he approaches a level in which his connectedness with the larger spirit world may become more apparent. However, I doubt if this shift ever happens without some kind of invasion of his privacy that appears to come from without. This phenomenon suggests a reversal that is reminiscent of the Wesleyan doctrine of rebirth. You will remember that, for Wesley, rebirth or regeneration is the reversal of the direction in which one's life is going when one is justified by grace through his faith. He is forgiven his sins and initiated into a new life of faith in the grace made available by the Atonement. In other words, he may have become increasingly alienated, but he now finds himself accepted.

Bishop Spong also believes self-awareness creates the awareness of our mortality because it appears to leave us vulnerable. What may happen is that, as infants, our self-awareness is embryonic until we have begun to recognize increasingly our separation from the rest of the world. In the earlier condition, the fear of death is going to be less. However, we eventually begin to identify our mortal bodies with our own reality and take our values from the mortal world. As we do so, the fear of death begins developing. We learn the natural body dies, and that means we die as well. Again, as we become aware of our connectedness to the spirit world, our fear of the death of our natural body decreases. I believe this fits with the findings of child psychologists as well and perhaps with those of gerontologists, too.

The first Genesis story of creation states that human beings are made in the "image of God." The literal sense of this expression suggests the human spirit is a mere reflection of God so that God himself remains a discrete entity as theism maintains. Clearly, I must prefer the second story of creation in Genesis that remarkably says:

> [T]hen the Lord God formed man from the dust of the ground, and breathed into his nostrils the breath of life (the Hebrew uses the same word for breath, wind and spirit); and the man became a living being.[16]

According to this account, the breath animating the human being is the same breath or Spirit who is God. One may read this to suggest (again) that, once a human spirit comes into being, it does so as a part of the self-aware spirit world that is God. In other words, God gives every single human being a part of himself. Therefore, the qualities or powers constituting the Spirit who is God are also present as parts of the human spirit, though defective. That is, the divisive powers are not yet subdued. Some of the powers of the Spirit who is God may not be present at all in a particular defective human spirit. However, some degree of self-awareness must always be present for spirit to exist. Furthermore, variations of self-awareness exist among human beings in relation to limitations their bodies may place upon them as well as in relation to their degree of personal development. Varied degrees of self-awareness must also exist on a million other levels throughout the universe.

The following incident proves nothing with certainty, but animal lovers have observed myriad similar phenomena. According to our veterinarian, my big, beautiful, tiger-striped, gray cat had a heart murmur. But no sign of a problem was visible to the untrained eye. Then, as I sat on the couch reading one evening, he walked up to me, stopped, and looked directly into my eyes. Ordinarily, he would have jumped onto my lap to be held, but he just stared at me this night. His eyes showed no slits, but they were like deep, black holes. He looked at me for the longest time before moving on to stare with the same intensity into my wife's eyes. When he was ready to go out, we let him go. The next morning, we found him lying dead on the lawn where he had simply stopped and placed his head on his outstretched paws. Did he know he was about to die? Did he tell us good-bye? I do not know, but I am sure he knew something was different. Moreover, it felt like he had told us something important, even though we were not sensitive enough to understand.

The entire natural world is suffused with spirit on an unknowable number of levels of self-awareness. Each spirit, at whatever level of awareness, is a property of the spirit world, potentially in spiritual communication with all the rest and an integral part of the spirit world who is God.

Perhaps the instincts of the animists were not as preposterous as we imagine. How far down the chain of being does self-aware spirit descend? For example, experiments have made it quite clear that plants respond to environments where human emotions are strong.

In any case, when the human person suffers or rejoices, God is also suffering or rejoicing. When the human spirit is torn and struggles and hurts, God also feels the struggle and pain within himself because human spirits are a part of God and his self-awareness.

It follows that the spirit world, that is, Spirit who is God, is both sovereign over the entire creation (in traditional terms, transcendent) and pervasive in nature (immanent, in traditional language). As a self-aware spirit, he is both separate from—above, below, or beyond—the created natural world and immersed within it. Perhaps we can say it like this: It is the Spirit's own self-awareness that transcends, and his presence and participation in the life of the spirit children he has produced out of himself that makes him immanent.

The Perfection and the Imperfection of God

The previous discussion implies the presence in God of destructive and pathological powers due to human participation in the world of spirit. It also affirms the presence of deficient spirits in the lower forms of life.

Therefore, when we speak of the perfection of God (of the self-aware spirit world), we are saying, in his self-awareness, the divisives exist as possibilities, but they are kept in submission by the unifying forces and exercise no power there. This is possible because of his perfect self-awareness and self-knowledge.

At the same time, all the negativity and toxicity present in those other self-aware spirits, which also form part of the spirit world, remain. That is, the alienating powers at work within the world of created spirits are clearly part of the life of the Spirit who is God and are exercising their power and producing results. Therefore, it is in the immanence of God that they remain still to be subdued. So, the Great Spirit is at work, subduing all the alienation and disease remaining within his immanence. In the same way, our divisives resist the healing of our spirits, the dysfunctions or illnesses in our bodies and spirits continue to resist his healing powers. Nevertheless, by his powers of unity, peace, and love, he is busy healing himself like the spiritual power of healing we seek to use to heal the illnesses of our bodies. He is healing us in healing himself. In healing ourselves, we are healing him. Thus, he is perfect in his transcendence, but he is imperfect still in his immanence. He is perfect in his purpose, but he is imperfect still in his parts.

Through this struggle, it is his purpose to create and sustain a world of cooperation and harmony, a world in which all the parts work together harmoniously. It is a world in which the freedom of all self-aware spirits remains intact. It is a world in which healing takes place and reconciliation bridges chasms and alienations. It is a world in which the destructive powers are subdued within the life of all self-aware spirits. Thus, the spirit world will be fulfilled in wholeness with only the potentiality of negativity remaining. However, the presence, even of potentiality, causes ongoing stress and will always require constant vigilance. That sounds a lot better than a static condition completely free of tension or struggle, that is, a condition in which one has no more goals and no more reason for being.

Perhaps an appropriate analogy for the perfection and the imperfection of God would be the spiritual struggle that Paul describes when he says:

> I do not understand my own actions. For I do not do what I want, but I do the very thing I hate...Now if I do what I do not want it is no longer I that do it, but sin that dwells within me...For I delight in the law of God in my inmost self, but I see in my members another law at war with the law of my mind, making me captive to the law of sin that dwells in my members.[17]

In other words, the human spirit may have a perfectly good will and purpose, yet it must struggle against the divisives that remain. Just so, the Spirit who is God, though completely in control of the negative powers within his own desires and purposes, must still seek to heal every part of his body, which means every other self-aware spirit. So again, we are responsible to cooperate with God in his self-healing. Is there not then a powerful poetic truth expressed in the title of Kazantzakis' book *Saviors of God*?

This aspect of our vision of God is not so far removed from some of our theistic traditions as we might imagine. One of those traditions is that Satan, once a member of the panoply of angels created by God, has fallen. While he has become evil, he remains a part of God's creation and does not occupy equal footing with God. He remains finally subject to God. There is a sure instinct at work in that myth. Evil is not only a part of God's creation, but he is finally subject to God's rule. While that myth thus remains true, our description of God provides a far less poetic and far more rational explanation of the presence of evil in God's world. It also brings God alive in a new way.

Furthermore, this vision of God means human life is inescapably a participation in God's struggle, either seeking to subdue the dividing powers or allowing them to gain ascendancy.

The Names of God

Having sketched a vision of God as all spirit and all spirit as God, I am now ready to suggest how this new perspective changes what may be said about the other speculative doctrines.

In AD 325, the Council of Nicea decided to declare specific doctrines of the Trinity and the Incarnation to be the official teaching of the church. Thus, the theistic God was said to be constituted of the Father, the Son, and the Holy Spirit. Greek philosophical concepts were utilized to describe the relationship between these three parts of the deity. Obviously, this was a major adjustment in the theistic image of God. However, the early legal characteristics of God as lawmaker, judge, and so forth remained. In fact, the doctrine of the Trinity, among other things, facilitated the characterization of God as both judge and the one who arranged for grace to be available through the Atonement made by Jesus.

As part of the Trinity, Jesus was declared to be the Son who was, therefore, of sufficient value to the Father so the Father could use him, in one version, as a ransom to be paid to Satan for the souls of men. In another version, he was sufficiently valuable to the Father so that he could be used as payment for the sins of mankind and thus satisfy the Father's demands for justice. The Atonement of Jesus met God's demand for justice, which, in ancient times, had been met by blood sacrifices throughout the year and finally on the Day of Atonement. Jesus' equality with the Father was necessary in order for his death to be a sufficient payment. Trinity, Incarnation, and Atonement were thus a required package because the basic image of God was still that of lawmaker, judge, prosecutor, and, sometimes, executioner. The doctrine of the Trinity actually facilitated the doctrine of Jesus' Atonement.

However, under the spirit vision of God, it is possible to identify a new set of presuppositions altogether for our doctrine of salvation by grace.

First, what shall we do with the Trinity? Of course, many persons who still use the Trinitarian formula have little knowledge of the Athanasian definition and often seek to explain the Trinity in other terms altogether. And it is possible, of course, to play around with the formula without accepting the original three-in-one doctrine. For example, either Father or Mother may be applied to the sovereign, magnificent, and gracious reality we have described. In either case, it is only a metaphoric name and remains inadequate, as does our use of the masculine pronoun. However, either name at least has the value of attributing to the Spirit who is God both creative power and the kind of love that freely and unconditionally gives.

Along with Spirit and Son, either Father or Mother may imply major features that characterize, again inadequately, the reality of the spirit world as it meshes with the natural world it emanated and emanates. However, this abandons the three-person characterization of the Trinity in favor of three major functions of the Godhead, an option that may not even have occurred to Wesley. In other words, if they name functions, they are not three things but three functions of the same one thing.

I once had a book on my shelf called *Spirit, Son and Father*. I think it was written by Henry Van Dusen. Though I finished reading the book and set it aside, the title has popped into my mind from time to time. It occurs to me that someone might even want to substitute that title for the orthodox Trinitarian formula. For example, first, Spirit is the fundamental reality. Second, the portrait of Jesus as the one in whom the Spirit was incarnate in all the fullness that is possible within the limitations of a finite body and who displays the process by which the Spirit makes peace may be called the Son. Third, Father is Jesus' favorite name for the Spirit, but such a rendering results in three different kinds of things pretending to be one. That is, Spirit is the real thing. Son is a pawn of the real thing. Father is the pawn's name for the real thing.

Disregarding Jesus' choice of a name, someone might prefer to speak of the Spirit, Son, and Mother. Here, the name Mother is one we might choose simply because we like the image of a female reproducing herself in the act of creating the world of self-aware spirits. However, that would leave us with the same problem.

As to the use of Son, it may well carry the connotation of the incarnation discussed subsequently, but, traditionally, it also tells us how precious Jesus was to his Father. He was so precious the Father could use him to pay for the sins of the whole world. It might be difficult to delete that connotation from the title of Son, even if he is the Son of the Mother instead of the Father. The difficulty with his role as pawn remains: If God used him as payment, he is a pawn. Then there is no compliance, merit, or righteousness made available by his death.

There is another risk in applying either Father or Mother to the Great Spirit. The risk is that we may be tempted to fall back again into the theistic picture of a being who manipulates and is manipulated. Furthermore, to use Spirit as part of the formula suggests that spirit is one among several qualities or functions belonging to God rather than the Spirit's identity with God.

For all the above reasons, any Trinitarian formula is highly problematic. My own preference is to refer to God as the Great Spirit. Of course, others have beaten me to that name, too, but it encourages me to use masculine and feminine pronouns interchangeably when referring to God. It usually depends on the context. However, such a practice is also likely to confuse and distract the reader or hearer.

While Wesley's traditional theological structure did not provide any explanation of the manner of God's tripartite unity, he said he felt comfortable using Trinity, but he did not feel it was necessary:

> I dare not insist upon anyone's using the word "Trinity" or "person." I use them myself without any scruple, because I know of none better. But if any man has any scruple concerning them, who shall constrain him to use them? I cannot.[18]

Essentially, it is Wesleyan to allow great latitude in the use of names as well as in explanations of the classical affirmations. Like Wesley, I would never think of insisting one use any Trinitarian formula to speak of God. Personally, I will stick with "Great Spirit" or, perhaps more awkwardly, "The Spirit Who Is God." Given our vision of the Great Spirit, we might even want to think of God as One and Many. But we must simply delete the orthodox meaning of the Trinity.

The Role of Jesus

1. Incarnation

I am well-aware we do not have a complete, unbiased picture of the historical Jesus in the Gospels. However, we have an image, a composite picture taken from the four Gospels, of him as the sinless incarnation of God himself who is, nevertheless, a real, live human being. In many religions, there are ideal individuals. They are sometimes gods in human form or "heroes," as Joseph Campbell characterizes them. They are ideals to be imitated as Thomas à Kempis suggests in *The Imitation of Christ*.

In this picture of him, we may see the positive, unifying, healing, reconciling spiritual powers in the process of subduing the divisive and alienating properties in all their manifestations. That is, the negatives of all unifying spiritual powers were represented as completely subdued in such a way that the early Christians could say, "God was in Christ reconciling the world unto himself."[19] In Philippians, Paul says Jesus "emptied himself and became obedient."[20] Even so, the story says he was tempted as we are. But these quotes also reflect a theistic presupposition.

However, we may be able to think of these affirmations in a nontheistic way. The picture the author paints seems to be of God as a discrete being while Jesus was another discrete being whose form was divine like God's. Then Jesus, who was already divine, gave up his divine form and was born in human form. Though divine, he was not too proud to submit himself to the cross in obedience to God who sent him. Thus, Jesus was divine, but he was not God because he became obedient to God who sent him. Of course, that may have left him short of enough value to pay for the sins of the whole world, but that does not seem to be the author's concern at the moment.

Obviously, this was written before the orthodox doctrines of the Trinity and the Incarnation came into being. The position of Arius, who opposed Antanasius at Nicea, was somewhat reminiscent of this view. However, it differed in that, for Arius, Jesus was never in a form equal to God's. He was a being on a level somewhere in between the human being and God. However, the view of him in Philippians more nearly fits that of Arius than that of Athanasius.

My suggestion now is, at some point or over a period of time, the fully human Jesus allowed the Spirit who was God to take over his own spirit, still divided like that of any other human being, and subdue all its negative powers. The story of his temptation in the wilderness suggests such an occurrence. In other words, because the Spirit who is God had perfected the human spirit of Jesus, Jesus had become the complete and ideal human person. His divinity and his complete humanity were one and the same. That fits nicely with our understanding that God is all Spirit and all Spirit is God.

This idealized biblical image of Jesus presents a picture to be imitated. That is, it represents the possibility that is open to every human being in this life or beyond. Whenever that possibility is being realized, it is as though an opening has been made in the dam. The water of the Great Spirit, by its own pressure, begins to flow in, widening the crack as it enters. Thus, all the negativities come under siege.

However we interpret the previously cited passages, we can affirm, from our spirit image point of view, an idealized biblical image of Jesus is of one in whom the Great Spirit lived and worked. This image is not in conflict with the laws of nature. Instead, it is in limitation and cooperation with them. In other words, the

Spirit who is God, in whom all the negatives were subdued and robbed of their power, is fully realized in this picture we have of Jesus.

Taken together, the Gospels do not present a totally coherent account of Jesus' teachings, life, and death. They do not submit to proof texting. However, I am inclined to believe the Gospel of Thomas, which was not included in the canon of the New Testament, may well have been rejected in favor of the Gospel of John, as Pagels suggested. It seems quite possible the choice was made as part of the resolution of the conflict between Athanasius and Arius because both were written in the same period. My point is: There was not a unanimous view of just who Jesus was during the ante-Nicene period and the choice finally made was driven by the need to put on a united front as the Church confronted the world.

To be sure, we would like to know as much as possible about the historic Jesus, but, in the end, that knowledge is not critical. The idealized biblical image of Jesus, which I have suggested, can still serve its role in our spiritual life.

On the human level, we all know the experience of suffering with those whom we love. Sometimes we call it empathy; sometimes we call it compassion. A low-level kind of spiritual communion or identification takes place. If we are to emulate the image of Jesus, then it means, as our connection with other spirits increases, we will also suffer with those who suffer and rejoice with those who rejoice. This is the foundation of all social concern and action. Can this power of spiritual communication be imitated? Perhaps it cannot be imitated, but it happens daily among us. Without a doubt, it can be nurtured and improved.

Through the Spirit the Scriptures say was in Jesus, the healing of bodies also took place. Is this also a power that may be imitated? I believe it happens in various degrees all the time. Constant prayer and contemplation can also nurture it.

Can the Spirit who is God empower our spirits to love, trust, reconcile, make peace, show compassion, rejoice, and be thankful? In other words, have the mind of Jesus? Of course!

Doesn't it make sense to think in this way of the incarnation of God in Jesus? I think it does for those who are able to delete the notion that Jesus was somehow a being with different potentialities than the rest of us poor humans and instead take him as the Pioneer of their faith, their Hero, and their Ideal.

2. Atonement

The story tells how Jesus was crucified by the destructive, alienating spiritual powers (the principalities and the powers) that ruled in so many of the affairs of humanity. Thus, by his submission to the cross, Jesus revealed to the world the fact that the unifying spiritual powers had destroyed in him the power of the divisive ones. The divisive powers in the world that crucified him could not break the creative and healing spirits of unconditional love in him. This was the grace to forgive his crucifiers, his trust in the goodness of the Great Spirit, or "the joy that was set before him" that enabled him to "endure the cross."[21]

That was possible because the Spirit who is God had wholly taken possession of Jesus and subdued the destructive powers in him as they were subdued in his (God's) own self-awareness. Then, in Jesus' resurrection, death, the ultimate form of destruction in the natural world, was overcome. That is, it was shown to be incapable of destroying the creative powers of the Great Spirit because Jesus lived again. In this way, the story of Resurrection shows how natural death was stripped of its destructive power by its opposite, the power of spirit.

The powers of unity, reconciliation, peace, and wholeness were shown to be more powerful than the divisive and destructive spiritual powers, both in individuals and in the world. That possibility is offered to all persons by the grace of the Spirit who is God in all persons. This is the case, and it is not because God has made some transaction. It is because this has always been the nature of God. He has always been struggling to subdue the destructive powers within and subdue those same poisonous powers as they exist in human society.

Those who look upon Jesus' death and resurrection, as the witnesses have remembered them and/or reconstructed them in the Gospels, are shown the spirit world at work. It is seen to be at work in the terrible struggle between the destructive powers and the creative powers the destructive could not destroy. It is seen in the creative power of spirit to destroy the destruction of death.

Therefore, Atonement is not necessary because the power of generosity (grace) has always belonged to God by reason of his transcendent perfection. We need finally to delete the Atonement. However, the picture of the suffering and death of Jesus, as it were, provides a microcosm of the cosmic struggle and victory of the Spirit who is God, a struggle into which all human beings are invited to enter.

This fresh, intimate vision of the reality of God, drawn from our knowledge of our own spirits and a major theme of the Old and New Testaments, allows us to delete the old theism, the Trinity, Incarnation, and Atonement. It then enables us to substitute new understandings of who God is, how he was ideally present in Jesus, and what the death and Resurrection can mean for us in the twenty-first century. These understandings will serve as the presuppositions for a different version of Wesley's essential message of salvation.

6

Things of the Spirit

What does this new vision of God mean for Wesley's doctrine of salvation? What will it look like without the theism that underlay all his preaching and teaching? This will be the essential Wesley we need to preach in the twenty-first century.

It presupposes the vision of God as spirit, a vision reflected throughout this chapter.

In Wesley's sermon on "The Circumcision of the Heart" preached at Oxford in 1733, he began focusing on the doctrine of grace. During the next thirty years, most of his preaching dealt with the topics of justifying and sanctifying grace. During the last twenty or so years of his ministry, his preaching seemed to focus much more often on matters of morals and lifestyle. Because he continued to assume the order of salvation, he saw them as a manifestation of the process of sanctification.

Those later years also saw the publication of sermons with a more developed treatment of his doctrine of prevenient grace. A few sermons sought to update earlier treatments of justification and his running debate with the Calvinists. Outler observes:

> This concern with the *ordo salutis* and his cumulative insights into its wholeness may be recognized in all the developments in his preaching and in his personal pilgrimage as well.[1]

Wesley understood the search for salvation is, in fact, the care of the soul. That is why he could affirm his desire to know the way to heaven and simultaneously focus his attention upon the present life of the spirit. This present life was not to be seen as a way to buy or earn one's way into heaven. It was a means of becoming what a human being is meant to become. Among other things, he called it "holiness." His doctrine of perfection, which we know he thought to have been his major contribution to Christian thought, was an integral part of holiness. The specific doctrine of sanctification by grace was his way of integrating holiness of life into his total view of salvation. Even the living of the Christian life in this world was possible, for Wesley, only by God's grace.

His view of the doctrines of salvation differs from his approach to the great mysteries. It is not that the speculative doctrines were unimportant, but they were simply assumed as necessary background. Therefore, his preaching is focused on the question of how one appropriates God's grace, both for forgiveness (justification) and holiness (sanctification). Many of his sermons exhort his hearers and readers to certain kinds of behavior, yet he never abandons his insistence that even one's moral efforts are possible only by God's grace. Over the years, he came to regard his entry into heaven as a matter he was also willing to entrust to God's grace.

The fact that Wesley saw grace as his essential message is attested, not only by the focus of his early preaching itself, but by the way he valued his early preaching. He required the preachers in his movement to preach no other doctrine. In 1763, the conference of preachers officially adopted a "Model Deed" after Wesley's original deed had appeared in 1746. It was a guide for the use of the Wesleyan "preaching-houses" and specifically provided that preachers in those houses should "preach no other doctrine than is contained in Mr. Wesley's *Notes upon the New Testament* and four volumes of sermons."[2] Later sermons dealing with many other topics—though they assumed his doctrine of grace—were never included in this requirement.

Clearly, Wesley intended his earlier sermons to serve indefinitely as the doctrinal standard for the Wesleyan movement. In his mind, preaching was fundamental to all else he did in the course of his ministry. Moreover, grace was the key concept.

We now need to reformulate Wesley's doctrine of salvation by grace through faith by examining it through the prism of our spirit image perspective. Our examination will take the shape of the four stages or gifts of grace identified by Wesley.

More Than Natural/Prevenient Grace

To use spirit image language, we are now talking about the unconditional gift of a life that is more than natural from the beginning. That gift is our life of spirit that gives us freedom to change directions and grow up into spiritual maturity. Even the living of the Christian life in this world is possible only by the free gift of the Great Spirit.

For Wesley, as for Protestantism in general, salvation is a gift of God's grace received by faith. That process begins with his gift of spirit to each person. Wesley called it "prevenient grace." We can think of it as the gift of our spiritual reality as self-awareness.

Though Wesley does not characterize God's gift of our natural bodies as an act of prevenient grace, we must also see that, as a free gift from the Great Spirit, the nature of the Great Spirit is to give all things with no preconditions. That is what Wesley calls grace and we may call the "spirit of generosity," or unconditional giving.

However, in our spirit image approach, giving is not an act of handing something off to someone else. Rather, if I try to form an image of the process, I see the Great Spirit who is God conceiving and giving birth within herself to self-aware centers of spirit for each of which she creates or "emanates" our natural bodies.[3] Conjure your own image for this, if you prefer. I find the feminine image quite compatible with the context. In any case, it is an act of unconditional love or grace.

Another way to speak of it might be to say that each of us woke up one day to find he existed as an individual spirit and possessed a body. So, both body and spirit are given with no strings attached. However, Wesley's prevenient grace applied to the spirit of the human being only.

Whatever we do with our freedom to choose, it can be forfeited only by our own choice to submit to habit, conditioning, or even to threat. But, even for that act of forfeiture, we are responsible. Therefore, we are both completely indebted for the power to choose and completely responsible for the choice. There is no contradiction involved here between responsibility and total indebtedness. They are not opposites.

Is there a better word than "grace" to denote the reality of our indebtedness? The closest I can come is "unconditional love." I also like "unconditional giving" or even "generosity." However, I confess that no term still evokes quite the same emotion in me that "grace" does. Perhaps the popularity of the hymn "Amazing Grace" suggests "grace" may continue to resonate with power for a very long time into the future. I remember entering the Student Center on a college campus on many occasions during the 1960s and hearing Judy Collins singing "Amazing Grace." It was not laden with other religious terms. Only one verse (not quoted here) even mentions "the Lord." The popularity and power of the hymn all rests on "grace."

> Amazing grace, how sweet the sound that saved a wretch like me! I once was lost, but now am found; was blind, but now I see. 'Twas grace that taught my heart to fear, and grace my fears relieved; how precious did that grace appear the hour I first believed. Through many dangers, toils, and snares, I have already come; 'tis grace hath brought me safe thus far, and grace will lead me home. Yea, when this flesh and heart shall fail, and mortal life shall cease, I shall possess, within the veil, a life of joy and peace.[4]

Whether we use the traditional term or not, it is by such unconditional generosity of the Great Spirit that we are alive. We are both indebted and free.

For Wesley, faith was to be understood as analogous to the natural senses of sight, hearing, and so forth.[5] It was a spiritual sensitivity that could perceive the reality of God and other things spiritual in a manner similar to the way the eyes can perceive objects presented to their line of sight. He distinguished this aspect of faith from assent (*fides*), trust (*fiducia*), and assurance. He held that faith was the spiritual perception of spiritual realities and preceded both assent to true propositions (which draws on reason), trust in the reality (perceived and understood), and the assurance of grace (which was an emotion attached to an idea). Therefore, no person ever had the right to take credit for his faith because the spiritual sense was a gift of grace. Even faith was by grace, and Wesley could subscribe wholeheartedly to the Pauline theme that "we are saved by grace through faith and that not of our own doing."

Wesley writes that the devil believes and trembles, but that:

> The true, living, Christian faith, which whosoever hath is born of God, is not only assent, an act of the understanding; but a disposition, which God hath wrought in his heart; "a sure trust and confidence in God, that, through the merits of Christ, his sins are forgiven, and he reconciled to the favor of God."[6]

In this passage, he seems to suggest that assent was possible, apart from saving faith. Even for Wesley, the analogy of sight was not quite adequate to express his meaning because a disposition of trust was also necessary. Moreover, that trust was added to the spiritual perception that created assent. Hence, spiritual perception + assent + trust = faith.

This grace/faith relationship is basic to Wesley's doctrine of prevenient grace. It is the grace or gift that is given to every human being by which he is made free to participate in his own salvation through his faith. Wesley's motivation was to find a way to preserve both "salvation by grace alone" and human responsibility.

I share Wesley's motivation. Our spiritual vision of God provides a ready-made solution to this dilemma because I find the most satisfactory foundation for understanding the meaning of faith is the common experiences of self-awareness and spiritual communication (ESP, thought transference, and so forth). It is more adequate because it has more nearly the meaning of an internal connection or mutual participation between the believer and the Great Spirit who is God.

Our primary awareness of God is our awareness of ourselves because we are part of God. However, what I want to call "faith" begins with the initiative of God (grace) as he seeks to impress his positive values/powers upon the consciousness of the individual human spirit through the power of spiritual communication. Our awareness of the rest of God, that is, the rest of the sprit world, is also a function of spiritual communication. In fact, such a relationship is precisely what one would expect to find within the spirit world. Such thought transference appears to include the transference of attitudes and emotions, as well as spiritual powers.

These powers, and therefore faith, are present in some degree in every self-aware individual, thereby fulfilling the function of Wesley's doctrine of prevenient grace in the sense they are spiritual powers in their early stages of development and growth. However, they are given as a spirit first comes into existence, not by the retroactive grace secured by the Atonement.

Coming Home/Justifying Grace

Wesley's doctrine of justification by grace involves the following pieces: Atonement, faith, sin, repentance, forgiveness, and decision, which total up to rebirth into a new life. The reality of sin depends on the reality of the lawgiving God. Repentance depends on the reality of sin. Forgiveness depends on faith in God's grace. God's grace depends on the Atonement. The Atonement is required by man's sin and makes faith possible through the gift of prevenient grace. The acceptance of one's forgiveness depends on faith in the Atonement.

Now, how are we to think about sin? Without the lawgiving God, we can dispense with the old notion of sin. Interestingly, when Wesley spoke of "sin in believers,"[7] he spoke of repentance as "realistic self-knowledge."[8] This is the way we need to think of the first step in preparation for the refocusing of one's life on the things of the spirit. We need to recognize the devastating presence of destructive and alienating powers in our own spirits and their conflict with our healing and reconciling powers.

Thus, we are replacing the concept of original sin and the "broken image of God" in us (Wesley and other theologians) with our normal human condition, which is the unsubdued presence of divisive and destructive spiritual powers in tension with the unifying and healing powers.

Therefore, the possibility of a new beginning does not depend on the theistic transaction of the Atonement. Rather, it depends on the nature of God himself, whose method has never been judgment. Instead, it has been transformation by the power of unconditional love (grace). It arises from the unrelenting pressure of the Great Spirit upon our spirits, that is, God's efforts to heal himself. The role of judgment in the old imagery is replaced by the inherent conflict between unitive and divisive powers within the human spirit, a conflict present in all the parts of God's body and potentially present even in the self-awareness of the head of the world of spirit.

Faith proceeds with the articulation or explanation of the idea (the power of thought or reason). Finally, it blossoms with the decision to commit or entrust one's life (freedom). In this way, grace and freedom cooperate to produce faith. Therefore, the fullness of faith is a combination of the powers of communication, thought, trust, and decision. Such faith accepts—even absorbs—the grace that is the Spirit's gift of himself.

Of course, traditional language refers to "repentance for sin." In the absence of sin, we must rethink that idea. Wesley always demanded repentance and drove the demand home with strong language, describing the inability of the natural human being to do anything good. In his view, nothing man does on his own can be good. Only if he is enabled by the grace made available through trust in the Atonement can his actions be good. Ironically, the repentance he demanded turned out to be repentance for a condition that did not exist because, in his system, all persons have been given a certain measure of prevenient grace. No one is simply a natural man.

In another context, Wesley did admit there were sometimes positive results from the acts of nonbelievers. Later, he even admitted there might be some small degree of real good associated with those acts because they result from the presence of prevenient grace. Nevertheless, the admission of one's total sinfulness was the first step to the new birth in his early preaching.

The replacement of repentance with self-knowledge requires the recognition that our focus is skewed and our aims distorted and off target. It requires brutal honesty with oneself. It also calls for an awareness of the complicated ways in which some positive powers may be unifying and whole-making in certain circumstances. In other situations, the same powers may be destructive.

However, the necessary honesty does not require one to identify all the mixed motives that have governed some of our decisions or track all the consequences of all our actions. That is manifestly impossible. To be honest about ourselves requires the recognition of the ambiguity of most of our actions and the ignorance that always threatens to vitiate even our best intentions. In our new perspective, repentance is not a matter of wallowing in guilt about this or that bad deed. It is a matter of confessing our ignorance and our mixed motives, thus avoiding the pitfalls of self-righteousness and the arrogance of judging others.

That refocusing requires the recognition of the possibility that the negative or divisive powers within our spirit can actually be replaced by the corresponding positive and healing powers. This recognition is something like what traditional language calls "forgiveness" and John Wesley calls the result of "justifying grace." Forgiveness promised new life in Wesley's scheme. We need to recognize this process is a kind of gift or change that occurs when we allow the Spirit who is God to take over our spirits and impress his powers upon ours, thereby enhancing our positives. It is this gift of grace or this pressing of the Great Spirit upon our spirits that enables the act or process of refocusing.

That is why the new life or rebirth is the product of justification or what I want to call this act of "coming home." It requires a decision. One needs intentionally to refocus his life on life in the spirit, not on the specific manner in which that refocusing occurs. This reversal of life might be triggered in several possible ways.

This decision is the act of entrusting oneself to the Spirit who is God and deciding to turn one's attention to the creative, healing, reconciling powers of the Great Spirit. This must be something like what Paul means in his letter to the Romans when he says that "to set the mind on the flesh is death, but to set the mind on the Spirit is life and peace."[9] Our responsibility is to open the cracks that will allow the Spirit who is God to flow in and impress, enhance, and empower the positive unifying powers and subdue their negatives in our lives. Elsewhere, it is called being "born again."

The ubiquitous but loose talk about being born again, which we often hear, actually has an honorable and revealing origin in a much used passage in John. Jesus tells Nicodemus "no one can see the kingdom of God without being born from above" and "no one can enter the kingdom without being born of water and the spirit."[10] In other words, he indicates such a rebirth depends upon "seeing the Kingdom" and "entering the Kingdom." I take the "Kingdom" to mean the realm or world of the spirit. To be born again or born of the Spirit, as Jesus tells Nicodemus, is both to see and deliberately enter that world. To see it is to become aware of the spirit world of which one is a part. To deliberately enter it is to become focused on and committed to the possibilities of growth in the life of the spirit.

This has always been a powerful story, but it has often been abused by making rebirth into a particular kind of emotional crying jag. Without these emotions, one is thought never to have been born of the Spirit and therefore never to have been saved. Of course, there is nothing wrong with weeping, but it only proves that one has been moved—and we weep for many reasons.

From the perspective of the spirit image of God, to be born again has nothing to do with the Atonement or weeping. It is a total reorientation from our focus on personal material or social goals toward the pursuit of spirit goals. For example, Wesley recognizes how strong our focus on material goals is when he urges, "Sit loose to all things here below, as if you were a poor beggar."[11]

God as Spirit works in mysterious ways, according to spiritual laws we do not fully understand. However, there are special moments of grace, which Paul, Wesley, and others have called "justification." I choose to call them "coming home."

A moment of truth is usually understood to be a life-changing event. Such is the act of coming home. As dramatic as these moments sometimes are, they are usually the result of long and often hidden preparation.

Sometimes, these moments of grace come in response to our own prayers. Sometimes, they come through a long night of struggle, the word of a loved one, or the touch of a hand or even a smile of understanding. They happen within, where God and we live together, but something external usually triggers them. That is, they come as if from outside ourselves.

As in the case of miracles, they do not usually occur simply through persuasion or by request. Instead, they happen by preparation of the way for the Spirit, who is always pressing to break through. If the breakthrough is sudden, a surfeit of joy may be experienced that can produce weeping.

However prolonged the period of preparation, and many events not of our own doing contribute to that preparation, the bottom line is always a decision to engage the life of the spirit in a totally new way. One does so with the purpose and expectation that wholeness and the fulfillment of one's human and divine potential will be someday and somehow realized.

There are times when one makes a deliberate choice to launch this journey. Of course, there are times when it is as though the choice were made for us. There are times when a person wakes up one morning and discovers, after a long struggle with the choice and without being fully aware of its happening, the decision has somehow already been made. In any case, it comes to us as a gift of the unconditional love or generosity of the Great Spirit, our true Head.

We are all at different stages of spiritual growth. However, the person who has seen the possibilities of growth and maturity is one who has received the power to put his past behind him and move on. Thus, it is also the source of hope in this life—even of hope for tomorrow and the next day—when the power of the Spirit can be manifested in ever greater measure. This can be an experience of great release and a sense of new freedom and joy. No wonder it has been characterized as the experience of being born again. No wonder we can appropriately characterize it as a matter of coming home.

However, coming home implies something further. It means we will still need to calculate the effects of our actions as we are able and assess our motivations, thereby fulfilling our responsibility to participate in the ongoing whole-making work of the Great Spirit. We will continue to have the model of Jesus as a guide, but the power comes from opening ourselves increasingly and continuously to the gifts of the Spirit who is God.

In the previous passage from the letter to the Romans, the spirit is distinguished from the natural world, and the refocusing of one's attention and desire is encouraged. However, from the perspective of the spirit world, the distinction is between the unifying spiritual powers and the divisive spiritual powers, not between the flesh and the spirit. There is no suggestion that the natural world is evil while the spiritual world is good. While the natural world puts certain limits on the spirit through the interaction of the two realms, the source of evil is the destructive powers found in human spirits.

For example, the old negativity toward sexuality, fostered by the doctrine of original sin and imbedded in our Western culture, is seen simply to have no more foundation when we look at the world in this new way. The creative, healing use of our natural needs and instincts, whether sexual, gustatory, or survivalist, is the task of our unifying spiritual powers. Therefore, stewardship of the natural world is a part of our responsibility as human spirits. The journey upon which rebirth sets us includes both the care of our bodies and the environment as well. Although the passage discussed above is not usually associated with the rebirth story in the Gospel of John, it fits rather neatly.

There remains the issue of Jesus' role in justification and rebirth. If we are to believe the story of Jesus' meeting with Nicodemus, he did not see his death as necessary to rebirth or salvation. But Paul, Wesley, and many others did.[12] How are we to think now of Jesus' death?

The story of the crucifixion and resurrection of Jesus declares to the world the possibility of spiritual victory. It challenges human beings to refocus their lives on the journey of faith and life in the spirit. Moreover, those who open their spirits to the Spirit that was in Jesus begin to participate in a totally new way in the life of God. They begin a spirit journey that can last as long as this life endures and into a future they can leave in the hands of the Great Spirit.

The recognition of this fact can have meaningful implications for the Christian's attitude to those of other religions. The biblical affirmation that "there is no other name under heaven by which one must be saved,"[13] has often been treated as an exclusive claim that one cannot be saved unless he becomes a Christian. Whatever the writer meant, we need to understand it is by that Spirit that the Christian story pictures in Jesus that human beings may grow into their full potential and thus be "saved." Salvation is the total process, beginning in this life and continuing into the life beyond. Each person's spirit is a part of that same Spirit by which he or she may be saved.

In other words, we need to treat the story of the life, death, and resurrection of Jesus as a particular witness to what is and has always been true of God who is Spirit, even apart from Jesus. In whatever manner a person comes to see the world of the spirit and focus his life on the struggle to subdue the divisive and exalt the unifying powers, he has become a seeker after salvation and wholeness. After all, the etymology of "salvation" is "soundness or health." No Atonement in the mode of the Old Testament or its adaptation in the New Testament and early church history is necessary.

However, the power of the story of Jesus' death and resurrection as both revelation of possibility and release from hopelessness remains. I am ready to witness to that power in my life while I simultaneously affirm there are other ways one may come to see and enter intentionally into life in the spirit world.

Surprisingly, John Wesley himself was open to that possibility. In one of his sermons, he writes:

> I have no authority from the word of God "to judge those that are without" (that is, outside the "Christian dispensation") nor do I conceive that any man living has a right to sentence all the heathen and Mahometan world to damnation. It is far better to leave them to Him that made them and who is "the Father of the spirits of all flesh"; who is the God of Heathens as well as the Christians, and who hateth nothing that he hath made.[14]

In effect, Wesley is saying those who know nothing of Jesus and his death and resurrection are clearly not responsible for responding to him (Jesus). In addition,

God surely has other ways of providing for them. I believe the spirit image perspective on God, which I have been proposing, suggests how that can and must be.

In summary, at some point, God the Spirit breaks through in the midst of a person's spiritual struggle with the negative spirits, shows him the possibilities, and sets him free from bondage to his past. Such freedom enables him to surrender himself to the life of the spirit, that is, to God. However, we can take no credit for any of it because it does not happen without the Spirit's gift of himself to begin with, both in our birth as self-aware spirit beings and in those decisive moments when our life is refocused.

We are now ready to consider how we might rethink, within the context of our spirit vision of God, what Wesley called sanctification, holiness, and perfection.

Growing Up/Sanctifying Grace

Sanctification or holiness was Wesley's major concern from the beginning. Theologically, he found he needed to set it up by describing the first two gifts of grace, prevenient and justifying. Not only does the first gift of grace, prevenient, give each human being the capacity for faith and free choice, it also makes the gift of justifying faith possible, which depends on both God's grace and man's faith. Even for Wesley, the two gifts of grace overlap and manifest the process nature of his understanding of salvation. They also clarify his understanding of the continuum of faith, that is, that faith grows from the smallest seed of possibility to its fullest blossoming as the process continues.

Also, when Paul lists the fruits of the Spirit in Galatians, he includes self-control. He says:

> The fruit of the Spirit is love, joy, peace, patience, kindness, generosity, faithfulness, gentleness, and self-control.[15]

Our power of self-control is—biblically as well as experientially—a function of spirit. It is not a product of the laws of the natural world, even though the chemistry of the body and brain impacts the degree of our power of self-control.

This implies the human spirit is, in the measure of his or her self-awareness, capable of faith and freedom to act. Both are gifts. Therefore, both are by grace alone. To this extent, we must agree with Wesley. However, the measure of our spiritual growth always limits the freedom to choose, decide, and act.

Our early capacity for faith must be used for our first stumbling efforts at prayer. However, as faith grows, even through early sporadic efforts, there comes the time in a moment or a lifetime when we are able to make the decision to commit ourselves to the life of the spirit, thus giving us a new birth into a new life. When that happens, spiritual growth or sanctification is already underway. In fact, it has been underway from the earliest use of prayer and the other means of grace. The new birth is given through the decision to commit oneself. Our freedom is involved throughout the whole process, not just from the new birth on, but from the first effort at prayer onward.

Because we understand the degree of our freedom is limited from the beginning, it is one of the gifts for which, as spirit persons committed to the life of the spirit, we need constantly to pray.

Wesley was also aware the border between justifying grace and sanctifying grace was somewhat fuzzy. He claimed that justification was the first step in sanctification, but some small degree of sanctification or holiness may have begun even earlier.

The new beginning will happen when the time is full and ripe and the way for the Spirit to work upon our spirits has been opened. Then the new gift of grace comes. It will enable our decision to commit ourselves (justification and new birth). Thus grace will continue to come throughout our life of prayer. Our own spirits will be sensitized to the pressures of God the Spirit and opened to the infusion of new strength for our struggling spiritual powers.

Therefore, the bulk of the Christian life was to be lived out seeking to allow God's grace to sanctify, make holy, and move us on to perfection. This is Wesley's third gift, sanctifying grace.

In the spirit image view, those breakthrough occasions when we see the way open to start a new journey in the spirit are the self-aware God cooperating with the laws of his own being and taking advantage of an opening afforded by some natural and/or psychological condition of ours. After all, our spirits are a part of his own being. It is in his own self-interest to tighten up his spiritual relationship with the children he has conceived and borne. It is a part of the spirit world's own self-realization.

Similarly, it is also the beginning of our own self-realization, that is, our becoming fully human as spiritual beings. Subsequent to the new beginning, the victories of the positive powers are made possible by our opening spiritual doors, that is, by us doing things to our own spirits through prayer and other means. This is the way we become not only fully human but also divine or, as Wesley might say, holy, sanctified, or perfect.

Wesley's spiritual disciplines that nurtured the sanctifying process were what he called the "instituted means of grace." In one place, he lists five:

> (1) Prayer; private, family, public...Do you use private prayer,...every morning and evening?...(2) Searching the Scriptures by; reading,...meditating...hearing,...(3) The Lord's Supper: Do you use this at every opportunity?...(4) Fasting,...(5) Christian conference (read conversation)...Is it always in grace seasoned with salt?[16]

It was the purpose of these disciplines to open the human heart to God's sanctifying grace. For us, as for Wesley, prayer is the primary means by which we can move our spirits increasingly toward the goal of a full union with the Great Spirit.

Of course, there are other "means of grace" or disciplines of spiritual growth. The nurture will not happen without the free exercise of spiritual disciplines, some of which may not yet have been discovered or devised.

However, I will add a few others that Wesley could have incorporated and that I want to recommend:

- The first is the reading of the mystical authors, whom the Moravians led him to reject early on, a rejection he later withdrew.

- Perhaps sometimes, even the simple quietness the Moravians recommended and which Wesley had rejected because they had insisted that waiting was all that was required.

- We might want to revise Arius' contemplation of the "obedience of Christ" by practicing the contemplation of Jesus' faithfulness to himself (which was also his faithfulness to God) on the cross.

- My final suggestion for a new set of spiritual disciplines is "aspiration" as the homilies of the English church taught, that is, desiring, longing for, and hungering for holiness. This last discipline may actually be a part of prayer.

The process of spiritual growth cannot be simply an internal process, such that our own spirits alone are sanctified. It includes the stewardship of our spiritual powers for the healing of all our relationships as well. Each movement of our spirit influences some aspect of the natural world, our own bodies, and the environment. As the measure of the powers of unconditional love and unity in our spirits increases, so will our care for the world in terms of the alleviation of hunger, violence, injustice, and suffering. The life of the spirit and our social relationships are not separate areas of our lives. They are constantly interacting. We will nurture our social relationships as we cultivate our spiritual growth.

Let me be clear. Such means of grace are not works of righteousness. That is, they cannot be used in transactions such as one might arrange between oneself and another being like the theistic image of God suggests. There is no *quid pro quo* involved. Rather, they are ways one uses the laws of the spirit world to allow the creative spiritual powers to go to work on the destructive powers. The difference between means and works righteousness is comparable to the difference between the act of striking the billiard ball with your cue just so it will go into the pocket and offering the ball a bite of your ice cream cone if he will just roll across the table and drop.

The purpose of prayer is not to persuade God to do something as though he were a magician who could wave his wand and make certain things happen if we were successful in persuading him. However, prayer does open the way through spiritual communication for the Spirit who is God to use the laws of the spirit world in order to affect the natural world. If the Great Spirit emanated the natural world, then he can influence the natural world. That is far easier to conceive than a theistic God being persuaded to intervene by fiat. I have no hesitation in affirming this because I believe there is no virtue in making things harder to believe than necessary.

In my experience, no practice is as important as constant prayer. In fact, it has become even more important as I reorient my thinking to the spirit image approach I am describing. As a child, I relished the opportunity to receive the sacrament. I still find it to be a powerful sign that holds the promise that the creative powers of the spirit may become strong enough to subdue the destructive powers I find in my own spirit. Out of such death to my destructive self, I can at last be given victory, even over death. To be sure, the liturgy of the Eucharist reflects the traditional understanding of the Atonement, which, of course, does not help my focus. However, I find it possible to concentrate on the sacrament as the sign and promise of God's victory and my participation in it. Can we rewrite the ritual and adjust the liturgy so that it reflects the new way of viewing and appropriating the story of the passion, death, and resurrection of Jesus?

What does Wesley's holiness look like? From Wesley's point of view, there is no doubt. Repeatedly in sermon and hymn, the Wesleyan movement affirmed love was the ultimate expression of sanctification, for of God it said "his nature and his name are love."[17]

What does spiritual maturity look like in our new vision of God? As important as are the fruits of the spirit, such as faith and hope, the greatest still is love. "Faith, hope and love, these three. But the greatest of these is love."[16]

In fact, the unconditional giving of the Great Spirit, that is, his grace, is both the source of spiritual growth and the principal product (our power to love). That perhaps explains why the "love chapter" remains the favorite passage of the Bible for more persons than any other.

This means all our social concerns, our political activism, and our advocacy for the poor and suffering are not to be something added on in order to make our faith somehow respectable. They are the fruit of our growing spiritual maturity, an expression of the Spirit's generosity within us. Therefore, the ultimate aim of all social activism, as well as of personal relations, should be reconciliation, peace, and healing. For thus, we participate in the purpose of the Great Spirit. Such should be the guiding principle of our stewardship of all the spiritual powers as well as the goal of all our unconditional giving. In fact, Christian morality is nothing other than the good stewardship of all our powers, to the end that peace and harmony should rule both in the lives of the people and in the natural environment in which we live.

We may exalt the value of love, but how can we express it? That is a technical problem. Right action must be determined by inquiring what actions will actually nurture the natural and spiritual life of the affected persons. The sentiment of love or the desire to nurture is never a guarantee of correct action because ignorance or miscalculation often makes our decisions unwise. For example, sometimes what is called "tough love" may be required instead of gentleness. It is a hard thing to know when that is appropriate, and it is often an even harder thing to make oneself practice it. I cannot imagine loving my sons more than I do, but they will tell you quickly enough there have been plenty of times when I could have done it better—if I had been smarter. The effective use of our unifying powers always requires the cultivation and use of our power of thought, that is, of wisdom.

In this life, not even perfect love can rule out technical errors in our efforts to discover how to love one another, how to effect reconciliation, or how to establish peace and justice. Some powers, including our power of thought, are limited by our immersion in the natural world.

A large part of the difficulty in knowing how to love is the two aspects of love that are often intermingled and cause confusion. One is the reality of caring for the spiritual and physical well-being of a person or persons by our nurturing actions and relationships. The other is the emotional overload that so often hides the real needs of those we have a strong passion for because it includes the desire to possess. Not only is this emotional overload present in erotic relationships, it is in the emotional bonding that is present among members of a family and with close friends. This intermingling is the source both of the confusion and the sacramental power of the sexual relationship to enhance the spiritual bonding.

However, like Wesley, St. Paul, and Jesus, I am convinced the principle marker of spiritual growth is the increase of love, the love that unites by unconditional giving.

The whole concept of stewardship rests upon the power of self-control. In fact, stewardship is the cultivation of all our unitive and creative spiritual powers, not just the use of our possessions, our time, and our sexuality. Therefore, it includes the cultivation of our power of self-control itself because that power is incompletely developed and the pressure to submit to impulse and conditioning without examination is always present. It involves our cultivation and use of the powers of hope, love, intelligence, creativity, healing, and so forth. We need to thank the Great Spirit for all our positive powers, both natural and spiritual. We then need to enjoy all of them, improve all of them, and share them in the service of unity and peace.

To what end do we seek spiritual growth? Wesley's own emphasis was on the process itself, even while he acknowledged the possibility of some kind of state of fulfillment or "entire sanctification." However, he rejected what he called absolute perfection in this life, that is, a life without any mistakes due to ignorance and so forth. Nevertheless, the process, which may have a very deliberate beginning in one's reorientation, may also have a fulfillment at our death or beyond.

The holiness movement, which has spawned a number of denominations and even some seminaries, traces its roots to this teaching of John Wesley. The spiritual growth emphasis in many mainline denominations can, just as well, trace its roots to Wesley's focus on perfection. We just need to remember that, while Wesley admitted early on that it might be possible in this life for certain persons to actually achieve perfection as a condition (what many holiness proponents call "the second blessing" or "entire sanctification"), Wesley repeatedly called the whole a gradual process.

However, I believe we must admit, so far as this life is concerned, spiritual growth always remains in process because the limits of our natural life cannot be ignored. Our goal must be the continued enhancement of our positive spiritual powers as long as we live. Such enhancement results in progress toward the Great Spirit's goal of a world in which all his parts abide in harmony and peace, fulfilled and complete.

Spiritual growth has its embryonic beginnings with the birth of new spirits, its intentional beginning in the new birth of justification, and its continuation in sanctification. Wesley believed his teaching on perfection was his most important theological contribution. It also remains, within our present spirit image of God, perhaps the most important feature. The bottom line is that, in becoming fully human, we also become divine. That is, we become fully compatible with the Head of the world of spirit.

This vision of God and our salvation can also help us deal with the vexing questions concerning unanswered prayer and complaints about God being not so good after all. For instance, "If God is good, then he wouldn't allow bad things to happen." God as Spirit wants nothing evil to occur, but he does not work in contradiction to his own purpose. That purpose is that human spirits should become fully human. To be human is to be free to open, by their own decisions, the way for the Great Spirit to enhance their spiritual powers and make them more fully human, therefore making them divine as he is divine.

On the other hand, someone says, "He really doesn't love me, or he would make my life a lot easier." No, if he loves you, he is pressing you by the gentle power of his grace to become more fully human, more responsible, more loving, and more patient as well as to find true joy in the struggle to grow in all the positive powers.

Many events not perpetrated by the divisive spirits of human beings also cause human suffering. For example, insurance companies and other humans consider earthquakes, volcanoes, storms, and so forth to be "acts of God." Such a designation simply reflects the insidious permeation of theistic thinking throughout all our Western languages.

Such events are quite obviously caused by natural laws in operation. They are not an angry God's way of punishing or taking vengeance on recalcitrant human beings. Why did God make a world in which humans are caused to suffer? That is a question right out of the theistic mode of thought. It is, we know, a world that has evolved, operates, and continues to evolve by means of natural regularities we call laws. Those events are not evil like the destructive powers of human beings. They are neutral, but people suffer when they get in the way. They do not suffer because God did it or was not paying attention. It is because he is a different kind of God, one still striving to make us responsible and fully human. Our problem often is that God just is not the kind of God we have grown up thinking he was.

Wasn't it Dr. Pangloss in Voltaire's *Candide* who insisted this is the best of all possible worlds? Nice try! Maybe it is—maybe it's not. However, we are affirming the Spirit who is God, by his creative energy, brought the natural world into being, including the animate bodies inhabiting it. He did so by a long process of growth so that the laws by which he grew this creation may well function much like the laws that govern the natural birth of a baby. Pain is a necessary part of that process. Suffering and pain result both from the destructive activities of human beings and when people get in the way of the natural laws in operation.

In our vision of God, he does not act by fiat. Instead, he acts in accordance with the interaction of spiritual and natural regularities. Only if we are able to block the operation of some natural regularity with that of another can we free up the pressure of his healing power to avert illness or avoid a natural catastrophe. Such an interruption can take place only when another law—natural or spiritual—comes into play. In that case, the interaction of natural and spiritual laws allows the healing to occur or the catastrophe to be averted. He does not suspend regularities, either spiritual or natural.

However, the more immediate problem is how to cope with the suffering that sometimes accompanies natural disasters. That is a matter of spirit, attitude, courage, trust, and hope. It is especially a matter of hope because our trust is in the purpose and ultimate victory of the Spirit who is God. It is a victory in which we will have a share.

Instead of calling this process of spiritual growth "sanctification" or "holiness," I prefer to call it "growing up."

Choosing the Future/Glorifying Grace

The spirit world is a world that encompasses, not only all those spirits inhabiting our natural existence, but all those self-aware spirits whose bodies can no longer serve their temporal existence. The difference is that the flesh, which has also been the Spirit's gift to us and them, no longer serves them. They are free beyond any freedom they were given or achieved during the course of their natural life.

Wesley called the state of our spirits after death by the name of "heaven." He also called it the gift of glorifying grace.

In the meantime, we will continue to grow, gradually subduing the destructive powers within our own self-aware spirits. In doing so, we will become increasingly like God in his perfect subjection of the destructive powers in his own transcendent self.

Beyond this, my thoughts all fall into the realm of speculation. For instance, Wesley suggested instantaneous sanctification, that is, the end of the sanctification process, could occur at the moment of physical death. That at least seems conceivable because there would be no natural body to block the way. Because we have learned that time and space belong to the natural world, we might assume that process in time has no opportunity to go forward beyond the death of the body.

Conceiving of life apart from space and time at all is pretty difficult. However, the notion that after death we would only need to keep the negatives at bay, as I suggested earlier, is a process that would have to proceed through time. Even to speak of something continuing to exist seems to be a contradiction. So we have a problem conceiving of a disembodied life.

At this point, a further speculation suggests itself. Because our self-aware spirits come into being in connection with the natural bodies to which they are attached, our self-awareness as individuals seems to depend upon some kind of body in which time, and maybe even space, continue to exist. The question is: What happens to our individual identities when the natural body dies? Paul's solution to this puzzle was to posit a resurrection body through which our self-identities continue to exist:

> But someone will ask, "How are the dead raised? With what kind of body do they come?"...You foolish man. What you sow does not come to life unless it dies. So it is with the resurrection of the dead. What is sown is perishable, what is raised is imperishable. It is sown in dishonor, it is raised in glory. It is sown in weakness, it is raised in power. It is sown a physical body, it is raised a spiritual body.[18]

What kind of body could this be? It would have to be the same kind of spiritual body the Great Spirit must have. That is, if a body in time and space is necessary for one to have a personal identity, then the Great Spirit in his transcendence must have a space/time body of some kind. If he has some kind of spiritual body, then time and space are not limited to the natural world as we ordinarily suppose.

If we insist time and space belong exclusively to the natural world, then perhaps we should think of the natural world itself as the body of the Great Spirit. This is what the pan-en-theists assert. That is no solution to our quandary because our spirits, after our natural death, in order to persist at all, would simply have to find another natural body. I suppose this is a thought that could lead to the Eastern notion of reincarnation.

However, there are other alternatives. If we limit the emanation from God to the world of spirit so that only the spirit world is a part of the reality of God, we could attribute the existence of the natural world to an act of creation *ex nihilo* by

God. This allows the dissolution of the natural world without losing God. It also eliminates the idea both of pantheism and of pan-en-theism. It also does away with the notion the spirit needs a natural body in order to exist, thus putting a crimp in the idea of reincarnation. But it leaves us without space or time in which spirits might continue to exist as self-aware entities.

Suppose we assume that, at death, our spirits are absorbed into the Great Spirit, and our personal identities disappear. That still leaves the Great Spirit with the need for space and time in which to operate, not only in his immanence within the perishable natural world of space and time, but also as the transcendent Head of the spirit world.

If we are going to assume the transcendent Head of the spirit world is able to operate within space and time, it is equally conceivable our self-awareness as individual spirits can continue in space and time, without a natural body. That is, we may speculate that time and space exist independently of the natural world. If so, not only does the Great Spirit inhabit space and time in a spiritual body, but our spirits can do so as well, thus retaining their identities as individuals.

This is possible if we are able to conceive the possibility that time and space are not things that are filled with change and motion, but rather are functions of change and motion as self-aware spirits experience them in both the world of spirit and the world of nature.

As continuing parts of the Great Spirit they would have to have the same kind of spiritual body that the Great Spirit must have. That is, if a body in time and space is necessary for one to have a personal identity, then the Great Spirit in his transcendence must also have a space/time body as a function of his own changing reality. And if he has that kind of spiritual body, then time and space are not limited to the natural world as we ordinarily suppose. In that way Paul's resurrection body solution works for us too.

One further thought occurs to me. Perhaps disembodied spirits can persist only in time, though not occupy space. After all, if we think of time as nothing more than the phenomenon of change, then the continued growth of our spirits will emanate time. In that case, we would find our continued identity in time but not in space. It is a rather different concept of body. Weird? Perhaps. Nevertheless, this is all speculation anyway. The one advantage of engaging in this kind of speculation is that it simply enlarges the mystery of life and leaves our mouths appropriately stopped.

Of course, the old question remains: What happens to those who have never turned their minds to the things of the spirit? They are still spiritual beings, and the positive powers as well as their negatives are present. The possibility would seem to be increased that, when released from the strictures of the natural body but while they are still living within space and time (or even in time only), they would be given a clearer awareness of the hope before them. It would also seem the immediacy of the Spirit who is God would assure a new focus and a new direction for their renewed spiritual efforts.

The common imagery associated with heaven is essentially spatial and temporal. However, if we believe the world of spirit can exist apart from the created natural world, we may also believe heaven is a spiritual condition which emanates its own time and space. Therefore, we continue to exist as self-aware spirits who still participate in the Spirit who is God in an immediacy of fellowship and unity that is scarcely imaginable.

The human mind has conjured up images of heaven, angels' wings, and golden streets. These can be powerful images. They can equip hymns and songs with their furniture, but they need to give way to the indescribable life of the human spirit in communion with the Great Spirit who is God. All this is an unconditional gift as well.

The correlative images of the bar of judgment and the prison of hell are also clearly powerful, though they also arise from the theistic image of God I described earlier. A young woman once said to me, "I'd be having me one whale of a good time if I weren't afraid of going to hell." It is a powerful image all right. Of course, John Wesley had his own vision of what he called "The Great Assize," that is, the final court of judgment.

We have no place for such an image because it assumes God sits in judgment at the Last Judgment, separating the sheep from the goats based on some set of criteria. It becomes a matter of keeping score. Even the vision of heaven is a consequence of that assumption. However, the Spirit who is God needs no such accounting because the spiritual state of each individual determines the quality of the relationship he has with God at any particular point, either before or after the death of the body. Each person is already a part of God's own reality by virtue of his existence itself. He is not cast out from God because he is spirit and all spirit is part of the spirit world that is God.

When all the above has been said, it becomes quite clear that, whenever we attempt to envision life with the Spirit who is God and begin to speculate about the possibilities after death, our tongues are finally reduced once again to silence.

Clearly, a certain amount of speculation has been involved in our reconstruction of Wesley's doctrine of salvation. This is the case in the positing of a transcendent self-awareness for the whole of the spirit world. It is also true of our discussion of various options for belief in life after the death of the body. However, an effort has been made to build those speculations upon the solid foundation of our personal knowledge of spirit through our knowledge of our own selves. I am convinced the result is a reasonable, believable picture of the realities and the possibilities of this phenomenal life we experience as self-aware individuals. The fact is that our speculative efforts all have some foundation in human experience, while the theistic constructions rest on little more than the claims of revelation, or less graciously, on the political machinations of the early church.

The hope that attends our decision to pursue the spiritual life includes the expectation we will grow a bit more tomorrow. It also involves the expectation there will be self-realization and fulfillment, healing and wholeness, and, finally, perfect harmony with the Spirit who is God at the last. Whether at the moment of death or somehow at some point further into the future, our potentialities as human beings will be fulfilled. We will then become fully human and fully divine. It also means our self-awareness will become complete and our positive powers perfect.

Our understanding now, like the rest of our spiritual powers, is weak and poor. We can expect no more for the time being. But our hope is also that at last we shall "see face to face…then (we) will know fully even as (we) have been fully known."[19]

Putting aside our speculations about the way life after death occurs, we can believe we will at last be made whole and at one with ourselves and the Great Spirit. I can ask nothing more because it is a vision out of which can be proclaimed a message of life and hope and joy that will speak to these new times.

This is my suggestion for our understanding, teaching, and preaching in the twenty-first century. It is a reconceptualization under the image of the spirit world of the major aspects of Wesley's theology. I see it as the true essence of the Wesleyan heritage.

However, this content must be focused on the universal human needs that Wesley addressed and that remain as deep in the human spirit in this new century as they were in his day. In the next chapter, I want to discuss some ways in which that connection can be made.

7
Addressing the Universal Needs

Personally, it is incredibly helpful to me to think in terms of the spirit image when I think of God, other persons, my spirit in relation to the Spirit's own self-awareness and especially when I pray. To think and feel all these connections is an amazing thing. To think of the possibilities for my own life and especially for my life with others is an exciting prospect. To think of the meaning of my death and the death of those I know and love is profoundly comforting. It gives me joy because it responds to one of the deepest needs my spirit feels, the need for hope.

However, hope is not my need alone. Hope is a universal human need. Moreover, there are other such universal needs as well. Universal human needs provide the targets for all effective preaching in whatever century and in every cultural context. Therefore, they are also the needs to which any spiritual message must speak in the twenty-first century. This is undoubtedly the most important connecting link between preaching in Wesley's time and preaching in the new time.

I wonder: What if the consequence of my effort to understand in a new way is to strip away the poetry of the spiritual experience? If I abandon the theistic image of God and the imagery that has been traditionally associated with it, will I have also neglected the power of the imagination?

T. S. Eliot's definition of what he calls metaphysical poetry is, though in different words, the marriage of ideology and imagination.[1] From time to time, he also refers to it as "the word made flesh."[2] For the intellect to acquire its greatest power, it must be clothed in an imagery the imagination constructs. I believe this is the second essential task to be accomplished if our new theological vision is to make a difference in peoples' lives. However, I raise the following flag: Beware lest the imagination come to mask the understanding.

Not only will we need the poetry, we will need the hymnody as well. Most people have learned their theology from the hymns and choruses they sing. Sermons are usually forgettable, but tunes and their words are not. Therefore, the message set forth in the last two chapters requires to be set to music.

Above all, our preaching and teaching in the twenty-first century must address the universal human needs of people, not only as Wesley's did in the eighteenth, but better. The list of universal human needs I identify and discuss in this chapter does not purport to be exhaustive, and you might well wish to identify them in some other manner. Nevertheless, I believe those I shall be describing are among those needs to which John Wesley's preaching spoke so powerfully. If we do not address those needs, we shall shortchange the message, no matter what it is.

Such needs are not identifiable by the creation of a list of wants because wants are mostly conditional and variable with the time, place, and the age of the individual. For example, at a certain age, I want Coke and hot dogs while I may later learn something about my health needs and begin to want better nutrition. On the other hand, I may be hoping for a job in cyber technology, but, in another age or on another piece of geography, that might not even be an option.

At any age, in any time, and anywhere, the human spirit has certain powerful needs. The following is my short list of the universal human needs that teaching and preaching must address: connection, hope, meaning or purpose, guidance, and understanding.

The Universal Need for Connection

The first universal need of the human spirit I want to discuss is the need for connection. The need is to be connected, to be an inseparable part, to be accepted, and to belong wherever we are. This need may be the most fundamental of all because the vulnerability of the self-aware individual demands connection to counter that vulnerability.

The reason for this is the fact the human spirit, at an early point in its development, becomes self-aware. That is, he recognizes himself as an individual distinct and separate from everything else around him. This recognition, suggests Bishop Spong, produces a trauma or a kind of hysteria because the individual finds himself alone and threatened from every side.[3] He must cope with a whole world outside himself. Everything is the other. Maybe everything is the enemy. So, he must either build up defenses or find some way of making friends with everything else. Perhaps he seeks to control the other or maybe he tries to absorb it. It is a constant struggle to cope with his own individuality because it is a fearful thing to be alone.

I believe this need is fundamental to every other need of the human spirit just because the essence of spirit is precisely its self-awareness as an individual. The need is for a way to connect that goes far deeper than superficial, casual, or temporal relationships provide. A powerful expression of this universal need appears in Bill Gaither's song "Where No One Stands Alone":

> Once I stood in the night with my head bowed low, in the darkness as black as could be. And my heart felt alone and I cried, O Lord, don't hide your face from me…Like a king, I may live in a palace so tall with greater riches to call my own. But I don't know a thing in this whole wide world that's worse than being alone…Take my hand, let me stand where no one stands alone.[4]

The expression of the need is powerful, but the song's response to the need is still inadequate because it pictures the Lord holding our hand and thus protecting us against everything else. In the end, the response to the need is exclusive, not uniting. However, the need for connection calls for a universal connection that excludes no one.

One of the continuities between Wesley and our reconstruction is the universal human needs he attempted to meet and that our preaching and teaching must address. In some measure, Wesley recognized and attempted to address the need for connection. It was an important part of his ministry. He used his organizational skills for the establishment of the classes and societies, which he saw as seedbeds of spirituality and sources of mutual support and accountability. He insisted upon the continuing importance of attendance at regular worship and the Eucharist. These activities provided some kind of connection, even community. Moreover, the message of his preaching included these disciplines.

Wesley's devotion to the community of the Church of England, in spite of his quarrels with it was the recognition of the need for connections with the past, that is, the traditions of the established church. The traditions provided the story, the imagery, and a vision that embodied the message he preached and taught. He was profoundly aware of the need to be connected with the past.

Furthermore, Wesley, though a man of his own time and place, was aware of the larger world. He traveled no farther than North America and Germany, but his curiosity ranged widely. In part, his fascination with the stories of the Indians of North America led him to make his ill-fated journey to Georgia. The reports of the Lisbon earthquake in 1755 awed and intrigued him. Thus, he wrote a treatise on "Serious Thoughts Occasioned by the Late Earthquake at Lisbon." Man-made boundaries did not impress him greatly. When the bishops of the church protested his labors within the bounds of their dioceses, Wesley responded, "the world is my parish."

Though his attitude toward the heathen was chauvinistic, for his time and place, his attempts at fostering a catholic spirit are still quite remarkable. His opposition to slavery has been well recognized. He believed both the Indians he went to North America to convert and the slaves being carried out of Africa had souls worthy of being saved.

He was willing to leave to the wisdom and mercy of God those who never had the opportunity to hear of Jesus. He believed God's grace, purchased by the Atonement of Jesus, covered them as well. Wesley's love for the poor and his willingness to spend most of his time with them is an object lesson in the universality of the human family. He wrote, "I bear the rich and love the poor; therefore, I spend almost all my time with them."[5] However, he also had the remarkable ability to connect not only with the poor, but also with the aristocracy, and the educated. (Samuel Johnson, the bishops, Lady Huntington, and so forth.)

Wesley's message and practice encouraged a connection with the broader world. His vision was not limited to his desire to "spread Scriptural holiness across the land,"[6] but it reached across the oceans as well. He addressed the need by announcing that God loved all persons so much that he gave his Son for the salvation of all. All this touched the need for connection, but the need for connection goes far deeper than Wesley understood.

So, we have this concern in common with Wesley, but I am reaching for a way to discuss something still more inclusive than those particular connections provide. Rather, I am thinking of a spiritual connection with the whole universe. We need to be connected, but not just to something. We need to be connected to everything in a special way.

Of course, many different groupings of people promise to meet the universal need for community, including such divisive communities as those created by political ideologies, nationalism, social goals, or religious conformity. Such communities are severely restricted.

Probably no American who lived through the first weeks after the 9/11 terrorist attack on New York City and the Pentagon will ever forget the powerful surge of patriotism, the pride in being an American that swept the nation. It touched the universal need of every human being to belong to some community in which all can share in a common pursuit.

I believe such connections on the level of human communities may have the potential to serve as a stage on the way to an ever-expanding bond of community embracing all peoples of the planet.

In this case, the community created resulted in hatred, suspicion, and a severe rejection and condemnation of the evildoers. This kind of connection cannot finally satisfy the human spirit's need.

The risk of such emotional communities and perhaps even of love relationships is they can so easily become divisive instead of unifying. The connection the human spirit needs is universal and spiritual. It is a connection with the world of spirit, that is, with all those spirits comprising the body of the Great Spirit. This connection already exists but it needs to be recognized, honored, and nurtured.

We find surprising connections with every other part of the universe in which we discern some measure of the spirit world. What, for example, is the basis of the bond we so often discover between ourselves and our pets? What is there of shared spirit there? To discern such connections all about us is like finding ourselves held safely in the womb of God. We do not stand alone with God, holding our hand in defiance of the rest of the world. That notion is only possible under the shadow of theism. Rather, we are not alone because we are together in God and he is in us inseparably.

In Carl Sagan's novel *Contact*, an astronomer receives messages from outer space and attempts to fly there. While gone, she meets her long-deceased father, who gives the answer to her question: "All we have is each other."[7]

He is right. All we have is each other. That is all there is, and it is enough! The world of spirit, God, is our home. Within our spirit image of God, we see ourselves connected to the Great Spirit through our connections with all other self-aware spirits.

Of course, the need for connection also includes our families, our villages, the whole human family, the animal world, the plant world, our natural environment, and, yes, the astronomical world as well. It includes connectedness with the spirit at every level, far beyond the bounds most religious institutions have defined and beyond our human communities of sharing, as important as they are.

There is a spiritual connection with the entire creation. I see a stranger, and I do not have to wonder about his religion, his attitudes, his heritage, or his ancestors. I do not need to know such specifics because I know he is a spiritual being, a person of spirit, a part of the spirit world, a part of God. He is my brother because both of us are inseparably and eternally united in the Great Spirit. His different beliefs, his different values, his different cultural dispositions, and even his enmity cannot change that immutable fact.

The things that make us different are important to our individuality, but they are indifferent to our brotherhood. That is somehow different from saying both of us belong to the same natural species or are bound together, perhaps unwittingly, by economic or national ties. The goal of connection may be said to be peace and unity in all things. Thus, we know we are never alone, and even the feeling of being alone is assuaged.

However, the intellectual recognition of that connection is still not enough. There must be an emotional component in our connection with other spirits and thus with the Great Spirit. Wesley recognized the need for such an emotional content when he emphasized Paul's words concerning "the witness of the Spirit with our spirits that we are the children of God."[8]

I think the need for love is a special case of the need for connection because love is a connection with emotional content. There is hardly another term in all of Wesley's writings that occurs more often than that of love. Many of Charles Wesley's hymns suggest its centraliy: "…anticipate your heaven below, and own that love is heavn," (O For a Thousand Tongues); and "My Lord, my Love, is crucified," (O Love Divine). Then, of course, there is "Love Divine, All Loves Excelling." Finally, perhaps the most explicit acknowledgment, "The morning breaks, the shadows flee, pure, Universal Love thou art. To me, to all, thy mercies move; thy nature and thy name is Love." (Come, O Thou Traveler Unknown).[9]

These hymns, though written by Charles, were published by John. They formed the hymnody of the early Wesleyan movement and reflected the preaching and teaching of John.

John's sermons reveal his focus on the centrality of love in his message:

> We must love God before we can be holy at all, this being the root of all holiness. Now we cannot love God till we know he loves us…And we cannot know his pardoning love to us, till His spirit witnesses it to our spirit.
>
> We love him because he first loved us. This is the sum of all religion, the genuine model of Christianity.[10]

John Wesley understood the people needed to hear about God's love for them and their responsibility to love in turn. It was the need for a connection that embraced God and, therefore, others as well. So, once again, we share the recognition of the universal human needs with John Wesley.

Love has emotional overtones and practical expressions that cannot accompany all of our connections with the rest of the world. Therefore, love has the potential to represent or symbolize effectively the need for a connection with the whole.

We may acknowledge we are connected with the rest of the human family through our membership in the species and our economic interdependence because the earth is our common home and even that we are connected with the whole spirit world. However, the recognition of those connections is not quite the same as the connection of love. Love for those we know personally—lovers, spouses, children, and friends—is emotionally charged. We all need that kind of love in which we feel valued, respected, cherished, and desired. We need to confirm and actualize our love by the gifts we give and the act of giving itself. Each gift must be given to nurture the life of the loved ones. Time, place, and opportunity limit such acts of love, but such love and such giving can be sacramental as symbols of our connection with the whole.

New images of connection may be necessary in the new times. For example, John Donne, the great poet and preacher in the seventeenth century, among others, has pointed to the sexual union of two persons as the most powerful symbol of the unifying power of the spirit.[11] We know how pervasive and powerful sexuality is in the human consciousness. Can we then treat sexual union as both strengthening our appreciation of the importance of unity and peace as an ideal and as an almost sacramental act in which the spirit of unity is not just symbolized, but reinforced and enacted? Many will respond to such a concept, but they cannot respond, whether for intellectual or cultural reasons, to the transactional interpretation of the passion story as the guarantee of God's love.

To treat sexual union as having sacramental power still risks confusing the passion of possession with the love that cares for and nurtures. Like other sacramental acts, it may become divisive rather than healing. For instance, the Eucharist, which is the great traditional dramatization of the reconciling death of Jesus, has been the source of more disagreement and division within the body of the Christian community than almost any other single issue. This has been the case even while the potential for unity and peace through the sacrament is so very great. However, these experiences of connection at least illustrate the strong human need for connections with emotional content in which we care for other persons and do those things that nurture their spiritual and natural well-being.

Beyond that, during a serious illness, when I am told persons I have never known are praying for me, there is a moving sense of connection with those persons. Thus, the power of intercessory prayer to reinforce our connections with other persons can also open the way, not only for healing and spiritual growth to occur, but also for strong emotional bonds to develop with those persons. To me, all of this suggests the basic need for love is the need for connections with emotional content of some positive kind. Therefore, there is a universal need to recognize our connection with all things spiritual and to do so with varying degrees of emotional content.

To be loved and to love is beautiful indeed. How each of us needs to be loved! How we need to be told and to know we are important and someone truly values and cherishes us, no matter how imperfect we still are. How we need that sense of self-worth that comes from seeing the lengths to which someone will go for us.

The kind of love we need is not warm fuzzies, as nice as they are, but it is a love that deeply cares for a spiritual union with us. To be loved and to love is beautiful indeed.

We have been told God loves us, Jesus loves us, and Jesus even died for love of us. That seems to mean Jesus knew we needed to be punished, but he loved us, so he substituted himself for us and took our punishment on himself. If we really needed to be punished for our sins, then he deprived us of what we needed. How does that prove his love? What does punishment accomplish anyway? If punishment is not good for us, then the God who makes the laws, judges us, and pronounces sentence does not really love us either? On the other hand, if it is good for us and he really does love us, he is not doing us a favor by punishing Jesus in our place. What we need is not punishment. What we need is his love.

When I think of the love I have in my spirit for those who are close to me, then I think again, how in Jesus, as the Gospels present him, the spirit of love, generosity, and giving or caring had become so strong it could subdue the spirits of division and alienation as well as of retribution and self-defense.

When I think of the length to which he went to preserve his own power to love even those who crucified him, then I may say, "Of course! Of course he loves me, wants to be close to me and wants to share the Spirit with me and all the world."

In the first place, he is connected with me and the rest of the spirit world by virtue of our common participation in the Spirit who is God. Because the power of love in him is victorious over the power of alienation, he does actually love me and all the world. That is the picture the Gospel stories present.

He did not go to the cross to pay off our debt or take our punishment on himself. He went to the cross to demonstrate that being fully human is allowing the Great Spirit to fill our spirits with the power to overcome. There it was where we see love and forgiveness coming out victorious over hatred and violence. They could not destroy his spirit. He would not bend to their ways, even in the face of death. The healing power of love overcomes the divisive, destructive powers that assail us, not only from within our own spirits, but from without as well. That was his love for us.

When I hold this picture of Jesus before me, it tells me how wise the Spirit who is God in him was to go about it in such an unexpected, powerful way. I begin to understand what it can mean to say Jesus loves me and every other human as a part of the spirit world. I then see the story of his death on the cross and his resurrection made it possible for all who read or hear the story to see the negative powers defeated by the positive powers and to finally see even the power of death destroyed. Then, those who see that can know the possibility that they also may share in that victory because, like him, they are a part of the Great Spirit. They can see the positive power that was manifested in Jesus and can begin to trust the Spirit who is God. That whole story was about the possibility that love, generosity, and peace, that is, the power of spirit, is the greatest power in the world and will finally subdue what the Bible and John Wesley called "the law of sin and death."[12]

I want to say this image of Jesus, irrespective of any elements in the story that may not be historical and ignoring any discrepancies in the chronologies of the four Gospels, has the power to produce unity and oneness just because the negative powers are there seen to be subdued by the positive power of forgiveness and love. He overcomes division at last.

Just like the potential for division found in the sacraments, patriotism, and sexual love, the central focus on Jesus has also produced division, alienation, and even wars. This has happened when Jesus' essential role has been taken to be that of providing Atonement as the only source of salvation for the world. That is, only those who trust the Atonement can receive God's saving grace.

That outcome can be avoided by taking and proclaiming Jesus as the ideal, the hero, and the exemplar. The patristic theory of the Atonement called "lutron" is akin to the role of the Jesus story. Gustav Aulen, the Swedish theologian, has called it "the dramatic theory of the Atonement."[13]

Can the dramatic power of the story of Jesus still change lives in the twenty-first century? It does pretty well for me as long as I remember the spiritual meaning of the crucifixion and resurrection and give up the transactional and/or magical explanation that theism has fostered.

What form of community will coalesce around a new vision of the spiritual journey in this new century? It will probably not be a replacement for the church. It was the church that produced and preserved the New Testament story with its imagery. That history somehow needs to be preserved. Perhaps the community required by the struggle for spiritual growth will be comprised of small groups of those who have "seen the Kingdom" and seek to enter it, who have glimpsed the possibilities of the life of the spirit, or who perhaps see and seek to join a band of pilgrims on the way to the Great Party.

In any case, the need for love can be seen as a special form of connection. It is as pervasive and universal as that need for a wider spiritual connection. We need someone who cares for our well-being, spiritual as well as material. We need to care for the spirits and bodies of persons who are close enough to us that our emotions are deeply involved.

Can our preaching and our special connection with all those forming our circles of human contact convey how deeply loved we are by the Great Spirit?

The Universal Need for Hope

There is nothing new about the recognition of our need for hope. For example, the Old Testament says, "Without hope the people perish."[14] I remember preaching from that text while I was in college, one of my very first efforts. Even then, I had an inkling of the profundity of the human need for hope. That was all in a different time, in circumstances quite foreign to anything John Wesley knew in the eighteenth century or we know in the twenty-first.

In yet another time, Dante drew his picture of the gates of hell, over which the following words were inscribed, "Abandon hope, all who enter here."[15] When hope flees, all is gone. The impact of those words never quite hit me until a seventeen-year-old girl, who had once been in my confirmation class but dropped out after two sessions, went home from school one afternoon, placed a gun in her mouth, and blew her head off.

I knew her well enough to understand a little of how badly she was hurting and how desperately she had looked everywhere for the kind of affirmation and purpose she needed. Nevertheless, she had run out of hope and had passed through the gates of hell. How could I speak a word of hope to anyone the day I had her funeral? Her parents, her siblings, her friends, and her pastor all needed to hear a word that day that offered a credible promise to aching hearts.

John Wesley recognized the universal need for hope. He also came to understand, if a person has no freedom either to choose his eternal destiny or the character of his life, he has no hope his present life and future prospects can ever be different. Only the person who believes that things can be different and that he has the freedom to do something about it, can live in hope. I am saying the universal need to which Wesley's doctrine of grace answered is a need that is present in every human life. That is the case whatever the culture, language, economic system or social class within which he lives.

In his time and place, he had found a way to speak to hopeless lives, that is, to those who made their livelihood, such as it was, from the mines and the fields of the aristocracy. There was no light at the end of the tunnel for them, no hope things would be better next year. The traditional message of the church could not be heard either, because they were largely unwelcome and uncomfortable in the churches of the land. Crime and drunkenness were rampant among those to whom John Wesley went. No less in his time than today, hopelessness produced antisocial behaviors. Neither hope for tomorrow nor hope for the hereafter illuminated their lives.

Whitefield (and most of the other Calvinist evangelists) catered to the rising middle class and the lesser nobility. Outler notes:

> It is true, of course, that Whitefield attracted huge masses to his outdoor services, and he had built a tabernacle in Moorsfield within sight of the Foundry. Even so his support came largely from the constituency of the Tottenham Court Road Tabernacle and from Lady Huntington's Connexion.[16]

These were those who had a sufficient number of smaller hopes to sustain them and were perhaps less sensitive to their need for a greater hope. Calvinism fit more neatly into the sense of security that their social position seemed to have guaranteed them. Perhaps that goes some way in explaining why Whitefield was primarily noted for his oratorical skills. Wesley's claim to fame, instead, rests with a spiritual movement that had wide social consequences because Wesley told his people there was hope.

He told them they did not have to live the way they did. They could do things differently. They were free beings in spite of their oppression. That was the gift of what Wesley, in his writings, called prevenient grace. There were things they could do to not only better their worldly estate, but there was help for their spiritual well-being. They were not doomed. They had the God-given freedom to not only decide on matters of behavior, but on the destiny of their own souls. Wesley told them God's justifying (forgiving) grace was for them because Christ had died for them, not just for the nobles. That is why, when Wesley went into battle against the Calvinists, he understood he was going to bat for the souls of the people—all the people.

Of course, Calvinism was not the only object of Wesley's disputation. Early on, he had begun honing his views of grace and responsibility in his various contacts with the Moravians. However, the nuances of his more mature positions were hammered out through his polemic with the Calvinists. Because God's prevenient grace had already given them freedom, when they turned their lives over to him, his sanctifying grace would continue to give them the gifts and fruits of his spirit as long as they continued to trust him and make use of the means of grace. They could grow in grace, even unto perfection at last.

Wesley spoke, therefore, not only to the need for hope in the hereafter, but to the need to be a free agent in some manner even now. That is, justifying grace forgives the messes we make and promises a new start. Only a word promising a new start can speak to the need for hope in this world. The word speaks. The human spirit (free by the gift of God's prevenient grace) responds.

Thus, the special power of Wesley's message of grace is that it is accompanied by the notion of accountability. The following is how the argument goes: By his prevenient grace, God gives each person a conscience. Conscience means the ability to decide between right and wrong. That ability implies freedom. Freedom implies accountability. Accountability implies responsibility. Finally, responsibility implies hope because it means you are not helpless, that is, there is something you can do.

One reason Wesley opposed the Calvinists was because he feared they could not offer hope to any except the elect. Of course, because no one knew ahead of time whether he was elect or not, one could always hope he might be. Still, there was nothing one could do about it. "Just wait and see" is not an attitude that provides much incentive. Perhaps Wesley was also temperamentally incapable of waiting for anything. Whatever the reasons might have been, it was his polemical engagement with Calvinism that provided him the occasion to polish a doctrine of grace that synthesized grace and responsibility so that his hearers were given reason for hope. That, perhaps as much as anything else, fueled the Wesleyan movement in the eighteenth century. They could respect themselves in this world and expect perfection in the life to come, if not before. So hope remains one of the most fundamental human needs in all times and places.

How can hope be embodied in a picture? If, as Vaclav Havel, former president of Czechoslovakia, affirmed, hope is committing oneself to a goal because it is good, but without an absolute guarantee that it will be attained, perhaps the image of running the race in the presence of those who encourage us can serve us with power. "Since we are surrounded by so great a cloud of witnesses…let us run with perseverance the race that is set before us."[17]

Of course, this is a biblical image, but it does not depend on theism for its power. Certain biblical images can still serve us in the new time while others simply do not. Of course, different people will always respond to different images.

The image of a footrace embodies the same essential elements as our version of the passion story's meaning. First, we are encouraged in the race by the witness of those who cheer us on, even as Jesus' life and death witness to us of the possibility of achieving daily victories by the positive powers over the negative forces of history. Second, the finish line toward which we race is a promise because it provides a vision of the goal itself, even as the picture of Jesus' resurrection promises the victory of spirit over death.

The hope that Wesley preached included the promise, in Peter's epistle, that we may come "to participate in the divine nature."[18] For him, that was the promise of divinization he had encountered in the teaching of some of the Ante-Nicene Fathers and the mystical union with God he had so avidly sought in his early years. In these new times, we are offered hope, not simply for victory over the negative powers in our lives, but for a real spiritual union, or harmonious participation in the life of the Great Spirit himself. As the individual uses her freedom to focus her attention on the things of the spirit and undertakes the spiritual disciplines of prayer (and perhaps fasting), she can create the conditions that allow the initiative of grace to operate.

Hope that pulls us through the race of spiritual growth also reaches into the future beyond our natural deaths. The victory of the positive powers over the negative powers, that perfect union with the Spirit who is God, is assured for us at some point beyond the death of our natural bodies, even if it is never attained in this life.

Those for whom it is hard to face each new day find it so because hope has grown dim. The little hopes associated with the pleasures of the day or the morrow are weak or nonexistent. But, no matter how dim our little hopes have grown or how difficult life has become, there can be hope, not simply for a better life beyond death, but hope for victories of the positive spiritual powers over the negative, today or tomorrow. Such hope for this life can feed our patience and restore our joy. Then hope for the life of the spirit beyond this life begins to take care of itself.

Is there an image to be found for this completion, this fulfillment? Or must we go back to that Negro spiritual I quoted earlier and try to remember the spirit world for which it stands? The following is how the whole of it goes:

> I dreamed of a city called holy, so bright and so fair. When I entered the gates I cried holy; the angels all met me there. They carried me from mansion to mansion. Then I said I want to see Jesus, the one who died for us. So I fell on my knees and cried holy. I cried holy, Thou art holy! I clapped my hands and sang glory, glory to the Son of God. As I entered the gates of that city, my loved ones all knew me well. They took me down the streets of heaven. Oh the saints, too many to tell. I saw Abraham, Jacob and Isaac, talked with Mark and Timothy...I fell on my knees and cried holy! Holy, holy, holy! I clapped my hands and sang glory! There was glory, oh glory! Glory, I clapped my hands and sang glory! I clapped my hands and sang glory! I sang glory, glory to the Son of God! I sang glory to the Son of God![19]

That song moves me deeply. I can play it repeatedly, but, unless I remember the spiritual explanation of the journey that takes me "down the streets of heaven," it is no more than a thrilling piece of music. Can we hold this hope with some powerful image that avoids the separation of sheep and goats?

What about the Big Party? In any case, those who are seekers can create their own poetry and share it with one another while the preachers' imaginations must provide the images and the witness that will address the profound human need for hope.

The Universal Need for Meaning and Purpose

Our time has been characterized as a time of crisis in meaning. Perhaps that is true. However, the eighteenth century hearers of Wesley's preaching found they also needed a purpose for their life. Their longing for a sense of the meaningfulness of life was met by the message John Wesley spoke to them. That longing was closely related to their need for hope. However, there is a difference.

The difference between hope and meaning is that hope is more directly focused on the future, either short-term or long-term. Meaning refers to the need for fulfillment in the present. Meaning is found in the doing, that is, in the process instead of in the anticipated result.

That distinction keeps us focused on Wesley's process of sanctification, the process by which one goes on toward perfection. The process is not only meaningful because the end is anticipated. It is meaningful because of the joy accompanying the struggle itself. The struggle is meaningful because it aims at the goal, not because it believes the goal will be attained. I suggest that joy is the emotional product of meaningful struggle, for example, something like love is the emotional product of a deep connection. Everyone, in all times and circumstances, needs to experience the joy of the struggle. Wesley gave his hearers that.

In some circles, the struggle for perfection has been disparaged as smacking of arrogance. It is also often suggested that it produces a judgmental attitude toward other persons. Moreover, it is sometimes blamed as the source of bitter frustration. I have even heard bishops suggest in ordination services that the Wesleyan question asking ordinands if they are going on to perfection should not be taken very seriously. Though Wesley did believe one should have instantaneous perfection as his goal, he strongly focused his emphasis on what he called the gradual process. For him, instantaneous perfection was simply that moment when the process of removing conscious sin would be complete, a quite legitimate goal.

According to Wesley, to pray for spiritual growth, for the increase in oneself of the "mind which was in Jesus" and to hope for the gift of holiness which is only possible by God's grace, provides no ground for arrogance or pride. In fact, the moment one starts to take pride in his holiness, as though it were his own accomplishment and not a fruit of his faith (which is itself not of one's own doing but a gift from God), he has stepped backward and lost some degree of spiritual growth that may have already occurred.

In the struggle toward perfection, there is no ground either for arrogance or standing in judgment on others. If the struggle results in either one or the other, it is because one has trusted in his own efforts and not in God's grace. It is because he has sought to take credit to himself, which is not the perfection that John Wesley preached.

As to the frustrations of the struggle, you will definitely flounder, slip, fall, pick yourself up, and move forward again. That is the nature of struggle, just as it is the nature of serious training for an athletic competition. If you talk to any serious athlete, you will learn of the pain, the sweat, the doubtful moments, the need to change training methods, and the need to keep one's aim clear. You will also likely discover there is a certain exhilaration in the effort. The result is never sure, but the aim is certain. The hope abides, and the purpose produces joy. Wesley responded to the universal need for meaning and purpose in the only way he knew, and the people heard him.

What is the meaning of life for human beings in the twenty-first century? I suspect every thoughtful person has asked this question, that is, all who have contemplated both the beauty and ugliness of life. The suffering that attends so many millions in the struggle for mere survival fills our minds with horror. Our own sufferings when we lose a precious someone or possession or when we experience failures and disappointments in the pursuit of success, honor, fame, celebrity, or power force the question into our consciousness. Universally, human beings need to find meaning in their lives. In fact, most of our daily activities are devoted to the attempt to wrest meaning from our mundane pursuits. Sometimes we try to settle for very little indeed, for example, hobbies, recreation, entertainment, artistic enterprises, and other pursuits such as those Kierkegaard attributes to what he calls the "aesthetic" stage of the human search. Yet, the testimony of the ages everywhere and among all people is that such pursuits provide only fleeting satisfaction and a very fragile and ambiguous *raison d'être*. We really need to be able to say, "The purpose of my life is to…"

Sometimes, perhaps out of desperation, we hear people report on some close call, some experience of survival. They conclude their story with, "God still had something for me to do," or "He wouldn't have saved me unless he had a purpose for my life." From our perspective on the spirit world, we want to affirm the purpose of each human spirit is to take the spirit journey toward what we may call spiritual maturity. In fact, I suspect Wesley might have approved of such terminology had he been able to find it in the Bible.

During a grief therapy session following my wife's death, the leader asked each of us to write two things on a piece of paper: our favorite name for God and the one thing that was of the greatest importance in our life at that moment. We were then to form those two things into a prayer and write it out. I wrote, "Father, show me a sufficient purpose for the rest of my life."

Until her death, I had been content to believe the purpose of my life had become caring for her. Now I had no idea what to do. However, I had no more than written the prayer down than understanding dawned. The purpose of my life had not really changed. The meaning of my life was still to walk the spirit journey, pursuing the perfection of hope and love as well as of peace and unity with God the Spirit. Of course, I still had the technical problems of how to do it, what steps to take, and what opportunities to grasp. Much of that depended upon the time and place in which I lived. The how-to lies in the details for any person anywhere or in any time. For me, the only things that had changed were the details. Before, I had focused my care on one person. Now I had to walk the spirit journey in a much wider context.

Wesley said he wanted above all else to discover "how to get to heaven."[20] That struggle, I take it, was the meaning of his life. Yet, I cannot think of heaven as a place to get to. The image of heaven has largely disappeared, along with the image of a theistic God.

I think it was almost gone by the time my mama died when I was eight years old. Perhaps, even then, the idea of God as a good guy up in heaven, tied as it was to the theistic image of God, had begun to crumble. I think I have struggled with it ever since, but the Spirit as God touches and holds me. And I want to find union with her or him.

This is a purpose sufficient for any life, and it is one that cannot be destroyed by its vicissitudes and setbacks. So, each human spirit needs to find meaning for his life, which is impossible except for the generosity and the loving initiative of the Spirit who is God. This is a good-news message for the twenty-first century.

The Universal Need for Guidance

What should I do? How can I decide what I ought to do? As free human beings, we need to make decisions and constantly act upon them throughout every day of our lives. We need help in making those decisions. Yogi Berra once said that whenever you come to a fork in the road, you should take it. But it is never that easy, is it? Some decision must always be made. Guidance is a universal need for each human being.

Wesley's treatment of what he called prevenient grace provided his basis for decision making. The gift of a conscience was a primary feature of God's gift of spirit to each person. However, the presence of a conscience does not provide guidance in itself. Instead, it is the power to discern and assess possibilities, weigh the options in terms of the values they embody, and decide on the actions that serve the values with the greatest weight, that is, decide between right and wrong.

The values giving weight to our decisions come from a variety of sources. Our parents teach us some, or they may come from our schools. Some come from our social or religious environments. However, because we have a conscience, we are free to weigh and decide.

According to Wesley, the source of true values is the Holy Spirit. Of course, he does not call them values. As we have seen, the Scriptures name a fair number of them, including faith, hope, love, joy, peace, patience, gentleness, kindness, and self-control. Of special interest in this context is the gift of self-control. Self-control is the deliberate use of our powers of conscience. There is greater value in careful deliberation about our actions than in ill-considered or thoughtless action. So, for Wesley, a conscience given by prevenient grace, along with the fruits of the spirit given by sanctifying grace, are the source of our guidance.

The freedom we are thus given makes us responsible persons. The struggle to open ourselves to the gifts of the spirit and make right decisions may well be understood to be what Paul referred to as "working out our salvation in fear and trembling."[21] The gift of freedom is a fearful gift, but it is part of what it means to be spiritual beings. Moreover, each time we exercise that freedom with self-control, we grow in self-awareness.

In the meantime, the fundamental universal need of the human spirit to find guidance for his decision making is all but self-evident. The question is: Where will he find that guidance?

We need to fill our spirit-given consciences with some kind of values, that is, some judgments about what is important and what is less important so we can make decisions about what we do and what we refuse to do. What values will we use? Conditioned social values? Learned rules of action? Someone else's system of morality? Some set of rules of conduct, like the Old Testament Law? A system devised by some other lawgiver? Or will the positive powers and the negative powers we have described earlier help to inform our consciences?

We wonder: Is a conscience unique to the human spirit? Is there any other animal that makes calculated decisions? The conduct of animals lower on the scale of spirit is mostly determined by instinct and conditioning, and it does not involve calculation and choice. However, the higher animals among them sometimes seem to demonstrate the ability to make simple, calculated choices. However, that freedom is pretty minimal, even as the level of self-awareness is correspondingly lower.

At the same time, many of our human activities are determined by our autonomous nervous system, for example, breathing, heartbeat, and so forth. Many of our values are reinforced in us by the culture of which we are a part. Usually, we have not examined those values very carefully. We assume they are valid and right and that our only job is to weigh them against each other and finally decide which are the most important and which actions will best serve to promote them.

Our spirit focus, however, requires a careful examination of inherited or conditioned values to determine if they can contribute to the goal of harmony and peace. These will be, usually, the positive powers. They are the grist for the mill of conscience. (Does this suggest a meaningful image?) For example, which powers will best contribute to the peace and harmony the Great Spirit is struggling to achieve in this situation at this time? Such decision making is not easy.

I want to suggest here some principles for making our calculations.

- First, we need to pray for the strengthening of the positive powers within us so the negative powers can be subdued.

- We then need to pray for a clear mind to make the technical calculations that will tell us which actions will best serve the goals the Spirit who is God seeks to realize.

- Very often, our calculations will also require a determination of intermediate goals to be realized before the more nearly ultimate goals may be achieved.

These few principles are available for our decisions regarding what we usually call personal morality. They are also available for our public or social morality, our community service, our political activities, and our advocacy for justice and peace.

Wesley preached a great deal on moral issues, but the central thrust of all his moral exhortation was that holiness was love. In the spirit image treatment of spiritual growth, we have focused on unity or peace as the ultimate value or goal. Is it not self-evident that the initiative of grace or unconditional love is the principle means by which forgiveness brings about reconciliation and reconciliation brings about healing, peace, and unity? Because we are in the Great Spirit and are part of his own ongoing struggle, we know our well-intentioned misjudgments and even our wrongheaded efforts are accepted and new opportunities for change are offered. No positive deed is ever lost, and no negative deed can ever condemn us to lose our real connection with the Spirit who is God, though it may result in feelings of alienation or guilt on our part.

We have not mentioned the idea of providence in our discussions, although it was a large item in Wesley's consciousness. For example, he believed he was spared from the fire that destroyed the Epworth rectory when he was a child to do some great work for God. Moreover, he devoted an oft-preached sermon to the subject called "On Divine Providence." It was not written until his later period when he was more inclined to deal with speculative subjects. So, Wesley did believe in the kingdom of God and his ultimate victory and preached late sermons on "The New Creation" and other themes related to the end of history as we know it.

Providence was much more central to Calvinism's scheme of things because the central idea there was the sovereignty of God. In addition, sovereignty suggests absolute control.

However, in the spirit image picture, a nuanced view of sovereignty and providence are implied. God has given each spirit a degree of self-awareness and therefore some degree of freedom. However, that freedom is never absolute, partly because one's self-awareness or individuality is always relative. It is partly also because the options available are always limited. Our natural space/time locations and the actions of other persons limit them.

The Great Spirit, as a self-aware individual in his own right (even though each of us is a member of his spiritual body), constantly seeks to impact our spirits in order to enhance the positive and subdue the negative. He does this through the power of spiritual communication that is always limited by the dams holding back the waters of his grace. That pressure sometimes opens those dams—weakened either by means of our spiritual disciplines or the impact of external events—allowing the grace to flow more freely. He is involved, but he is no Big Brother.

Guess what! Another analogy comes to mind. I see the shepherd with his dog. They have ultimate control of the flock, but they do not have absolute control because the sheep move this way and that, sometimes trying to escape the flock and sometimes trying to hide themselves in the midst of the flock. When one sheep moves too far out of line, a command is given. The sheepdog cuts him off and brings him back, limiting his choices. Piece by piece, the flock is moved gently but surely to a fresh new pasture and flowing water.

Thus, the Great Spirit is constantly bringing his pressure to bear, and it is always positive, seeking openings and opportunities we may provide or, in the case of physical healing, may be opened by medicine, surgery, or therapies. Thus, the final outcome is assured, and there will be a million times in the course of everyone's life when that pressure will impact our lives, bring about unexpected results, and inexorably shape the future. Some of those occasions are the events we call miracles or acts of providence. However, whether we recognize and name them or not, they are occurring every day and every hour, and God continues healing himself.

Our decisions and actions are moral in the degree to which they cooperate with the Spirit's self-healing. Our preaching and teaching can provide guidance for needy consciences.

The Universal Need for Understanding

Aristotle said philosophy began with awe, or something like that. Rudolph Otto wrote a whole book on what he called "the numinous," that is, something out there (or in here) you cannot put a name to, yet is real. Certainly, the need to understand has a similar beginning. The human being is not only self-aware, but he is aware of that which is not himself. At a very early age, he learns there is something out there that he is curious to discover. At some point, he learns the toes he finds nearby are really a part of his own body, but the blankets covering him are not. When he finds himself trusting someone that is not himself, he becomes curious to learn about that which he trusts, the object of his faith. Therefore, the man of faith must also ask what it is he trusts and what it is he fears and why.

He needs to understand what he hopes for, what he is connected to but not identical with, the object of his love and his passion, the meaning of life and of his own life, and what is really important in life. He needs to be able to organize these things in his mind, to be able to think about and discuss these things. Unless he attains some level of understanding, he can neither anticipate the consequences of his actions nor weigh the values involved in possible actions. He cannot decide and act on his decisions.

Wesley was often accused of being an enthusiast, that is, his accusers claimed he was governed by his emotions instead of reason. However, he had a very high regard for reason, even while he insisted its limits needed to be observed.

For instance, certain things were to be believed without full understanding:

> Let him firmly believe, there is but one God, the object of any Divine worship whatever; and think and speak of him under that plain, scriptural distinctivity of Father, Son and Holy Ghost; leaving the incomprehensible nature of that union and distinction to the great author of our faith himself. Let him believe Christ to be the only begotten Son of God, in the obvious import of these words, and leave the manner of that inconceivable generation to the veracity of God. Let him believe, that Christ did as truly make an Atonement to God for us, as one man atones for another to a third person; and leave the unintelligible part of that Divine operation, for the subject of future praise and contemplation. Let men, I say, believe as far as they thus clearly understand, without perplexing themselves or others with what is incomprehensible, and then they fulfill the whole purpose of God in all his revelation.[22]

One should seek to understand as far as he is able, remembering the spiritual powers, including thought, are given us to be used, enjoyed, improved, and shared.

> Let reason do all that reason can: Employ it as far as it will go. But at the same time, acknowledge it is utterly incapable of giving either faith, or hope, or love; and consequently, of producing either real virtue or substantial happiness. Expect them from a higher source, even from the Father of the spirits of all flesh. Seek and receive them, not as your own acquisition; but as the gift of God.[23]

I confess I want to understand some other things besides those Wesley was anxious to understand and explain. I want to understand the nature of that reality I call God. To be more accurate, I want to understand what I mean when I engage in God-talk. I want to understand what in the world one can mean by saying God was in Jesus reconciling the world to himself. I want to understand why the story of Jesus' crucifixion and resurrection has been such a powerful story for millions and continues speaking to me. I want to understand the spiritual reality involved there. I want to understand how my sense that there is something more than the natural world going on relates to the burgeoning interest in unnatural phenomena.

Finally, like Wesley, I want to understand something about how I can work out, with fear and trembling, my salvation, my wholeness, and my maturity as a spiritual being. I might as well admit right here that the whole process of writing all this down is probably as much for the clarification of my own thought as it is for my readers.

I know there seem to be some people who could not care less about understanding, but that is not because they do not want to understand. Rather, they do not want to have their current understandings questioned or exert themselves to wrestle with issues—political, social, or religious—about which they have already made up their minds. They have their own understandings and simply do not want to exert themselves to answer objections or listen to alternatives. They want to understand, but they are content to rest on their existing notions. (These may turn out to be nothing more than prejudices—or they might turn out to be true after all.)

When it comes to speaking of God, I believe it is hugely important for people to understand what image or idea of God they are affirming or rejecting. Without such understanding, their speaking becomes unintelligible.

John Wesley was not much concerned with understanding the "manner" of the Trinity, the Incarnation, or the Atonement. These were mysteries he preferred to take for granted because he assumed understanding them was not directly relevant to the living of the Christian life or the ongoing pursuit of salvation. However, he was profoundly interested in understanding and helping others to understand the nature of grace, the gifts of grace, and the responsibilities of those who received those gifts. For him, an understanding of salvation was the most important thing any human being needed to grasp.

Wesley's message served to meet to a significant extent in his time and place the universal human need for understanding, but the most important thing of all to be understood was that salvation was not the product of our own reasoning. It was the gift of God.

The universal human needs to which Wesley's message was addressed were powerfully met in the lives of the poor, the lost, and the hopeless of eighteenth-century England. Can his message, his language, and his understanding speak to these new times? I do not believe it, but I do believe the universal human needs he so effectively addressed in those times still remain fundamental for all of us. With a new theological vision, a new understanding of God, and a recast language, we can meet those same universal needs in these new times with new power.

You may find it strange I have not identified faith or trust as a universal human need. I have not specified trust because it is so intimately related to the need for understanding. However, it might be helpful to describe that relationship.

Certainly, there may be an attitude or spirit of trust that does not arise from a definition of God or an explanation of the world of spirit. For example, one may experience a feeling or sensation of oneness with all things, such as some mystics seek, perhaps a deep contentment or rest. After all, no theory and no product of reasoning, as Wesley himself often insisted, can produce salvation or spiritual growth and wholeness by itself.

Several years ago, I was invited to stop to have ice cream and cake at my niece's birthday party. This happened just when I was ready to start a four-hour drive home. While sitting at the table over a bowl of ice cream, a huge headache began gripping the back of my head. I rose and began walking about, thinking it would ease up. It did not, and I lay down on the couch. That did not help, and I sat in a soft chair. I was scared and confused. My niece saw my distress and called 9-1-1. Within minutes, the door opened, and four paramedics walked in with their equipment. The instant I saw them, an immense feeling of relief overtook me. My fear simply melted, and my confusion quieted down. I knew everything was going to be just all right. I still did not know what was wrong, and I did not know what they were going to do. I did not even think, "Well, I'm not going to die after all." I just knew, whatever happened, it was going to be okay.

I think of that experience as one of utter trust. I still did not understand I was about to have brain surgery, but it was all okay. Such an experience of trust cries out for some kind of understanding of that which is trusted, some explanation or theory. My understanding of the events of that day came much later. So, trust is not simply believing an explanation or a proposition.

However, trust may also come after one has heard and believed an explanation. For example, it may be a matter of entrusting one's life to the spirit world of which one has acquired some understanding, either prior to the rise of trust or after the trust has stimulated the search for understanding. In one way or another, the need to trust is always involved with the desire to understand. It needs to come before or following understanding. In this way, I believe we may include the human need for trust within the universal need for understanding.

My image for this search is that light awaiting me at the end of the tunnel and promising such brilliance of understanding that I may end up blinded by it all. Such is the mystery toward which the journey takes us. Finally, that brings me to reaffirm, however long I have struggled to understand the implications of the spirit image of God, I have still ended up with the overwhelming mystery, one leaving me without words to properly praise, thank, and rejoice in the Great Spirit. Still, without trying to understand, I cannot even come to that conclusion.

This, then, is where I have come out. In these last three chapters, I have attempted to set forth the outlines of a reconstructed message for living, preaching, and teaching in these times. It draws strongly, but selectively, from the Christian Bible. It uses the traditions of Christian antiquity and the classic terminology of orthodoxy as filtered through the theological prism of John Wesley's mind and experience. It follows his example of eclectic theological reformulation to freely set forth a new vision of God and a description of spiritual maturity that, I believe, will resonate with the cultural sensitivities of the twenty-first century.

Using this message in these new times will require constant attention to living the Christian life, its reinterpretation in terms of the focal image of the spirit world, and an openness to new images, new poetry, and new music that may well arise as we carry this incredibly good news into the new future.

Part II

I'm beginning this section without apology, but with a considerable measure of humility. The first section represents the culmination of personal study and reading and not a little struggle with what has been happening in my spiritual and theological life from its very beginning. This part is the result of a very intentional effort to write sermons out of the results of that struggle. A certain number of those sermons began in hit-or-miss experimentation during the past twenty years. In retrospect, I found they reflected the very struggles that gave rise to this book in the first place. As they appear here, they have been heavily edited and, in some cases, largely rewritten. A majority of these sermons have been written as an intentional expression of the positions I have worked out in Part I. In this respect, I am following Wesley's lead. Therefore, the sermons are intended to be theologically instructive both for those who preach or teach and for any who seek a fresh way of viewing the faith.

The comments for each sermon are an attempt to clarify in what ways I understand the sermon in question to illustrate the kind of appropriation of Wesley's message for this century that I am proposing. I believe these sermons are less convoluted than my earlier preaching precisely because they rely on a radically different image of God. The positions adopted in Part I are assumed in these sermons and are often restated. However, I believe they retain the essential spiritual message for which Wesley strove in his preaching and respond to the same universal human needs.

They are ordered within the framework of Wesley's doctrine of salvation, even though each is given a name more in keeping with the new focal image of God as Spirit. With two exceptions, I have used the masculine pronouns for God in these sermons. In the two exceptions, the context seemed to require the feminine. Though the image of theism itself is the source of divine masculinity in the Christian tradition, I have chosen not to make this an issue because there seems to be no good way to be systematically gender neutral in reference to the deity.

8

More than Natural—Sermons on Prevenient Grace

Sermon 1
In the Beginning God
Genesis 1:1–5, 26–27 and Acts 2:1–17

Comment:

The biblical reference for this sermon is:

> *In the beginning when God created the heavens and the earth, the earth was a formless void and darkness covered the face of the deep, while a wind (alternatively read "spirit") from God swept over the face of the waters. Then God said "Let there be light";…and there was evening and there was morning, the first day.*[1]

Doesn't this suggest a picture of a potter and his clay? Or does it feel more like the sensation that Morris West speaks of in his novel **Navigator** as: *"—the voice of God—the rumbling at the deep foundation of things?"*[2]

Or perhaps it is that which one can only address as "Thou." Remember Dag Hammarsjold's prayer? *"Thou Whom I do not know But Whose I am. Thou Whom I do not comprehend But Who hast dedicated me To my fate. Thou."*[3]

Most doctrines of God are attempts to reduce some image or other sensation—visual or auditory—to an intellectual construction. For Wesley, God was described by the classical theistic and Trinitarian categories rooted in antiquity and his ecclesiastical heritage. He did preach one sermon on "The Attributes of God" and another on "On the Trinity." However, the only reason the sermon on the Trinity was ever written down and published was because his hearers asked him to write it out so they could have it to study. So his treatment of God did respond to the universal need to understand something about the beginning of things. It answered a need that some recognized. But it was not, Wesley believed, of great significance for most of his hearers, especially early in his ministry.

In this sermon, I do attempt to respond to that kind of question, a question that may be of greater interest to people in this scientific age than it was to the poor among eighteenth-century Englishmen. But, like Wesley, I am more interested in beginning to deal with the universal need for purpose and meaning. Each individual needs to feel and believe he or she has some purpose for his existence. I am saying here that each person is, in fact, crucial to the working out of the final destiny of creation as a responsible participant in the cosmic purpose and activity of God. The principal target of this first *sermon in the context of Wesley's notion of prevenient grace, therefore, is the need for purpose. The question of beginnings is used to introduce the issue of meaning.*

For Wesley, the idea of prevenient grace also served as a rejection of predestination and an affirmation both of free will and of faith as a gift. I have tried here, as did Wesley, to find a way to affirm both the responsibility implied by free will and the humility that grace makes necessary.

You will note the great word "grace" is never used, let alone the term "prevenient." Instead, I speak of God's free gift of himself as the spirit given to every person, thus rendering them spiritual human beings who participate in his being and his destiny as well as in their own. This concept of the relation of God and the human being is presupposed by all the following sermons.

◆ ◆ ◆

Before the worlds began, before the stars and moons, the trees and fields, the rivers and the seas—before chaos became ordered and each thing was divided from every other thing—it was probably one enormous mess! No one really knows just what it was like. But, at some point, in some fashion, something happened. And it began to take form, shape, and order.

How do you explain that?

Well, some thing, some intelligence, or some power there moved over and through it and gave it form. And here it is, what we call creation.

The biblical story says it was God the Spirit who did it! It was God who took all this chaotic mess and gave it some kind of order. It does not bother to answer the question: Where did all the chaos come from? It just says the spirit of God moved over it, sorted it all out, and put it in order.

Well, I am not about to attack the several different scientific theories about the beginnings of the world. After all, none of those theories says anything, one way or the other, about God. So I really have no problem with them.

What we do know is there is a system by which all this stuff works together, laws governing the movements of molecules and atoms, billiard balls, and falling leaves. And that in itself is a miracle.

This whole idea of order, of natural laws, tells me all this stuff we live with, what we call creation or the universe, is something more than an accident! We humans have this incredible power of observing the regularities in the natural world and of formulating laws we use to understand and manipulate the world. So, I would like to know, where else do these regularities, which we are able to formulate into natural laws, come from except the same kind of intelligence that makes the laws?

<u>To tell you the truth</u>, <u>the only place I experience intelligence</u> <u>is as a power of the human spirit</u>. Ergo, the ordered natural world must be a product of some intelligent spirit.

It appears to me the book of Genesis, where the word for spirit and the word for wind are the same, was right on target when it said the Spirit of God swept over the "formless void," and, thereafter, the chaos took shape.

But so what? What difference in my life and yours does all that make? The spirit brought order out of chaos?

Well, the most amazing thing in all of creation is the miracle of the human spirit itself, the miracle of you, the miracle of me, and the miracle of all the huddled masses who also struggle to survive, strive to bring order into their lives, and reach their hands to grasp their goals and their dreams.

We all are bodies, but we all are spirits, too. We have no problem speaking of the spirit of love we find within ourselves, the spirit of hope or joy, the spirit of enthusiasm or peace, or even the negative spirits of jealousy or vengeance. We know the spirit of curiosity. We are not blind beasts without powers of observation or the ability to make scientific theories. We are not mere animals without questions about how we came to be, without questions about how to live what we have been given, or without some vision of what might be or some dream of what we might become.

This amazing human spirit—this power to think, imagine, dream, plan, choose, and create—this phenomenon of consciousness is unique. It is unlike the mind of the beasts, even though we sometimes sense the presence of spirit among them.

Our self-awareness is that center around which we find all the powers of spirit gathered. Therefore, nothing is more real, anywhere we look, than the reality of spirit in the human being. For it is by that spirit we both know the natural world and we imagine and plan how to change it.

So spirit is here! Spirit is real! And all that which we observe within our consciousness that strikes us dumb with wonder, we call it spirit. Direction and purpose, the power to hope and dream, the power to wonder and ask questions, the power to choose, and even the negative powers within us that resist the positives, we call it all the human spirit.

Moreover, we have a name for this entire spirit world of which we are also a part. We have a name for all those positive, creative, unifying powers, along with their negative, divisive counterparts inhabiting the earth. They are the powers that brought it first into being and that now keep it real, that live, distorted and confused, imperfect and at war within us, making us uniquely human, and like no other creatures upon the earth. We call it all "God," this world of spirit.

God is that Spirit who moves in and through the whole of creation. It was God who is Spirit who moved over the chaos and breathed order into it. It was God who is Spirit who breathed his life into you (and into me), giving us some portion of himself and making us into spirit people.

Or perhaps one might say, like a mother giving birth out of her own fertility, she brought us into the world as parts of herself. Either way, "In the beginning was God!"

So, the spirit in each human being is a gift, God's gift of herself. We had nothing to do with it. We just received it, the spirit that is our life and our consciousness, which gives us curiosity and the power to dream and to choose.

So, before God was known as Father, before he was known as Son, before the doctrine of the Trinity ever came into the mind of man, God was Spirit. And all Spirit was God.

Every thought of our minds leads us inexorably to the original reality of Spirit. Even the ancient story of creation, there at the beginning of the Old Testament, affirms it.

So today, we know that Spirit is real! There is a spirit world with its own laws, and that world is in constant interaction with the world of natural law, even as our spirits are always in interaction with our bodies. Even so, negative and divisive spirits within each of us contend against the positive and creative spirits that are in each of us.

Within each of us, there is a mighty struggle for control. As light struggles against the darkness and knowledge against ignorance and wholeness against brokenness, the contest goes on through the nighttime, in the daytime, in our dreams, and in our waking.

How then can we ever come out of this cauldron, out of this spiritual turmoil? How can God, who seeks always to subdue the negative powers, come out victorious within us?

John Wesley often talked about the natural man. He said the natural man could do no good, and we may add "no evil either." The natural man, the animal in him, the beast apart from spirit, could have no power to choose, to decide between good and evil. He could never have the power, apart from the gift of spirit, to believe in God, trust God the Spirit, or decide to live by the spirit. He could not pray for God's spirit to possess him in all its fullness or pray for the fruits of the spirit to live in him and overflow him into the lives of those around him.

So, we humans, who never have been simply natural beings but who have all been given our spirits, our self-consciousness, by the gracious Spirit who is God, are thereby capable of deciding to trust the Spirit. That is why even our faith, our trust, is not something we can take credit for.

By trusting the Spirit, every victory of ours over the negative spirits within us, every time we put down and trample beneath our feet the powers within and around us that divide and destroy, we are participating in the victory of God. So, as we are saved, made sound and whole, and made fit for life in God the Spirit, God himself is saved and made whole. God himself is healed.

So, we will live in God through all the ages to come by our trust in the power of the Spirit who is God. We will be saved and made whole, not by our good deeds, not by obeying a bunch of rules, and not by believing all the correct doctrines. We will be saved by living in the Spirit and entrusting ourselves to God who is Spirit and who will rule at last. We are saved by participating in God's own struggle against all that alienates and builds walls of hostility and by becoming makers of peace and practitioners of healing.

We will be part of God's struggle to bring to reality a new creation in which the spirit of unity has subdued all the spirits of discord in what the Bible calls the Kingdom.

For God the Spirit is more powerful than the creation he brought into being. And all the healing powers of God the Spirit are more powerful than all the negative spirits that are also operating in the world, more powerful than the spirits of destruction and alienation, of division and envy, of hopelessness and despair, of apathy and hostility, or of violence and vengeance.

For in the beginning was God who is Spirit. And at the end it is God the Spirit who shall reign victorious over sin and death!

Amen.

> *O You who before the beginning were already old,*
>   *unseen,*
>   *unknown*
>   *and unimaginable:*
> *Still we imagine You,*
>   *Spirit before the beginning,*
>   *old before the new came into being,*

self-knowing,
dreaming,
longing,
anticipating,
preparing,
planning for the new,
    for the beginning of all natural things,
    for the birth of all spiritual things
    and for the wholeness of the community of all spirit,
        even the perfection of ourselves in You.
You it is we love and praise,
  in whom we live,
  move
  and have our being.
Amen. Saf

Sermon 2
Where No One Stands Alone
Genesis 2:4b–9 and John 17:20–26

Comment:

This sermon uses Jesus' prayer for unity as its biblical reference. Though the prayer itself speaks of the unity still to be achieved, I am affirming both a unity that already exists and the possibility of its more perfect realization. This represents a change on Wesley's prevenient grace that the spirit doctrine of God allows me to make. Because the Spirit who is God is not a discrete entity whose union with the human spirit must be manufactured, the relationship is already a real one, even as a cancerous cell is already a part of the larger body.

Of course, Wesley himself often used the passage from John when he preached on perfection. For him, it was the promise of a possibility. I have used it less literally to suggest the ideal goal of union with God already involves the foundational reality of our oneness in the spirit world.

Wesley's recognition of some insignificant measure of goodness that attaches to the deeds of an unjustified or unconverted person was necessary given his postulate of the gift of prevenient grace. But, when a human spirit is understood to be the Spirit's gift of himself, any deed that furthers the movement of that human spirit toward its proper goal of complete compatibility with the spirit's purpose of unity must be seen as good. Therefore, the reality of human participation in the spirit world, that is, in God, needs to be recognized by human beings in order for the connection that exists to begin meeting our universal need for a connection that consciously bridges the appearance of separation created by our individuality. This sermon is intended to sensitize the listener to the connection that already exists and thus meet his or her fundamental need for connection.

Wesley tried to satisfy his passion for union with God, first through his reading in the mystical writers and his devotional life and later with his efforts to achieve it through his good works. Finally, he found reconciliation between God and man through God's gift of justifying faith. Beyond that, his promise of perfection or instantaneous sanctification was a promise of "participation in the divine nature."[4]

The difference between Wesley's connections and those of a spiritual theology is that his were based on a legally acquired guarantee of the gift of grace by way of the Atonement. On the other hand, the spiritual view is that the essential gift or grace of spirit belongs to humans simply because of their creation as spirit beings. Even before our perfect reconciliation with other persons, there exists our spiritual connection with them through our mutual participation in the Spirit who is God. This provides the foundation for the kind of growth and deepening of our connections that satisfy the need we all possess. It is nurtured and perfected by the disciplines of prayer.

◆ ◆ ◆

> Once I stood in the night with my head bowed low
>   in the darkness as black as could be.
> And my heart felt alone and I cried,
>   O Lord, don't hide your face from me…
> Like a king I may live in a palace so tall
>   with greater riches to call my own;
>   but I don't know a thing
>   in this whole wide world
>   that's worse than being alone.
> Hold my hand all the way,
>   every hour, every day
>   from here to the great unknown.
> Take my hand,
>   let me stand where no one—
>   where no one stands alone.[5]

Is there such a place, a place where no one stands alone?

Yes, there is! In the meantime, in the night with our heads bowed low, our hearts feel alone, and we cry, "Oh Lord, don't hide your face from me."

Now, I know these feelings and thoughts are not just mine. I know every one of us starts his life (this is what our child psychologists tell us) without any sense of "I" and "you" or even of "me" and everything else that's "not me." But, very soon, we begin to pull our toes, look at our fingers, and touch our mother's face. Then begins to dawn the incredible fact we are unique and different.

Finally, we become aware of ourselves and discover that what is not "I" often goes away and disappears. And we are left alone. So, we learn to talk and begin to communicate with what is not ourselves. But we cannot always count on what is not ourselves to be there. Still, we ourselves are always present.

Thus, we experience our individuality, which means we discover we are alone and always subject to being separated from the rest of the world.

There is nothing wrong with that, of course. It is part of growing up human, a part of being a spirit being. However, everybody experiences it a little differently and differently at different times.

Here is something I wrote down the other day after hearing a Negro spiritual on the car radio. It was a song that triggered memories and caused my tears to flow again.

This is what I wrote:

> Sometimes I feel like a motherless child.
>   (My mother died when I was eight.)
> Sometimes I feel like a rudderless ship.
>   (I've struggled all my life with my calling as a pastor.)
> Sometimes I feel like the only star
>   in the vastness of the heavens.
> And sometimes I feel like the only snowflake
>   left in the sunshine.
> Sometimes I feel like a vagrant along an empty road.
> Sometimes I feel like a fortress without windows.
> Sometimes I feel like crying for my mother.
> And sometimes I feel like calling for my dad.
> Sometimes I feel like I've been looking for my brother all my life,
>   when I've never even had a brother at all.
> Sometimes I feel like I am running in the street again
>   behind the car
>   that carries my parents down the road,
>   out of town
>   and beyond the horizon.
> And the terror wells up from my chest
>   and makes my throat to ache
>   and fills my head with a child's terrible panic.

These things I remember. You remember your things, too. And I do not know a thing in this whole wide world that is worse than being alone.

Without that aloneness, there are no individuals. Without it, there is no personal freedom, no human life. Without it, there is no competition, no retaliation. There are no cycles of violence, and there is no war. So what a mess this is, being a spirit human being! We cannot live without our individuality, so we are stuck with our aloneness.

No, of course, we do not always feel alone because we spend so much of our time compensating. We are always looking for connections, creating links of one kind or another. We join churches, lodges, political parties. We join theater groups, choruses, and study groups. We go to dinner parties and bowling. We spend hours on the Internet, talking with somebody—anybody.

Now I am not about to put down any of that. We need connections just because we are individuals. In the night, when the office has closed, the meetings are over, the parties have shut down, the children are tucked in, and the spouse has gone to sleep, then you know. Then it is that you know there is only one person in all the world who can experience your experience, think your thoughts, and feel your pain and your joy. Only you.

Then you know no one else can ever understand everything about you that you know. Nor do you know the interior of any other person's real life. You know—no matter how sociable you are, how well you can express yourself, and how much time you spend with other people on projects you all enjoy—you are still alone.

So, is there no hope for this bind? Is there any such place as a place where no one stands alone?

Yes, there is. Yes, there is. In fact, the Gospel of John has it that Jesus prayed with his disciples just before his death. And in that prayer, listen carefully to what he said:

> I ask that they may all be one. As you, Father, are in me and I am in you, may they also be in us…I in them and you in me, that they may become completely one.[6]

Now, I want to say to you, for me, this shines a whole new light on the reality of God. I have read it a hundred times before, but now I begin to hear it. It speaks to me of a connection that can never be destroyed. It cannot be broken when we shall no longer see one another with these eyes. It cannot disappear in the darkness of the night, when the party is over and conviviality has dissipated in the air. Even when the most precious possessions of our lives are lost, this connection cannot be lost.

For God is not a guy upstairs. He is not a guy at all. God does not come and go. God cannot be manipulated. He is not a lawmaker, judge, executioner, or dealmaker.

John said, "God did not send the Son into the world to condemn the world, but that the world might be saved through him." Then he explained himself, saying, "Those who do not believe are condemned already."[7] That is, they cannot receive the benefits of believing God is in Jesus and God is in them and they are in God and Jesus is in God and all are one because all are spirit.

So, if I do not pray and do not set my mind on the things of the Spirit, then I am condemned to feel all cut off. If I remain unaware of the connections that are always, already there, I am driven to create relationships, and I become desperate to make some kind, any kind, of connection.

You see, all Spirit is God, and God is all Spirit! It is like the fish in the ocean. The ocean is so close to them they do not see it. It is their life; it flows through them, and they move through it. The world of spirit is the ocean in which we live, move, and have our being. Mostly, we do not see it, do not know it is there until someone calls our attention to it. That is just what Jesus did.

So, I walk down the street alone one day and brush shoulders with someone hurrying by. I know I have touched one in whom God lives, not fully, not perfectly, but just like me. I am not alone on the street anymore. If she glares at me and does not smile, I can smile at her because I know she often feels alone, too. Sometimes my spirit seems to reach out and touch her spirit, and, perhaps, she smiles, too. Then I know we both stand where no one stands alone.

After the supper hour, I sit by myself before the television screen and listen to some important person being interviewed. The longer I listen to him, the more frustrated I grow. I then become angry because I just know he is wrong, and everything he says is like hearing the chalk screeching across the blackboard. And I want to shout at him!

But, if I take a moment to calm myself, I know he is a human being just like me, filled with positives and negatives. They are just different positives and negatives than mine. And he is also alone. I do not know the things he suffers, the hurts he bears, the hopes that have been dashed, or the secrets he carries. So he's pretty much just like me.

I know we share, both alike, in the life of the Spirit who is God. And so, I know, even in the time of my anger, I stand where no one stands alone, and so does he.

Last summer, I spent four days driving all alone about my home state of Nebraska. One morning, I found myself driving down its western border where it touches the state of Wyoming. I had left Harrison in the farthest northwest corner of the state and headed south. For more than fifty miles, I drove before coming to another village.

For thirty miles, I saw not one car on the road, not a single ranch house, nor even an outbuilding. I saw not one tree, not one windmill, nor even the usual meadowlarks on the fence posts nor pronghorn antelopes on the distant hills. Nothing. Just nothing, for miles around me. Only the dry brown grasslands of the high plains engulfed me. And I felt so alone, so alone in all that emptiness. I felt like I had never been quite so all alone in my life Then, slowly, I began to exult in the stark beauty of the empty plains and the immensity of the blue sky. I began to pray as I drove. I prayed for everyone I could think of for the next thirty miles. I prayed:

> Lord Jesus Christ, son of God, have mercy on me; have mercy on my sons; have mercy on Jack; have mercy on Mary; have mercy on Arlene; have mercy on Mike; have mercy, have mercy—

My spirit touched theirs, I'm sure of that, across the spaces and through all the times. It touched the Spirit who is God in me in that strange alchemy that binds the spirit world together in one. My loneliness was gone, and I knew I was in touch with every spirit. You were there, with my mother and my father, with Anita, with old college friends, and with former colleagues from Brazil. With all of them.

I knew my spirit was in God, and God was in me. I was in you, and you were in me. We were all one, right in the midst of that emptiness. And I stood where no one stands alone.

Amen.

> *Lord of creation, Spirit of all spirits,*
>   *moving through us into one another,*
>   *connecting,*
>   *binding us in one,*
>   *making sensitive our spirits,*
>   *alive to one another,*
>   *exercising compassion and care,*

> *touching with a touch beyond that of words, or of flesh,*
> *with the joy of silent laughter*
> *and the gentleness of dove's wings.*
> *Take from me now the terror of being alone*
> *and comfort me with the awareness of our oneness in You.*
> Amen. Saf

Sermon 3
Free at First

Lesson—Galatians 5:1, 13-25

Comment:

This sermon draws quite directly on Paul's letter to the Galatians, one of Wesley's favorite books and one of mine. The theme of freedom for Wesley was not one he treated as a topic in itself. Instead, it was an essential gift of prevenient grace. It was also important in his debates with the Calvinists in which he vehemently resisted the doctrine of irresistible grace that denied the human being participated in any way in his own salvation.

Freedom was essential if the human being was to have any active part in determining his spiritual future. Wesley's discussion of this issue appears primarily in those places in which he is dealing with the doctrine of justification by faith, for example, in the sermon by that name. That was due to freedom's role in receiving the gift of justifying faith. However, I am dealing with it under the heading of prevenient grace because free will was one of the gifts of prevenient grace in Wesley's doctrine of salvation and it is part of the gift of spirit that is the birthright of every human being in our spiritual theology.

I have not introduced the philosophical issue of free will because Wesley dealt with it philosophically. Instead, I introduced it because it is implied by Wesley's resistance to irresistible grace. It is important for my spirit image of God because it is a necessary aspect of my definition of spirit. Freedom can exist only for a self-aware subject because freedom requires deliberation and the weighing of alternatives. That is, without it as a real part of spirit, both God and man are rendered totally subject to the laws of the natural world and the distinctive reality of spirit is ignored. I do not attempt to develop the philosophical arguments for free will but only to describe a common sense understanding of the term.

My treatment of free will is tied to the notion of freedom from oppression, which is the biblical concern with freedom, by the following thesis: Freedom is the power of a spiritual individual to resist outward influences upon his actions. Oppression originates in outward influences, including genes and other natural forces as well as social and political pressures.

By dealing with freedom in the context of prevenient grace, I want to make it clear that freedom is not something available only to Christians. It is available to every human being by reason of his or her birthright. This is the foundation of all morality, whether in a primitive society or under more sophisticated moral systems such as philosophies and religions have set forth.

This sermon is an attempt to respond to the universal need for hope because it tries to clarify how the free human being is a participant in the cosmic purpose of God himself. For Wesley, the assumption of freedom was essential for the hope he preached to those who had no hope for a better future. It thereby gives meaning to the struggle against external social, political, and economic pressures.

◆　　◆　　◆

When I was a kid, I discovered a great mystery. I thought I had stumbled on a question no one had ever asked before. In high school, I argued with my friends and teachers about it. I did not know it was one of the questions that human beings had been arguing about for as long as they could ask questions.

It was the question about whether the individual had free will, whether he had the ability to decide and choose. Was he predetermined by his genes, that is, controlled from inside his body? Or was he determined by his environment, that is, controlled from outside by his surroundings?

Are we human beings free to make our own decisions? Or is every choice we make predetermined by some other force? That was the question that fascinated me, and arguing about it was sometimes more a game than a serious search for an answer.

But, I wondered if I was really free to decide in the morning if I would have oatmeal or cream of wheat or, in the afternoon, if I would go out for football or band. It felt like I was free to make the choices I did. But was I really? When we think or act in the ways we do, is it an illusion to think we are ever free to choose differently?

I can almost hear us arguing still, "You can do anything you decide to do."

"No, I can't."

"Yes, you can. You're free!"

"No, I got a bunch of genes down in here messing me up and telling me what I can do and what I can't."

"But you can tell those genes off any old time."

"No, I can't. I can't help it if I got red hair."

"Well, of course not. But you can decide if you'll dye it or how you will wear your red hair. Are you going to put it in a ponytail, or will you spike it?"

I think the question had probably come up in the first place because I hated the idea of not being in control of my life. I wanted to think it was I who decided the career I would pursue, not my genes, my parents, my environment, or just plain dumb luck. I wanted to have something to do with the choice of the values I would use in making my decisions, determining the passions I would allow to influence me, picking the friends I would cultivate or the organizations I would join, or the God I would believe in.

So, actually, this question is not just a cute philosophical exercise. It is not just a game. It is an issue of the utmost concern for each human being on this planet because it has to do with the dehumanizing effects of oppression on people who were born free, but are no longer able to choose freely.

The oppression I am concerned with is not the oppression of our genes, however real that may be. It is the oppression of rules and laws that prevent the fullest development of the human potential for creativity and growth. It is the oppression of cultural values and practices that rob women of their humanity. It is the oppression of systems of government that rob citizens of their rights and their dignity. It is the oppression of racism, ghettoes, and apartheid. It is the oppression of blind nationalism and narrow class distinctions. It is the oppression of social and political systems, the kind of oppression that forced the impassioned cry of freedom from the throat of Martin Luther King, Jr.: "Free at last! Free at last! Thank God almighty, we are free at last!"[8]

That was the resounding cry, not of freedom already achieved, but a cry for freedom yet to be realized. It was a cry for freedom from prejudice and the economic oppression of a people oppressed by laws and deeply rooted social mores.

But it was not an original cry! It was a cry prefigured throughout the third world countries where exploitation had oppressed and enslaved vast populations. It was the universal cry for freedom that goes back at least to the time when the Hebrews fled Egypt, crossed the Red Sea, and entered into the pathless wilderness where there were no markers, no signposts, and no weather vanes to point the way out. It has always been the cry for freedom from oppression! A freedom yet to be won, won by struggle, political action, voices raised in protest, and prayer.

This really is an old story, isn't it? But, tell me again. How is freedom once lost to be won again?

Well, let's try Paul's version in Galatians! Paul was addressing the question of freedom from oppression when he wrote to the churches in Galatia, proclaiming "Christ has made us free!" He was talking about the oppression that burdened the lives and the spirits of the people. For the Jews living in Galatia, their oppression was the burden of the Law of Moses. They lived under that Law, and it was a load!

Remember how the story says that happened! It tells how Moses had once led the people out of Egypt, to freedom from the oppression of the Pharaoh. But they had no direction and wandered aimlessly in the wilderness until the day Moses finally went up Mount Sinai and received the tablets of the Law, called the Decalogue. There they were, the Ten Commandments.

All the rest of the Law was added later, hundreds and hundreds and hundreds of rules and regulations all telling the people how to obey the Ten Commandments, what the exceptions were, and how they could atone for their disobediences by a whole system of sacrifices.

The whole meaning of life and every hour of every day were given over to the struggle to obey those laws. So, what had first started as the search for freedom from oppression from Pharaoh had turned into meaningless wandering in the desert. Then, in order to solve that problem, they had submitted to a new oppression, the oppression of the Law. That was the burden under which the people had been living ever since. That was the oppression from which Paul said Christ had set them free.

Here is exactly what Paul wrote to those Galatians: "For freedom Christ has set us free. Stand firm, therefore, and do not submit again to a yoke of slavery."[9]

It had happened to them so many times over the centuries. "Just don't do that again!" he told them. But it is not easy to throw off oppression and keep it off, is it?

Now you and I probably do not take all those rules and regulations found in Exodus, Leviticus, and Deuteronomy very seriously. We may give lip service to the Ten Commandments, but we do not give much recognition to the Old Testament rules about how to obey them.

Or do we? Maybe some of us do get all tangled up in those old rules. Maybe they have become burdensome. But, in any case, we really do get oppressed by other things.

Haven't you ever found yourself plodding along in a rut? Haven't you ever become tired of the rat race? Haven't you ever said "Thank God, it's Friday?" or perhaps "I just wish I had some time for myself? Too many people are depending on me. Others are just expecting too much of me. I'm trapped."

Well, there is always one very obvious response. When we find we are living under external demands, under some law not our own, we can just go ahead and settle into the lifestyle and the little duties that are expected of us. We can do that. We can conform our lives to somebody else's law and decide not to make any waves, that is, to live a life of mediocrity. We can grin and bear it because "that's the way it is."

But there's a second option. We can decide to kick over the traces. We can say to ourselves, "I've got to look out for myself for a change! I've got to find myself, find out who I really am."

Maybe I have been oppressed because I am a woman, Chinese, Irish, gay, poor, or Middle Eastern. And so, I decide to throw off the yoke, demand my rights, take my case to the courts, and struggle to change the laws and the prejudices of my society.

Or maybe I become a revolutionary and go to war! And I think, in the end, I'll be free at last. Free for myself!

Did you hear that? Did you hear what I said? I said, "free for myself!" For myself?

Is that what this is all about? So I can be free for myself?

Well, let me tell you how it was with me. I retired, and I had a blast, doing a lot of different things. And I loved it! I thought I had it coming, that I had earned it! And so I had. I was free! So, I spent a few years just doing the things I wanted to do. Until I realized my freedom had very little direction to it. The rat race had sometimes been oppressive, but the freedom train was going nowhere!

You know, I think that is not so different from those rebellious youth we sometimes decry these days who seem so intent on flouting convention and propriety. Or even Abbie Hoffman, who wrote a book called *Revolution for the Hell of It* back in the 1960s.

But freedom for the sake of freedom only results in aimless wandering and becoming lost all over again. I think that is just the bind in which the Hebrews found themselves when they had become free from Pharaoh and begun wandering in the desert. They were free. But free for what? So now they had fallen back into slavery once again, this time under the Law. It was more comfortable that way.

Well, when I discovered my freedom train was going nowhere, I realized I had yet another major choice to make. I was free all right! But free for what? I could fall back into the old ruts again, like the Hebrews had done in the wilderness. Or I could use my freedom for something new!

The Galatian Hebrews had cast off the oppression of the old Law of Moses into which their ancestors had fallen. In fact, theirs was the spirit we see blazing through the entire life and death and resurrection story of Jesus. They had made the choice to be free of the old Law.

Now they were in danger of falling back again into the old slavery because freedom is scary. And Paul was telling them not to fall back again into the old rut, not to be conformed again to the expectations of their peers.

You see, it is a fearful thing to be free and responsible, and it is easy to dive back again, like prairie dogs, into the safety of our old holes. We need to be saved from the terror of that freedom somehow, saved from the meaningless wandering that so often issues in antisocial, destructive behavior.

That is why Paul did not stop with the exhortation not to fall back again, but he went on and said, "Do not use your freedom as an opportunity for self-indulgence, but through love become slaves to one another."[10]

To stop our pursuit of freedom when we have put off the yoke of oppression short-circuits the intention of the Spirit who is God and leaves us lost in the desert of self-indulgence. However, the Great Spirit calls on us to use our freedom to love one another. That is the only justification. The *only* justification. That is the only justification for rising up against oppression in the first place!

That was true for the early Christians of Galatia. It is true for modern youth. It is true for you! And it is true for—for old men and women like me!

This Christ of whom Paul wrote was that Jesus whom the story displays as a free man, free from the burden of the old Law of the Jews, free from the demands of the religious authorities, free from the law of the Romans, and even free from the expectations of his own family in order to love us unto death.

So Paul said, "Neither circumcision nor uncircumcision (that is, neither law nor no law) counts for anything; the only thing that counts is faith working through love."[11]

At first, we are born free in order to resist every oppression. We become free from every oppression in order to be free to work the works of love. And then we shall be truly free at last! Love will drive out fear. Self-control will drive out self-indulgence. Patience will drive out dissension. Kindness will drive out jealousy. Generosity will drive out greed. Gentleness will drive out cruelty. Peace will drive out quarrels and strife. Every act of forgiveness, every act of reconciliation, will bring the Spirit who is God a step closer to his perfection.

Oh, yes! We were born free! Oppression came later. Because we were free at first, we can be free at last!

Amen.

Dear Spirit, dear Wind,
who has blown me into being
as a flame in your own greater fire:

I long to be free as You are free.
But You have placed me in this body,
    in these communities where pressures burden my spirit
    and threaten to destroy it.
Now I need You to blow upon my dying flame
    and ignite the fire of freedom within me.
Empower me to throw off the inhibiting and suffocating conventions
    and debilitating powers
    in order that I may freely love
    and find myself in compassion and care for my fellows
        in their struggles for freedom too.
Amen. saf

9

Turning the Corner—Sermons on Justifying Grace

Sermon 4
Be Honest with Yourself
Exodus 20:1–3 and 18–20

Comment:

A whole cluster of themes circle around the idea of justifying grace in Wesley's framework, including sin, repentance, faith that justifies, rebirth, and the beginning of sanctification. Therefore, for this chapter, I have written four sermons.

For this sermon on a new understanding of the old terms, sin and repentance, I use an Old Testament passage that sets forth the classic theistic image of the lawgiver God. This is the source of the idea of sin and foundation for repentance for sin. My task is to ask what happens to these notions when the image of the lawgiving God is replaced with the spirit image of God I am proposing.

In his early preaching, Wesley relied largely on preaching the Law, as he called it. His preaching on sin and repentance were focused on breaking down the resistance of the hearer to the point of anguish so that his need for grace could be enhanced. The result was often the embarrassing phenomena of weeping, falling down in faints, and so forth. However, by driving home the inability of human beings to obey the Law, he sought to bring about repentance for sin in preparation for the announcement of the saving grace offered to those who believed in the sacrifice of Jesus.

The notion of sin must change when your God ceases to be the lawgiver. When sin changes its character, so must repentance. Therefore, I am preaching here first to the need for understanding. Because the human individual is himself spirit and therefore a part of God, he becomes his own judge. At the same time, the example of Jesus can serve as a light to illuminate his own spiritual reality. I want to commend Jesus for that role without saying that such honesty about oneself is impossible apart from Jesus. After all, we are treating Jesus as a kind of iconic model, not as the exclusive author of either honesty or faith.

This sermon also seeks to meet the need for hope and guidance. Honesty can produce hope in the possibilities that reside in the spirit of the hearer as well as guidance for the journey of faith. Therefore, simple self-honesty and the affirmation of freedom and responsibility found in the human spirit (see sermon on "Free at First" in the previous chapter) must replace Wesley's repentance for sin. Honesty about oneself and a clear grasp of the possibilities of one's own spirit are sufficient grounds for making a decision to actively engage in the spiritual pursuit.

◆   ◆   ◆

> Then God spoke all these words: For I am the Lord God, who brought you out of the land of Egypt, out of the house of slavery; you shall have no other Gods before me.[1]

And then he gave Moses all the tablets of the Law. But...

> When all the people witnessed the thunder and lightning, the sound of the trumpet, and the mountain smoking, they were afraid and trembled and stood at a distance, and said to Moses, "You speak to us and we will listen but do not let God speak to us or we will die." Moses said to the people, "Do not be afraid for God has come only to test you and to put the fear of him upon you, so that you do not sin."[2]

Have you ever had a friend with the irritating habit of making you feel small? A friend of mine always sees himself as an authority on sports, almost any sport. He has never played a sport in his life, but he is a great spectator, and he knows exactly what is wrong with every team and every player. He knows their strengths, but he especially knows their weaknesses.

I love sports, too, and played some of them. And I have my opinions. But I've learned never to express them to my friend because I will always be wrong. And I'll come away saying, "Gee, I feel so dumb."

Of course, it works the other way, too. One day, an acquaintance of mine and I started to discuss the theater and acting. He and his wife regularly attend movies, musicals, and other theatrical events. I expressed my views on those actors whom I thought were superb craftsmen and on some popular actors whom I thought were run-of-the-mill. He obviously did not agree with me, but he said nothing until he suddenly stood up and walked away, saying, "I can't stand to be wrong. I just can't stand to be wrong." It was apparent he had felt put down by the forcefulness with which I had expressed my views and took me to be attacking his views, though I had never heard him express them.

Every human being is sensitive to what others think of him because he or she really wants to think well of himself. The more oppressed we are by forces outside ourselves, the more put down we feel, and the less likely we are to think well of ourselves.

I will tell you what really makes me feel small and out of control of myself. It is when I hear a siren coming up from behind to tell me I am speeding, breaking the law, just doing something wrong. I once went to court to protest a traffic ticket. As I stood before the judge to explain, I looked up at him. He looked down on me from his high bench, and I felt like God had caught me in something evil.

You know the word "sin." It is a religious word, and it speaks of a mighty law-making God who is also the judge, prosecutor, jury, and one who passes sentence. He is like that one who gave Moses the Ten Commandments. Finally, he is also the one who appoints the defense counsel. Before the judge, all must cower and await his disposition of their cases while they feel smaller and smaller. That is the picture of God most of us have grown up with, even though we have often found ways of rounding off the rough edges of God's rule.

Of course, in the Christian era, we have "an Advocate, Jesus Christ the righteous"[3] appointed by God to defend us. In that way, you see, we still do have a chance against God. Maybe Jesus can affirm us, give us some sense of self-worth. That is about our only hope. But God himself is still the lawgiver and the judge. And God himself can intervene, especially if we, for some reason, have failed to give our case to the Advocate.

For example, if many of a nation's citizens displease God, he can send a pestilence, say AIDS maybe. Or, if some poor soul steps out of line, God can pass sentence and execute justice without waiting for the Advocate.

Apparently, that is what happens when some self-proclaimed prophet on a stage somewhere announces, "I swear by the Holy God that I speak the truth. If I am wrong, I call upon God to strike me dead on this very spot!" He waits, and nothing happens. And so, it appears the prophet is vindicated.

Or, maybe, some poor woman thinks God gave her cancer, so she must be a bad woman.

I know you do not think this way, do you? Most of us do not. We find ways of making God seem softer. We find ways of excusing him for the outrageous behaviors that some people have charged him with.

We do not want that Old Testament picture to muddy up our hope for a benevolent, patient, loving, and manageable God. So, in order to avoid that happening, we appeal to Jesus and his mercy and compassion. For example, if dad's the disciplinarian, we go to mom when we are in trouble. We do that because we need to be affirmed. We need to think better of ourselves!

In fact, we have taken the old picture of a lawmaking judge who demanded blood sacrifices as payment for the sins of the people, and we have claimed the blood of Jesus as the payment required by God the judge. Even in the language of the Eucharist, we pray:

> O Lord God, heavenly King, God the Father Almighty. O Lord, the only begotten Son, Jesus Christ; O Lord God, Lamb of God, Son of the Father, that takest away the sins of the world, have mercy upon us.[4]

The Roman Catholic mass is said to be a repetition or reenactment of the crucifixion every time it is said, and that is how we have dealt with our need for affirmation and a sense of self-worth within the Christian context. If we keep the old picture of God as the lawgiver and judge without depending on Jesus' sacrifice, we are lost. We have to have Jesus paying the price for us, or we lose all self-appreciation and self-respect and therefore live under a burden of guilt.

Maybe, of course, we just reject the whole idea of a God entirely and call ourselves atheists. We can always do that, but it leaves us dependent on our own efforts to measure up to someone else's standards in order to find any degree of self-worth at all. And that, at best, is pretty shaky business.

Even when we keep the notion that God cannot have mercy on us without Jesus dying on the cross, it seems we are still nobodies as far as God himself is concerned. All the credit still goes to Jesus. The church once tried to deal with this puzzle, of course, by saying Jesus was also God, so God himself paid the price for our sins and thus manifested his grace toward us. But that introduces a whole new set of problems by robbing the human Jesus of his humanity and his freedom. Therefore, we are lost unless—unless we dare to see God differently.

So what if we try to look at God in a new way? What if God is, in fact, the whole world of Spirit in whom all the positive and negative, the creative and destructive, the reconciling and divisive, the healing and chaotic spiritual powers are present.

What if he is that creative Great Spirit who, out of his spiritual fertility, conceived and gave birth to all the human spirits living in these natural bodies of ours? Weird idea? Well, not really. After all, we know, in the natural world, there is the phenomenon of self-reproduction. What if thereby every human spirit is a part of that Great Spirit world whom we call God? What if God himself is involved in the struggle to subdue all the negative and destructive spirits within himself by the expulsive power of his positive and creative energies?

Then everything we human spirits do to subdue the negative and divisive spirits within ourselves is a part of God's own struggle. And nothing, nothing can be so affirming as the belief we are ourselves participants in God's own struggle to subdue the power of the destructive spirits that are a part of his life and ours.

So, in such a view of God, what has happened to judgment and mercy? What has happened to sin and repentance? Sin, as the breaking of the laws of the lawgiving God, is replaced by the reality of the negative spirits within each of us, including the powers of chaos and disorder, the powers of despair and hopelessness, the powers of disease and dysfunction, the powers of envy and resentment, the powers of greed and acquisitiveness, and the powers of enmity and hatred. These things must be subdued in us because they inhibit the growth of unity and peace. They block the growth of the spiritual powers of hope and health, love and generosity, and harmony and beauty.

And repentance? Repentance is replaced by the honest recognition of the presence of all the negativities in our lives, of all those things that destroy harmony, love, compassion, and peace. Without such honesty with ourselves concerning this unhealthy state of our spirits, we can hardly turn our minds to the things of the Spirit.

Only when we have seen ourselves as we are will we be able to see the possibilities of new life and healing that the Great Spirit who is God seeks constantly to enable us to achieve. That is when hope becomes possible. Tomorrow does not have to be like today. Life can be better every day. Our spirits can grow because we can nurture the positive and put down the negative. We can open our spirits to the positive power of the Spirit who is God within us. And so, the way begins to open for the burgeoning of new life within us.

Then what happens to the old lawgiver? The Great Spirit who is God replaces him. This is the Spirit who has sought from the beginning, not to judge, but to heal us. This is the Spirit who has sought from the beginning, not to condemn us, but to seek to overcome everything negative and nurture and give growth to everything positive. This is the Spirit who struggles within himself for the harmony that is his own perfection and our perfection as well.

Now, Jesus does not have to be the one who persuades God to have mercy by paying the price that God demands, but he can be seen as the one who reveals to us what this whole business of life is about. He shows us it is about allowing the Spirit to make us whole. It is about becoming like God in the measure in which we realize our own human potential for peace, harmony, and love. It is about sharing in God's work and purpose for creation.

So, look on Jesus, and behold this one who reveals who God is because "God did not send the Son into the world to condemn the world, but that the world might be saved through him."[5]

Amen.

O God, who, like us, is spirit, too:
We may be spirit,
>*but we find so many negative powers in us,*
>*threatening to put down the good within us.*

Hope is dimmed by doubt;
>*love is weakened by self-defensiveness;*
>*generosity is shortened by greed;*
>*the grace of peace is disturbed by toxic anger, resentment, and guilt.*

Put down these insurgent powers,
>*and heal us, O God,*
>*You who desire only our wholeness and our health.*

Amen. Saf

Sermon 5
Coming Home

Hebrews 11:1–3 and 12:1–2

Comment:

The theme of justification by grace through faith raises the question what we mean by the term "faith." It is variously understood today and was a question among the Church Fathers from the earliest times. John Wesley was familiar with their writings and was actually indebted both to some of the Church Fathers and the philosophical empiricists of his own time. Of course, his sermons on faith used the familiar verses from Hebrews that I am using here.

I might have written a sermon on faith for inclusion within the section on prevenient grace because the capacity for faith is, in Wesley's scheme, one of the gifts of prevenient grace that is given to each human being. However, this sermon affirms, not only that everyone has the capacity for faith, but, actually, in some degree, is a person of faith in virtue of being a spiritual being. To show how this rudimentary faith becomes justifying faith, to use Wesley's term, is the purpose of this sermon.

For Wesley, justifying faith was the acceptance of pardon by the believer, but it was accompanied by the new birth and, sometimes, the "assurance of grace." This sermon is an invitation to the hearer to see in Jesus the possibility of a reversal of focus from one that is directed to the goals, ambitions, and purposes of the natural life in space and time to one focused on the things of the spirit. Thereby, one becomes an increasingly fulfilled embodiment of the Spirit who is God. That is, justifying faith as a new focus is necessary for the rest of the journey of faith to proceed.

Wesley's view of salvation as a process beginning with the gift of the capacity for faith, along with what he admits is a small modicum of faith (perhaps the seed of faith), and moving on through justifying faith and sanctifying faith to glory is replaced here with the view that faith is already a property of the human spirit. It gains a new focus at a certain point so that hope, purpose, and peace begin filling one's life. Thus, the continuum of faith is present, but it is not up front in Wesley's four-part scheme. However, it is a strong theme in our new vision of God. Justifying faith is treated here as a refocusing and a clarifying of faith rather than as a necessarily temporally identifiable event.

Target needs here are understanding, hope, and connection. Coming home is the ultimate connection. Peripherally, the sermon also addresses the need for meaning and purpose.

◆   ◆   ◆

Thomas Wolfe said you can never go home again, right? Well, a few years ago, we had a family reunion in Nebraska. That is where I grew up, but I had lived in nine different towns while doing that. I had already lived in three towns before starting school in Huntley. In second grade, I lived in Hildreth. Then, there were three years in Archer and three more in Bassett. Finally, I started high school in Atkinson and graduated in Hemingford.

Anyway, following the reunion, my wife, my three sisters, and I took a van and spent several days visiting every one of those towns where we had lived while growing up. During those four days, I saw only one person whom I had known during all those years, only one. I saw buildings I remembered. In Wallace, I walked down Main Street and saw the old bank building. I remembered walking there with my dad as a four-year-old and looking for the crack in the building and the falling bricks because I had heard my folks say at home that the bank had gone broke. I saw houses I had lived in and churches and schools I had attended. But I saw only one person I had known.

Wouldn't you know, people sometimes ask me what my hometown is. And I can't tell them. I finally began saying, "Lincoln is my hometown." After all, I have lived there three times: once before I started school, once while attending college, and once while serving as pastor of a church. But, really, I have no hometown. So I can never go home again.

Still, I get homesick. I am homesick for a place I have never yet been. There is something out there. There is some place I want to go. I do not know where it is, and I do not know how to get there. I do not just hope it will happen or even just wish it would happen. I want to get up and go there! There is something I need to do. There is something I need to find. There is something I need to see, experience, or become. It calls. It beckons. And I've got to go!

It happens to everybody, this longing for a home. If you are living in the same house where you were born, you still want to get up and go somewhere else. There is something more. But maybe it is too scary. The longing is there, but not the courage. There is a real home for you somewhere!

Bob Herbert, the columnist, writes about the kids of Watts in LA:

The kids who are running wild and frequently killing one another have, in almost every instance, been abandoned in some way. They've been left to their own devices by adults for reasons that in some cases are unforgivable, and in others, unavoidable...Gang members who are willing to talk will tell you about neglectful or physically abusive parents, fathers or mothers (or both) who have taken off or died, parents who are alcoholics or drug addicts, single parents who spend most of their waking hours working, and so on and on. The welcoming arms of street gangs are an almost irresistible lure for such youngsters.[6]

They are also looking to come home. They are homesick for some place that is their own because they are human spirits just like you and me. And you are looking, too! You also want to go home. Some place where you will be comfortable, where you will truly belong. Some place where, no matter where you have roamed, they have to take you in when you return. Some place that is sure and permanent that is not filled with questions and doubts. Some place where you can rest in peace, where you know you are loved and there is no threat of separation ever, ever again.

But how can we ever go home, go home to a home when we have never been truly at home before?

Well, what I am talking about here is faith. That is what I am talking about. Faith! Once, we thought faith was perhaps a set of correct doctrines or true beliefs. But we cannot think that way anymore because we have learned the search for true beliefs is the task of what we call theology. Theology is simply the effort to make sense out of our faith. But faith comes before theology, not after. Faith is something else.

Once, we perhaps thought faith was a kind of mysticism. The mystics are those who think God is somewhere else and we have to find him, get in touch with him somehow, rope him in, and maybe even find some kind of mystical union with him from whom they have been separated. The mystics want to come home again, too, but they do not know whether they ever can.

That is why my biblical reference for today is from that unknown author of the letter to the Hebrews. He wrote, "Now faith is the assurance of things hoped for, the evidence of things not seen."[7]

In fact, he implies that faith is a kind of homesickness:

> They confessed that they were strangers and foreigners on the earth, for people who speak in this way make it clear that they are seeking a homeland.[8]

He suggests the journey of faith begins with "the assurance of things hoped for." They are things not yet understood. They are not yet seen or possessed. They are not yet in hand. It is an experience of deep trustfulness there is another world I do not see—out there, down there, in here—but somewhere! It is the assurance there is another reality that lives, throbs, and strives, perhaps a home even, where I belong. And that is "the assurance of things hoped for." That is the beginning of faith!

That is not all. There is more. The author of the letter to the Hebrews continues, "Faith is the evidence of things not seen." But what kind of evidence can this be? He was saying, in faith, there is not only an assurance, but there is something to be hoped for. There is an actual pull toward something ahead, beckoning, calling, and drawing us. Faith is homesickness, and homesickness itself is evidence of something more.

Further on, the author of Hebrews illustrates this homesickness when he says, "Abraham died without having received the promises; but from a distance he saw and greeted them."[9] That was "the evidence of things not seen."

That was faith! And it changed the whole focus of his life.

Martin Luther King, Jr. remembered Moses that night before he was killed in Memphis. He said: "I may not get there myself; but I have looked over Jordan. And I have seen the Promised Land."[10] That was faith! And that vision informed his life.

Each human being feels this longing for a home. Each of us feels this tug toward a greater fulfillment, perhaps some place where we will truly feel finally at home. Each human being wants to come home, wants to find the Promised Land.

Augustine prayed, "My soul will not be at rest until it find its rest in thee."[11] No one is yet fulfilled or complete so that he wants nothing more. He may think what he wants is more money or property, more leisure or recreation, more time or more space, more love or more goodness, more peace and joy, or more of God! And he thinks finding it will bring him home!

So, yes, I think faith is homesickness. And our homesickness is an evidence of things not seen.

We look wherever there is a promise, whether religious or secular, and life is just full of homecoming promises! The problem is that none of them ever seems to pan out. And so, we ask, "Can we never go home then?" And the answer is, "Yes! You can go home!"

Everyone longs for home. Therefore, every person is a person of faith, but there can come that moment when the longing turns to vision and we see! There is a gift that comes from that home for which we long. For me, at least, it is Jesus who points it out, who reveals it to my blind eyes, who reveals to us that, closer than our hands and feet, is the world of Spirit who is God. He reveals the Spirit who is God is so close that he is the very spirit within us that makes us human.

He reveals to us that we are already home and we did not know it! He reveals to us the possibility that every destructive or divisive impulse or purpose within us can be driven out by the influx of spiritual power from the Great Spirit who moves within us, through us, and around us.

So, I look to that picture of him I know so well from the Gospels. And I see the possibilities offered to each human being. It is in that moment, or perhaps that period of months or even years, when we catch the vision of a new connection with each human being on the planet. We see undreamed of possibilities for growth and change and for wholeness and fulfillment. In the time of that new vision, homesickness turns to confidence we are already at home in God. Longing turns to understanding God is already at home in us. Hope in things unseen becomes the decision to allow the Great Spirit in whom we live, move, and have our being to make us fully human and therefore fully divine. In the time of that new vision, with the gift of a faith differently focused, we see the promise. We see, beyond these limits of time and space, that fulfillment of our longing and completion of our journey will give us perfect peace and an abundance of joy!

Faith is homesickness for what we do not yet see, and that is given in some form to each human being. But the gift of a deeper faith, a faith enhanced by the Great Spirit in whom we live and refocused by the picture of Jesus, gives us a vision of our true home, because we are already at home in the world of spirit.

It gives us the joy of setting our feet upon the way to the fulfillment of our destiny, a destiny as spirits made perfect by the Spirit who is God. It calls us to focus our mind and our will upon the imitation of that One who appears as one so fully immersed in God and God in him that the ages have dared to call him Immanuel, "God with us."

It changes the direction of one's life! It changes our relationship with all other persons! Bit by bit, day by day, and year by year, it will fill us with an abundance of life and an assurance that we are already at home.

Amen.

> *Spirit who is God,*
>   *I long for what I do not know until You touch me*
>   *and say to me:*
>   *I am here!*

*I think sometimes if I could know the answers to all my questions,
   I should be content.
I think a perfect job, a perfect family, the admiration of the world
   would set my heart at ease
   and fulfill my longing for a home.
But show me now where my true home really is.
Turn my eyes within where You abide.
Let me see that happiness and peace never can be found
   except in the life of the Spirit.
And You are that Great Spirit.
Let me find my home in You.
Amen.* Saf

Sermon 6
The Day the Glass Shatters
John 3:1–8

Comment:

In John Wesley's scheme of salvation, the coming of justifying faith is also the beginning of a new life, that is, rebirth or the experience of being born again. In this sermon, I want to focus, not on the gift of faith itself, but on the results of this new gift described in the previous sermon on "Coming Home." It produces a whole new focus of purpose and a new direction for the spiritual struggle.

So, I focus on the beginning of actual changes in the life of the believer, not on the moment of reorientation itself, which may also take place over a period of time. In other words, we are looking at the new direction the believer's life now takes.

The traditional Scripture for this occurrence is the encounter of Jesus and Nicodemus. In that story, the new life is not attributed by Jesus to any Atonement made under the Law nor to anything Nicodemus himself does. Instead, it is attributed to the unpredictable movement of the Spirit. It is a gift and it includes two occurrences in the life of the believer: seeing the Kingdom and entering the Kingdom.

The notion of rebirth or regeneration remains crucial to our reformulation of Wesley's message. If a change takes place in the life of someone, it necessarily begins at some point. It is the opening of the new life that I am looking at here. It is perhaps something like the opening of a chess game in which God makes the first move, but black must make the second move for the game to be underway. The opening seems to have both the character of a gift (God's first move) and an act of the will (man's second move). This is the point of overlap between grace and responsibility with which Wesley always struggled.

In my perspective, the power to decide was given to us when we were made as human spirits in the first place. Therefore, because all spirit is also God, when we decide, it is also God who is deciding, and the whole process is therefore a gift. At the same time, we have chosen to use our freedom to make the second move. So we retain responsibility. Such a view is possible only because the theistic image of God is abandoned and we understand our own spirits to be like organs in the spiritual body of God.

The universal need for understanding is, as always, addressed. Hope is given by the promise of a new beginning and purpose by the affirmation the individual has some responsibility for undertaking the journey.

◆　　◆　　◆

I know a man who said, "I'm in a bind. I'm what I am, and I'm stuck with it." This reminds me that Jeremiah asked, "Can a leopard change his spots?" Remember?

The man went on, "There are all those genes I hear so much about. Then there's the family I grew up in, the bunch of friends I've collected, and the lifestyle I've inherited. I'm a white, middle-class American living in rural New England. So I have some hang-ups and habits I really don't like a lot. There's my temper, for example. And I know I have some prejudices. I really don't know what to do with myself. I'm not very happy and I don't know where I'm going. I'm sort of disappointed with my life. The truth is, there are moments of happiness in my life. But, in general, I know something is missing."

Well, all of us could probably tell some version of this story. When we are honest with ourselves, we wish we could be better. If we could change certain things and direct our lives in a different direction, how happy we would be!

Maybe we have tried to find something we could pursue with a great passion. For example, I see these great athletes who are driven to become great. I see these CEOs who are driven to accumulate, by any possible means, obscene amounts of money. And I see those remarkable persons who have devoted their lives to some great cause, like Martin Luther King, Jr.; Sergio de Melo, the great Brazilian negotiator killed in Iraq; or maybe even Jesus. Then I think, "That's fine, but that's just not me. Those aren't the spots on this leopard."

Other less ambitious persons have said, "I'm not having much fun. There's something wrong with me. I'm bored to death. I need excitement, adventure, something new! It is just the same old thing over and over again. I'm in a bind and trapped. And I don't know if it is possible to remove these spots."

I think this is the kind of thing the Bible talked about when it spoke of the "law of sin and death."[12] It is a kind of downward spiral whether it is being caught in mediocrity or the roller-coaster pursuit of fun and thrills. And it feels like leopard spots!

There is a story in the Bible about just this very thing. The antihero in the story is a man named Nicodemus. He is a perfectly proper man who has kept all the rules, but he is not at all satisfied with his life. He has been watching a kind of renegade fellow about the city from time to time. He is a rustic country chap from up north, but the gossip is that he has been doing some pretty remarkable things, including healings of the blind and the crippled.

Nicodemus, who is anxious to preserve his reputation as a good Pharisee, comes secretly to Jesus one night. He asks Jesus what his secret is because he seems to be a driven man. Yet, he seems to be having fun and enjoying life all the same. Moreover, everybody thinks him to be a pretty good sort of fellow.

However, poor Nicodemus has lost his drive and his passion for the Law. He is not having any fun. He has been saying, when he sees the criminals being hanged on the crosses by the Romans, "There, but for the grace of God, go I."

Well, the answer Jesus gives him is, "Nicodemus, my friend, you need to be born again, reborn, not of the flesh, but of the spirit. First off, you have to see the kingdom of the spirit. And then you have to enter it."[13]

Nicodemus thinks, "Hold it there, Jesus! The kingdom of the spirit? What is that?" But, he says, "I haven't ever seen a spirit. I don't believe in ghosts! I think you've just spaced out."

"Okay," Jesus says, "You say you've never seen a spirit. Look at yourself, Nick! What do you see? What difference do you see between yourself and a rock?"

"Well," says Nicodemus, "a rock will last a million years, and I won't."

"What else?"

"I can think, and a rock can't."

"What else?"

"I feel pain and frustration, and the rock doesn't."

"What else?"

"Well, let's see—I want to change. I want to be different, and the rock doesn't."

"And you can look at yourself and think about yourself, and the rock can't, right? Pretty amazing, huh?" says Jesus.

"Yeah, that is amazing all right," says Nicodemus finally.

"Well, that's spirit," Jesus explains, "and the world is permeated with spirit. Wherever there is thought, hope and despair, love and hate, peace and turmoil, there is spirit. Wherever there is imagination and dreaming, order and creativity, there is the kingdom, the world of spirit.

"Look and see the kingdom of the spirit, Nicodemus! It is everywhere! All of us human beings are spirits and bodies, too. It is our spirits that feel the pain when our hopes are dashed. They feel the joy when they are fulfilled. They dream, plan, and struggle because they have this sense of themselves, this awareness that they are spirit—not stones, trees, soil, or seas.

"And this world of spirit is a world that encompasses every spirit and connects us with each other through lines of spiritual communication. And this world of spirit is that world in which we live, move, and have our being. We call it the Spirit who is God. And, within this world of spirit, all the negative and destructive powers are striving against the powerful spirits of love and reconciliation and peace.

"Look and see! I'm telling you the kingdom of the spirit is within you! You are already a part of this spirit world! And, in this spiritual kingdom, all the great powers of love and reconciliation and peace are struggling against the negatives and the destructives. All are a part of God's struggle to subdue and neutralize everything that opposes his purposes of peace and harmony, love and joy. He wants you to let him enhance your powers of good.

"Just look and see the kingdom of the spirit, Nicodemus!"

Well, I am going to leave this conversation with Nicodemus now. But we know Jesus also explained it is not enough just to see the kingdom of the spirit in which you live.

In the opening pages of his book *If Beale Street Could Talk*, James Baldwin has the character named Tish telling her story:

> He's in jail. So where we were, I was sitting on a bench in front of a board, and he was sitting on a bench in front of a board. And we were facing each other through a wall of glass between us. You can't hear anything through this glass, and so you have to have a little telephone. You have to talk through that.
>
> I don't know why people always look down when they talk through a telephone, but they always do. You have to remember to look up at the person you're talking to. I always remember now because he's in jail and I love his eyes and every time I see him I'm afraid I'll never see him again. So I pick up the phone as soon as I get there and I just hold it and I keep looking up at him. So, when I said, "—Alonzo?—" he looked down and then he looked up and he smiled and he held the phone and he waited.
>
> I hope that nobody has ever had to look at anybody they love through glass.[14]

It is not enough to see the kingdom of the spirit, no more than it is enough to look at someone you love through glass. You must reach out. You must touch. You must become engaged. You must enter the struggle to defeat the powers in you that divide and destroy.

The good news is that we can deliberately and intentionally enter the world of the spirit. We can welcome the spiritual struggle. We can open ourselves to the positive spirits. We can decide to pray, meditate, and pray again, breaking down the walls that block out the powers of love and creativity, of peace and hope and joy. We can plead with the Spirit who is God until the glass wall breaks and we can reach through and touch the hand of God.

Through that touch, his power enters us, reinforces all our positive powers, and begins to destroy all our negatives. We can allow the positive spirits to crush out the negative. We who are spirit ourselves can begin a new life! We can be reborn.

We no longer have to feel we are trapped. The leopard spots can be moved. A new passion can take hold of our life. Our passion does not have to be to lead some worldwide movement, to make some dramatic sacrifice of our life upon a cross of love, or to achieve some great feat of athletic or artistic prowess. Our passion can be to see the spirit world at work and engage in his work of rooting out and subduing the spiritual powers of destruction and division, alienation and hatred, prejudice and resentment. Having such a passion means to work, first, on ourselves—by prayer and openness to the Spirit who is God, and second, on the world around us that we touch every day of our lives.

This passion is not subject to defeat or failure because this is the work that God who is Spirit has been engaged in from the foundation of the world and will be until the last day of creation and beyond. This is the new life!

Jesus was a pretty smart guy, this carpenter from the hills of Galilee. He told his disciples, not just Nicodemus, to seek first the kingdom and its righteousness. Then he promised the other things that are necessary for life would be given them.

You see, the point is that we can start. We can decide to refocus our vision and our efforts on a goal that cannot fail because it is the goal of the Great Spirit who is God. It cannot, at the last, be defeated because the powers of love and peace are greater than the power of hate and division. It is the power of the Great Spirit who fights within us and around us to build the kingdom of love.

You may have been deciding for a long time. You may have been aware for a long time that there is a better way. You may have been longing for a better tomorrow. Today may be the day the glass shatters and you reach through and take the hand of God.

Amen.

> *I want to extend my hand to You,*
> > *Spirit in whom I live and who lives in me.*
> *I want to touch your hand*
> > *and receive your power.*

I know You are closer than my own body
  and that I can begin a new life
  only when I begin to use your positive powers
  in the struggle against the negatives within me.
Receive me, O God,
  and purify me in love.
I pray this, remembering that One
  in whom You lived in fullness,
  my beloved Jesus.
Amen. Saf

SERMON 7
I, IF I BE LIFTED UP

John 12:27–36

Comment:

The role of Jesus in the Christian tradition is central and needs to be. What that role is has been as much at issue as has been the incarnation itself. For Wesley, his role occupied center court because it made God's grace available through the mystery of the Atonement. Therefore, justifying grace, with its attendant benefits, forgiveness, and a new life, all depended on the Atonement of Jesus' death. For this reason, I include this sermon, which focuses on Jesus' death, in the chapter on justifying grace. However, Wesley also rested heavily on Jesus' life and teachings to expound the features of a holy life or sanctification. He did this preeminently in his series of thirteen sermons on the Sermon on the Mount. Perfection was also frequently described as "having the mind of Christ.

This sermon on Jesus' role keeps him at the center of our tradition while acknowledging there are many ways by which the new life in the spirit may be initiated and its blessings received.

In fact, this acknowledgment is made necessary if one takes seriously the story of Nicodemus (with which I dealt in the previous sermon). In that story, Jesus does not make the new life dependent upon his death or upon any theory of the Atonement at all. He speaks of seeing and entering the kingdom of the spirit. He points the way by both his example (that is what drew Nicodemus to him in the first place) and his teaching. His final example, of course, was his willingness to die rather than compromise his integrity and adulterate his courage.

In this sermon, I also treat Jesus as the iconic hero of our tradition, not as either an historical or a cosmic administrator of the world's salvation. His portrait is that of a human being who was possessed by the Great Spirit, that is, he was divine. In the biblical picture of Jesus, we see the positive powers holding victorious over the negative—right through his execution and beyond. He is, for those who see him thus, the ideal human being just because his spirit is portrayed as the image of the divine.

The role of his death is shifted completely away from that of Atonement by his blood to that of ideal representation of the possibilities of the human spirit when subjected to the positive, unitive, and reconciling powers of the Spirit who is God.

Therefore, this sermon, primarily addresses the universal human needs for understanding and guidance.

◆   ◆   ◆

In <u>Robert Bolt's play</u>, <u>*A Man For All Seasons*</u>, Thomas More uses every device he can think of to save himself from execution. First, he uses the protections of the law because he is a lawyer. Second, he uses his silence before the demands to support the desire of King Henry VIII to put away his queen and marry Ann Boleyn. Nevertheless, nothing works for him, and he is finally faced with the choice of giving his support to the king's proposition on one hand or, on the other, losing his head.

He makes the choice, maintains his own integrity, and is executed. At the end, just before he goes to the block, he says:

> To avoid this I have taken every path my winding wits could find. Now that the Court has determined to condemn me, God knoweth how, I will discharge my mind...I do none harm, I say none harm, I think none harm. And if this be not enough to keep a man alive, in good faith I long not to live.[15]

In his introduction to the play, Bolt explains:

> Thomas More...became for me a man with an adamantine sense of his own self. He knew where he began and left off, what area of himself he could yield to the encroachments of his enemies, and what to the encroachments of those he loved...But at length he was asked to retreat from that final area where he located his self.

> Set like metal, (he) was overtaken by an absolutely primitive rigor, and could no more be budged than a cliff.[16]

There is something admirable and powerful about such a death. It is a choice each human may be called on to make. Under some circumstance, he may have to decide if he will keep inviolate that sacred place at the center of his being or if he will save his life and allow himself to be compromised, violated, and therefore spiritually destroyed.

In other words, one who chooses to protect his own soul is seen as a saint, like Sir Thomas More or, at the very least, as a hero of human courage and integrity.

Of course, the Christian tradition has its own hero, its ideal, its model of human integrity and courage. Jesus of Nazareth died rather than compromise himself, rather than destroy his own soul and violate that sacred place at the center of his being.

In the story that has come down to us, he is quoted as saying, "I, if I be lifted up, will draw all men unto me."[17] Of course, not all have been drawn to him. But many millions have.

We have been drawn to the picture of him as painted in the Gospels. We have been fascinated by him, mesmerized by his example, and claimed by the beauty of his character. We have been captivated by his words and haunted by the persistence of his image through the last 2,000 years. We want still to sing, "Jesus, Jesus, Jesus. There's just something about that name. Jesus, Master, Savior. Like the fragrance after the rain."[18]

Over all his words, his deeds of compassion, and the stories of his healings, the image of his death on the cross still hovers. His death and resurrection dominate the picture. Very early on, his story was written down by eyewitnesses and those who had heard it repeated. Four versions of his biography still appear in our Bibles. In each of them, the major portion of the story is devoted to his death and the events surrounding it.

Perhaps the favorite verse of the Bible for more persons than any other is the one we all learned as children in Sunday School: "For God so loved the world that he gave his only Son so that everyone who believes in him may not perish but have eternal life."[19]

When I go through the hymnal searching for hymns to sing on a Sunday morning, I find, out of 676 hymns in that book, most of them mention, in one way or another, the death or the blood of Jesus.

Moreover, the sacraments of Baptism and Holy Communion are both built upon the foundation of Jesus' death, not on his teachings or good deeds. Just listen to the prayer we make each time a child is baptized, "He called his disciples to share in the baptism of his death and resurrection…"[20] Listen to the liturgy for the Eucharist, "The body of Christ given for you. The blood of Christ shed for you."[21]

At the center of the Roman Catholic mass is the miracle in which the host and the wine are said to become the actual body and blood of Jesus. Even so, late in his life, John Wesley complained about the so-called "gospel preachers" who wandered the countryside:

> I find more profit in sermons on either good tempers or good works than in what are vulgarly called "gospel sermons." That term is now become a mere cant word. I wish none of our society would use it. It has no determinate

meaning. Let but a pert, self-sufficient animal, that has neither sense nor grace, bawl out something about Christ, or his blood, or justification by faith, and his hearers cry out, "What a fine gospel sermon!"[22]

Clearly, Wesley, who put great stock in the doctrine of the Atonement, found an excessive emphasis on the blood and death of Jesus to be misleading. Nevertheless, it is Jesus' death and the surrounding events that continue to draw people, rather than the life he lived or even his teachings. There is still something about Jesus' death that takes hold of people. There is something that fires their imaginations. There is something that draws them to him and won't let them go. "I, if I be listed up, will draw all men unto me."[23] What is it that draws us?

We have tried all kinds of explanations, but why cannot we see it as something that Jesus did to preserve and protect his own integrity as a human being, that is, something that happened when he refused to bend under the pressures to conform himself to the ways of the ruling powers.

That is how he himself talked about it. "What does it profit a man if he gains the whole world but loses his own soul?"[24] Why isn't it his integrity and courage, simply the presentation of the way a human being can live and die like human beings are able to do when the Spirit who is God is allowed to possess them, that draws us?

That is what makes sense to me. But we have not been content to let Jesus be human. Here is what we have done with his death, his magnificent manifestation of the possibilities of human life and death. Sometimes in the history of the church, we have treated it as a great dramatization of the depth, width, and height of the love of God. Maybe that is the interpretation implied by the line in our communion service that says, "Christ died for us while we were yet sinners. That proves God's love toward us."[25] It is as though God had staged a play with Jesus as the star in order for the audience to see the greatness of his love. But that puts the whole burden of his death on God and strips Jesus of his part and the integrity and courage of his humanity.

What kind of God would that show us? We would have a playwright for God, and Jesus would be reduced to an actor on the stage who had been fed his lines and his movements.

So we have sometimes tried to explain it differently. We have posited an enemy who is intent upon harming God's children. Satan, remember? So God makes a deal with Satan, whereby Satan can have Jesus while God gets to keep us. In other words, Jesus is the ransom payment. What kind of a God would it take to work that way? Well, at the very least, he would be a trader and a dealmaker. In today's world, he would be charged with negotiating with a terrorist.

The most popular theory about this strange business is adapted, quite understandably, from early Hebrew practices. The Old Testament Law contained a whole system of blood sacrifices. They were designed to make Atonement for those who broke the other laws. That is, lambs, doves, and goats were sacrificed, and their blood poured out upon the altar to pay off the debt the people owed God for their disobedience.

What happened, according to this system, was that a deal was struck between God and the people, whereby God could have mercy on them if they made the right blood sacrifices. Then, the early Christians decided the blood Jesus shed when he died was precious enough to pay all the debts for everyone who had broken or would ever break the laws of God. So, he was called "The Lamb of God who takes away the sins of the world."[26]

Haven't you ever wondered about that? Wondered about what in the world it could possibly mean? The only way it makes any sense is if we have a certain picture of God or a certain way of thinking about God as a lawgiver and judge who makes deals with people and is a trader in mercies as though they were merchandise. His mercy and grace have to be purchased by Jesus' blood. What kind of love is it that has to be purchased?

No, such pictures of God deprive Jesus of his humanity and God of his grace.

Clearly, what we need is a new image of God, a new way of thinking about God. We can no longer think of God as the divine playwright, the lawgiver and judge, or the dealmaker and tinkerer. We need to see God as the Great Spirit in whom all human spirits live, move, and have their being.

Furthermore, we need to see Jesus as that human hero in whom the human spirit has been perfected by the influence and power of the Great Spirit, of whom he is a living part. We need to see him as "the pioneer of our faith" and as "the author and finisher of our faith."[27] It is quite appropriate for Jesus to be represented as saying, "I, if I am lifted up, will draw all men to myself."[28] We will not only be drawn to him because of his teachings, deeds of compassion, and healing. We will be drawn to him because he represents the possibilities each human being possesses just because he is a part of the Spirit who is God. We will be drawn to him because, in him, we see God can overcome the negative powers within us by accentuating the positive powers.

Most of all, we will be drawn to him by that powerful picture of his death through which he protected his own integrity as a human spirit who is a part of the Spirit who is God. We will be drawn to him when we see, in his death, his absolute refusal to bend before the destructive forces in his society.

We will be drawn to him when, in the stories of his resurrection, we see the promise that the Spirit who is God in us will survive the natural world of the body and be liberated from the limits the human spirit in this life is heir to.

If we read the stories the Gospels tell and if we hold up before us the picture of him they paint, we must still want to sing, "Jesus, Jesus, Jesus. There's just something about that name. Jesus, Master, Savior. Like the fragrance after the rain."[29]

You may wonder about those who have neither read the stories nor seen the pictures of Jesus. Are they then lost and without hope?

Of course not! Rather, whoever anywhere enters upon the life of the spirit and cultivates the positive, healing, uniting powers of the spirit begins a new life. Whoever by the power of the Great Spirit within himself or herself subdues the negative, divisive, and alienating spiritual powers grows ever more perfect. Thus, his spirit imitates ever more completely the Great Spirit himself.

What do I say of this Jesus? I say only that his story is the one that points me to the life of the Spirit. He is the one who offers the promise that, when I open myself to the power of the Great Spirit who already resides in me, I shall become more and more like him in whom I see that the fully human and the divine are one.

I say it just so happens in the economy of the Great Spirit who is God that because Jesus has been lifted up, I have seen him, and he has pointed out the way of the spirit to me. That is why I commend him to you!

Amen.

Lord Jesus, my ideal,
  you reveal the grace and power to heal,
  the spirit that forgives,
  the love that comforts and encourages,
  the strength that bends to no other power
  and keeps faithful to himself
  and the honesty that casts a light on all my weakness
  and my failure to fulfill my destiny.
In You I see first the bud.
And then, Lord Jesus, hero of my life,
  I see in You the flower when, upon the cross,
  You demonstrate how one may live,

> with neither fear nor favor,
> and so defeat the powers that intimidate
> and seek to destroy.
> Then by your rising,
> You reveal that nothing in heaven or on earth
> can crush the spirit that feeds on that Spirit
> which shall prevail at last.
> Make me whole and keep me safe.
> Amen. saf

10

Growing Up—Sermons on Sanctifying Grace

Sermon 8
Pray Without Ceasing
John 15:1–11

Comment:

In Wesley's scheme, sanctification or holiness begins already with justifying grace. In fact, he came to admit, because of the presence of prevenient grace in every human life, some good works might even occur before justification. But, as we have seen, justifying faith is just the door that opens the way for grace to work in its fullest measure. This is the real beginning of intentional, personal spiritual growth. Faith that continues and, over time, allows the greatest fruits of grace to be produced was called sanctifying faith by Wesley.

The sermons in this chapter deal with the "means of grace" and the ongoing fruits of grace. Wesley preached about both, so I shall do so here. While justifying faith has often been associated with rebirth as the heart of the Christian experience (and was so considered by Wesley at one point in his journey), his focus on holiness earlier yet and then again later actually made sanctifying grace to be the heart of the Christian experience.

Of course, it has to start some place, but the gradual growth in grace and spiritual power that lasts as long as faith and grace endure is the great sine qua non *of the Christian life for Wesley and this reinterpretation. Nowhere does the process nature of salvation become so clear as it does when we look at the continuum between justifying and sanctifying faith and the corresponding gifts of grace. The move from the one to the next is often nearly imperceptible so that the nature of both faith and grace does not seem to change at all. What changes is the refocusing of attention and the increase in the fruit. With justifying faith, the fruit may be said to be in the bud stage, while, in sanctification, the flower blooms, and the fruit takes form. The fruit then ripens, is picked, and is finally eaten. In fact, there is a spiritual progression that runs from the birth of spirit in the human being (see prevenient grace) through recognition and decision (see justifying grace), the nurturing disciplines of prayer, fasting, and so forth (see sanctifying grace) to perfection at last (see glorification). This process is comparable to the natural process beginning with germination, flowering, and fruit. In fact, D. A. Reily, the Brazilian scholar, has argued that this natural process is one of the major sources of Wesley's theology (see our discussion of the Quadrilateral in chapter two.)*

This first sermon on sanctifying grace seeks to expound what I consider the absolute foundation of all the means of grace. It is through prayer that faith grows. It is through prayer that grace feeds our spiritual growth and is released into our spirits. It is by prayer that the power of the Great Spirit takes possession of our lives and all our relationships. This sermon seeks to meet the universal human need for connection with others and, in that very act, connection with God the Great Spirit. Indirectly, it also touches the needs for hope, guidance, and understanding.

Such prayer is not institutional, even though I find prayer in the congregation to be real and important. It is not circumscribed by any set of theological opinions, even though I find it enhanced by a theological vision that makes sense of prayer and places it at the center of one's life. It does not take the place of the other means of grace, for example, the sacraments understood in their spiritual rather than their legal connotations, Christian conversation, fasting, or the study of the Bible. Rather, it supports them all and makes them real and effective. That is why this sermon stands at the beginning of our chapter on sanctifying grace.

◆ ◆ ◆

No question about it, prayer is just about the most universally accepted religious practice going. Think about it! Very few people suggest the Ten Commandments should be taught in the schools. Even fewer think the Apostle's Creed should be recited or Bible stories should be placed in readers. Prayer, silent or spoken, that is the ticket. Prayer is offered as the universal cure-all for irreligion in our schools. Only those of us who hold out for separation of church and state oppose the use of prayer in the schools. For some reason, prayer is not only seen as the least likely practice to meet opposition. It is also seen as the surest religious practice to make a real difference in peoples' lives. In fact, it is often equated with "putting God back into our schools." Opponents are charged with wanting to take God out of our schools. But what kind of God is it that can be pushed around like that?

Not only that, but routine prayer speckles our public life. It opens Congress. It blesses inaugurations. It is formalized at White House prayer breakfasts. Even now, it is rarely missing at public functions. It is a highly touted exercise.

I suppose the reason for all this is that prayer is seen as nonsectarian. It is usually religiously neutral, and it is not nearly as controversial as other forms of religion. Of course, I am not for prayer in the schools precisely because I think there is nothing neutral about it. I believe it does make a difference. Plus, it can be dangerous as well as beneficial! And that's not what the state should be doing.

But, you are not sure it really does work. Well, that depends on what you are looking for. What should we expect from prayer anyway? The disciples asked Jesus to teach them to pray, so he did. But, he had some other things to say about prayer, too. First, he said it is dangerous to mess around with things of the spirit.

Prayer is spiritual power. Spiritual power is something like electricity. It depends on what it is used for. For example, the story says Jesus once cursed a fig tree. Then, when he and his disciples passed by it, the next day, Peter said, "Look, the fig tree you cursed has all withered up."

And Jesus said:

> Have faith in God. Truly, I tell you, If you say to this mountain, "Be taken up and thrown into the sea," and you do not doubt in your heart, but believe that what you say will come to pass, it will be done for you. So I tell you, whatever you ask for in prayer, believe that you have received it, and it will be yours.[1]

That's pretty heady stuff, isn't it?

What was Jesus' point in all this? I think his point was a warning about the misuse of prayer. Even prayer for things that are not important or maybe even questionable (like destroying a fig tree) can be powerful and therefore dangerous! To play around carelessly with prayer and things spiritual is like playing with electricity.

Years ago, in Brazil, my seventy-five-year-old neighbor, Dona Maria, came breathlessly to my back door one day. Her eyes were wide, and her face was wracked with fear. She had found a small cloth doll lying on her kitchen doorsill. It was filled with pins. It was a fetish left there by someone who wished her ill.

Though she was a Christian, she retained the popular belief in the evil power of fetishes because they often seemed to work. I talked and prayed with her in order to counteract the spirit of evil in the fetish with the spirit of good which was God (as I explained to her). Thus she was comforted.

There is spiritual power abroad in the world into which we may tap, even if it is the spirit of evil, alienation, or destruction. As spiritual beings ourselves, we have access to all the spiritual powers.

Maybe we are still not sure that prayer is always really that powerful. You have offered prayers that did not produce the desired results. You have prayed sometimes when it seemed like there was a cement roof separating you from God. Your prayers went nowhere. They simply fell back to earth unheard.

Remember how Hamlet comes upon King Claudius at prayer? Hamlet wants revenge upon Claudius for killing his father. He holds a knife raised to strike, but he then withholds his hand, lest Claudius die while at prayer and therefore go to heaven. And he doesn't want that.

Then, when Claudius has finished his prayer, the king says, "My words fly up, my thoughts remain below. Words without thoughts never to heaven go."²

Our prayers sometimes seem as futile as his, and this has been the experience of the race in spite of the promise Jesus made. It almost seems sometimes as though God has reneged on Jesus' promise. We face that reality every day. Even Jesus faced it. The story says, when he prayed in Gethsemane for the cup of death to pass him by, he ended up submitting himself to God and accepting his death. Clearly, the promise Jesus had made earlier did not mean we were to pray for and expect God to give us just anything our hearts desired, even though it sometimes seemed to happen that way.

So what's going on here? Sometimes, it may seem God is that great judge who simply overrules us on some of our petitions, saying, "Hey, I've got something better for you."

An unknown Confederate soldier once wrote:

> I asked God for strength that I might achieve.
> I was made weak, that I might humbly obey.
> I asked for health, that I might do greater things.
> I was given infirmity that I might do better things.
> I asked for riches, that I might be happy.
> I was given poverty, that I might be wise.
> I asked for power, that I might have the praise of men.
> I was given weakness, that I might feel the need of God.
> I asked for all things, that I might enjoy life.
> I was given life, that I might enjoy all things.
> I got nothing that I asked for—
>   but everything I had hoped for.
> Almost despite myself
>   my unspoken prayers were answered.
> I am among all men most richly blessed.³

Maybe prayer is a conversation with God in which we tell him what we want and he tells us what we can have. I think that is getting a bit closer to the heart of the matter. It is something like a conversation, something like sharing stuff. It is just opening our spirits, our human spirits, to the impact and influence of the Spirit who is God.

Maybe it is like sharing with him everything we are, what we are feeling, what we are thinking, what we are wanting, what we are doubting, what we are believing, and what we are hoping. Maybe it is like allowing God to share with us what he is thinking, feeling, and wanting. It is not like a long-distance telephone call or going online with our computers. It is not like a trade-off, making a deal, or bargaining. It is more like something magical happening when two persons fall in love, and a change takes place within us, right where God and we meet.

Maybe the power of prayer is that there is something going on behind the asking and receiving. Maybe something else is going on here. Can it be that God, after all, is not some being up there or out there who is in the business of handing out gifts or withholding them according to some secret agenda of his own?

What if he is a lot closer than that? What if prayer is something that goes on within us where both God and we are a part of each other? What if, when we pray, we are simply throwing the switch for the electric power of the Great Spirit within us to flow and something happens inside of us, something changes?

Maybe it is like the sap flowing into the branches when they are grafted onto the vine because the branches have become part of the vine. Then life is given! And the branches put forth blossoms of beauty and bear fruit that is sweet and nourishes.

Actually, that is what prayer is always good for, whether or not we get what we might ask for. Prayer is the way we engraft ourselves onto the vine that gives life and bears fruit. Prayer is the medium through which that life flows. Prayer allows the Spirit who is God and who lives as spirit within us to break down the blockages and close the broken circuits so he can flow through us and make us new.

Our spirits and the Spirit who is God get tighter bit-by-bit through time and as long as prayer persists. The fruit of the merging is joy and peace, faith and self-control, patience and mercy, and hope and love. The goal of prayer is not getting God to do our will. Instead, it is becoming more and more like that One whom we hold up before ourselves as the ideal man and the image of the Great Spirit himself.

Let me now make some suggestions for your prayer life as you move out on your faith journey.

First, praise God for his presence and his power, for his beauty and his goodness, for his mercy and his love. Do this because admitting your dependence upon him is to open the way for gratitude.

Second, thank him for every blessing. Count them, one-by-one. In a conscious, sincere way, daily refocus your attention on the things of the spirit because the heart of all spirituality is self-surrender.

Ask him to give you the grace and love to forgive whomever has offended you because resentment festers and stops the sap of the spirit from flowing.

Pray for someone you dislike that he or she may be blessed in abundance. It is hard, but it takes away an unnecessary, hurtful burden.

Pray for someone you love, and tell them you love them. Perhaps try sending them that message by spirit telepathy. You may want to think of that as sending it on the wings of angels.

Confess your needs to God, and ask him to meet them. Then pray, "Nevertheless, not my will, but yours, be done."

Finally, just let his peace and love fill you, so they overflow you and engulf those around you.

Prayer is powerful, and it can effect changes around us, either for good or evil. However, it will always change us inside so that, when focused on the positive, we may become, moment-by-moment, day-by-day, and year-by-year, more like that one whose name we adore, Jesus the holy one.

> Prayer is the soul's sincere desire,
>   unuttered or expressed,
>   the motion of a hidden fire
>   that trembles in the breast.
> Prayer is the burden of a sigh,
>   the falling of a tear,
>   the upward glancing of an eye,
>   when none but God is near.
> Prayer is the Christians' vital breath,
>   the Christians' native air,
>   their watchword at the gates of death,
>   they enter heaven with prayer.
> O thou, by whom we come to God,
>   the Life, the Truth, the Way,
>   the path of prayer thyself hast trod,
>   Lord, teach us how to pray.[4]
> Amen.

O Great Spirit,
    You who are all in all, the beginning and the end:
I want the full blossoming of the power I feel within me.
    I know you are here.
    There's something great inside me, the tiniest seed of faith,
        the bare bones of something beautiful;
        there's a butterfly, seeking to break forth;
        there's a majesty here, the bud of an overwhelming love,
        a power to heal and nurture and feed,
        and a glory to be revealed.
I want, O God, what You have promised.
    I want to be holy.
    I want to be a flowing stream
        that waters the ground where I flow.
    I want to be your beauty,
        your compassion,
        your light,
        your grace.
Amen. Saf

Sermon 9
Tomorrow Is Another Day
Luke 11:5–13

Comment:

Prayer is the fundamental means of grace, but what does prayer do? It opens the lines of communication within us that are blocked and thus inhibit the infusion of the positive spiritual powers of the Great Spirit into our human spirits. It subdues the negatives within us. Its goal is to give us the mind that was in Jesus, that is, a spirit in which all spiritual powers are devoted to the end of peace, healing, and oneness. Then all the powers that stand in the way of that result are rendered ineffective, though they continue to exert pressure on the positive powers.

This sermon focuses on the necessity of persistence in prayer and how that works. In Wesley's scheme, this is the process of sanctification with the goal being perfection or holiness.

The Scripture used is Jesus' story of the midnight friend who gives what his friend asks. He assures his disciples, if they persist in prayer, "the heavenly Father will give the Holy Spirit to those who ask."⁵ Hope in tomorrow's fulfillment encourages persistence in prayer.

The process of sanctification takes time, patience, and persistence. The short-term hope in change and growth tomorrow and the next day serves as an interim hope that keeps us focused on the ultimate goal.

The universal human needs to which this sermon responds, besides understanding, are, therefore, connection, hope, and meaning. The connection it reinforces is the connection of the human spirit with the Spirit who is God himself. Implicit is our connection with all other spirits who, like us, are parts of the spirit world, that is, of God. Through all these connections, the powers of the Spirit who is God are assisted in their effort to influence and enhance the spirits of others and to build the community of spirit that is part of the goal of sanctification

◆   ◆   ◆

Last New Year's, I paid very little attention to New Year's celebrations. However, I did make a couple of New Year's resolutions. Two were, I figured, probably two more than I would end up keeping. The fact was, I knew, I did hardly anything at all without having decided to do it, that is, without having exercised my willpower.

So I tried again—and I failed again. There is nothing unusual about any of this because every one of you has done the same.

Here is something else I knew: I knew the power to decide is a power of the human spirit. Nothing else in creation of which I am aware, with the exception of certain of the higher animals, has any such power of the will. Only spiritual beings have such power. We decide what to order in the restaurant, what to wear when we get up in the morning, what to say when we go for an interview, what to do on our day off, or what gift to give our sweetheart on our anniversary. As self-aware persons, we are using our wills to make a thousand little decisions every day.

So what happens to our New Year's resolutions? Why do we so often fail to keep them? Is it, perhaps, because our New Year's resolutions usually involve major changes in our character, our habits, our defense mechanisms, or our deeply ingrained ways of doing things?

Willpower is a great spiritual power, and each spirit has some measure of the gift due to the grace that gives each human being his spiritual nature. But willpower is never absolute in any of us, just as patience is rarely very highly developed in most of us.

Still we try to do better. We try to be better. We try to integrate our internal character with our external appearance. Sometimes old outward habits can be changed. We can sometimes break the smoking habit or the habits of cursing, gossiping, or putting others down in order to build ourselves up. More often than not, however, we end up with a cosmetic improvement of our outward appearance, leaving our inner life untouched.

To change our attitudes, to conquer our fears, to experience the joy of life, to know the peace that passes understanding, or to love the enemy and have compassion for the suffering (that is, to suffer with the sufferer rather than merely dropping pennies in the alms box) is often beyond the power of the will.

Why? Why can't we pull that off, too? Just look at the human spirit, at your own. Don't you see? The reconditioning of the spirit, the internal life, is beyond the power of the will, just because why? <u>Just because the will itself is a spiritual power that must be fed and nurtured along with peace of mind, love, and</u> patience. It is as much beyond the power of the ordinary human will to feed itself as it is impossible for the body to grow stronger by consuming itself.

That was Wesley's problem when he sought by the deeds of his own will to be assured he was saved. You can sometimes deal with the externals by the power of an imperfect will, but you cannot change the internal powers of the spirit in that way.

Listen to the lament of a man considered to be a saint. Paul writes:

> For I do not do what I want, but I do the very thing I hate…I can will what is right, but I cannot do it…for I delight in the Law of God in my inmost self, but I see in my members another law at war with the law of my mind.[6]

For Paul, the destructive and divisive powers were always at war with the constructive and unifying powers of his spirit. Hatred, envy, revenge, and resentment are always struggling against love, generosity, forgiveness, and compassion. If the positive powers are not strong enough in us to begin with, new power must be found.

It is like you have a stalemate going on inside you. It is like a tug-of-war in which the good guys start sliding, but they try to dig in to stop the slide. Maybe they make some headway for a while. But it doesn't last—and you start sliding again. You want to cry out, like Paul did, "I'm losing it, O God! Wretched man that I am! Who will rescue me from this body of death?"[7]

I say, if you care at all—if you have decided to live your life in the spirit—if you know that deep inside you are untapped powers that can make your life a thing of beauty and a power for good—if you have seen the possibilities of the human spirit in Jesus—if you've seen his life and listened to his words—if you have seen him stand up to the evil, destructive powers of his society—if you've seen him hanged on a cross with nails in his hands and feet and a crown of thorns on his head and a bleeding hole in his side—if you have seen how he revealed and displayed the glory of which the human spirit is capable—*then* that is when you know that new power can be found.

If you have seen the empty cross on which he hanged—if you have come to the door of the empty tomb through which he emerged—if, somehow, in the imagination of your mind, you have seen him walk in glory away from the hill of Golgotha, down the road to Emmaus, and out across the hills toward Galilee—*then* you will have seen the power of the spirit over the threat and terror of death. You will have heard the promise that this is your heritage, too, because, as a human being like him, you are a fellow heir with him.

Where will you find the power to supplement your own weaker love and compassion, your more fragile peace and joy, or your own trembling courage?

Maybe we cannot turn up the heat beneath our spiritual boiler and build a head of spiritual steam by which to conquer the world. However, we are free to use the means of grace. That much we have the power to do. That much our wills can be trained to accomplish. That much has been given all of us by the amazing grace of God, who has made us spiritual beings in the first place.

Listen to what we can do. First, before and after, behind and within everything else, we can pray. If we cannot pray, we do not have a prayer. Second, we can use the Sacraments. We can remember our baptism in which the water was placed upon us as a sign of the unbidden, unmerited love of God that precedes everything else in our lives. Then we can eat and drink the symbols of that victorious death that Jesus died and thus remember the possibilities of human life his story reveals.

We can converse with one another about these things, about life itself and the possibilities with which it presents us upon this journey between birth and death. This is conversation about the deep things of life and the sharing of our hopes and struggles.

We can also fast as a way to loosen our hold on the promises of money, possession, and the accumulation of pleasures, thus allowing our focus to concentrate on the growth of our spirits in grace and power.

Such spiritual disciplines (and many others that may be devised) are within the reach of our powers of will. But each of these fails unless a new vision makes it clear that all this can do is open up the lines of communication so God, who is already in us, can break through and nurture, strengthen, and enrich the positive, creative, and healing powers already there. So even before we are able to take up these means of grace, God is in us praying for us, bringing the pressure of his love to bear against all our barriers.

Such breakthroughs sometimes happen suddenly. A miracle occurs, a healing takes place, or a person's life is turned around. Such events can rarely be attributed to this prayer or that or to any particular exercise of one of the means of grace.

Rather, we may usually attribute such an occurrence to the weight of many prayers by many persons in many places, perhaps over a long period of time. The pressure of God's grace that is always there within us begins slowly, slowly, slowly to wear away and weaken the barriers. His grace comes seeping through some tiny opening, eroding it bit-by-bit, until finally, almost imperceptibly, our spirit grows stronger, more positive, more creative, and more peaceful. Or, perhaps, under the wearing pressure of many prayers, a dam breaks and, with a mighty rush, grace finally starts us on a new journey of renewed longing and prayer, spiritual discipline, and the use of the means of grace.

But it rarely happens all at once. Some dam may finally break and set a person in a new direction, but it does not happen until events and the prayers of others have conspired to break the barrier down.

Even the power of the will can be strengthened by our prayers. And, for those who pray and are faithful in all the means of grace, the victories over the destructive powers may be few and far between. But, for those who are faithful to the journey they have set upon, the victories will come. They will come.

The important thing is the positive powers will be enhanced and the negative powers will be subdued at last, even if only in the time of our final freedom.

Mostly, changes will be slow, two steps forward and one back. However, the promise is, if you cast your bread on the waters, it will come back.

So here is what we must do. First of all, pray for an increase in our powers of hope and patience because these are also spiritual powers. It is very hard to have patience unless you also hope in the relentless pressure of God's grace. Otherwise, so-called patience is nothing more than resignation. True patience is to wait for God to do his work while we persist in prayer and attendance upon the means of grace.

Remember Jesus' story about Henry, whose friend arrives late one night at his house asking for something to eat and a night's rest? He has nothing in his cupboard, so he walks down the street to the house of his good friend, Joe.

He knocks on Joe's door. "Joe! Joe! I've got a guest who just got in from the big city, and he's hungry. Do you have a loaf of bread I can borrow?"

Joe is groggy with sleep and is not at all happy about being roused in the middle of the night. He calls back from under the covers, "Henry, don't bother me in the middle of the night. Go away! I'll talk to you tomorrow."

But Henry won't go away. He asks Joe repeatedly. Then he pleads with Joe some more. "Finally," Jesus says, "even though he will not get up and give him anything because he is his friend, at least because of his persistence, he will get up and give him whatever he needs."[8]

Then Jesus says, "Ask and it will be given you; search and you will find; knock and the door will be opened for you."[9] Now, maybe that sounds like God has to be begged, cajoled, and finally persuaded, maybe even annoyed, before he will give in and give us what we demand.

The reality is that persistence finally breaks down the barriers and gradually subjugates the negative powers so that God can do in us what he has always wanted to do and has been trying to do all along. We do not have to persuade him. We just have to find a way to allow him.

Now listen to the way Jesus finishes this story about persistence in prayer:

> If you then who are evil know how to give good gifts to your children, how much more will the heavenly Father give the Holy Spirit to those who ask him.[10]

Maybe what God gives in response to our prayers will not always or immediately be just what we think we need or at least want. Always though, he will give us his spirit when we ask. The barriers between will always be weakened. We will always grow a little. We will always experience a bit more immediately the presence of God who is always waiting within us. There will come a time when we will become so open to God who is Spirit that our own spirits will be made wholly whole, we will be healed of all ills, and the destructive and divisive in us will be subdued and crushed under our feet.

We need not worry about whether we are good enough yet or whether we will get into heaven. The gifts of the spirit will become ours. Generosity and care will grow. Resentment and hostility will be dried up. Reconciliation will begin to heal our alienation from others. Justice for others—sometimes at the expense of justice for ourselves—will begin to demand our attention and our efforts.

More and more, the beauty of Jesus will be seen in us, and the mind of Christ will rule our spirits. And, as we labor, peace and joy will attend our way.

Amen.

> *O Lord, why do You delay so?*
> *I hunger and thirst and I pray and pray*
>   *and still my demons rise up.*
> *Resentments once put down show up unbidden.*
> *Uncaring settles over me like a shroud.*
> *If I move one inch today,*
>   *it seems tomorrow I slide two.*
> *But I want to grow up, put away my childish things,*
>   *become a man like the One who beckons me.*
> *Am I a better man than I was one year ago?*
>   *I pray I am.*
> *Just hear me; just listen, and feed me on yourself.*
>   *And tomorrow I shall be a bit closer.*
> *Amen. Saf*

Sermon 10
Sitting Loose
Matthew 19:23–26

Comment:

My biblical reference for this sermon is: "It is easier for a camel to go through the eye of a needle than for someone who is rich to enter the Kingdom of God."[11]

Wesley was highly sensitive to the seductive power of money and possessions. For instance, he preached sermons from Matthew 19:24 on "On Riches," from I Timothy 6:9 on "The Danger of Riches," and from Luke 16:9 on "The Use of Money." In his sermon, "On Riches," he wrote, "Sit loose to all things here below as if you were a poor beggar." He is clearly referring to our addiction to money and possessions. However, it may have a far wider application. Therefore, the title I am using for the present sermon comes from this passage.

The discipline of fasting was one of Wesley's important means of grace because it strikes squarely at our attachment to the natural pleasures and blessings of this life while simultaneously recognizing they are good. They just are not God. In other words, fasting was an anti-idolatry discipline. While it is rarely emphasized in the contemporary church, fasting calls our attention to the necessity for spiritual disciplines that loosen our hold on "all things here below" and aid us in focusing on the things of the spirit.

Therefore, this sermon also deals with some other means of grace as ways by which we break down the barriers to spiritual communication. They help us loosen our hold on the ephemeral pleasures and blessings of life in the natural world in favor of spiritual blessings or graces and the pursuit of spiritual perfection. They are idolatry fighters.

Thus, my expectation in this sermon is double-edged. First, I want to encourage anything that loosens our ultimate dependence upon such natural blessings as a way of focusing our attention on enhancing the powers of the spirit. Second, I also want to encourage a certain detachment from such blessings as a way of freeing us to be grateful for them as gifts, enjoy them as gifts, improve them as gifts, and share them as gifts. As gifts of grace, they are sheer blessings instead of the source of our salvation and our happiness.

Primarily, this sermon aims at providing practical guidance for our spiritual lives. Understanding and hope are touched as well.

◆   ◆   ◆

We have heard it said that, "What the flesh desires is opposed to the Spirit and what the Spirit desires is opposed to the flesh."[12] We have heard it said the world is evil and only the spirit is good. In fact, the word was put out that the "works of the flesh are obvious: fornication, impurity, licentiousness, idolatry, sorcery, enmities, strife, jealousy, anger, quarrels, dissensions, factions, envy, drunkenness, carousing, and things like these."[13]

In fact, everything negative or evil was attributed to the world and the flesh. Everything good was attributed to the spirit. Paul wrote, "By contrast, the fruit of the Spirit is love, joy, peace, patience, kindness, generosity, faithfulness, gentleness and self-control."[14] That was Paul's attempt to explain how things worked.

The result has been a strong tendency in Western society to put down worldly pleasures and natural passions and desires, blaming the natural world for the terror and suffering and all the unspeakable evils confronting us daily.

At the same time, the Bible has affirmed the world. The first Genesis story says, "God saw everything that he had made, and indeed, it was very good."[15] That included both the natural world and the world of human beings. Not only that, but human beings were given dominion over the natural world to care for it and use it well because it was good, good, good.

So, where does all the evil come from? Is the world evil and the flesh corrupt or not?

Well, here is one possibility: In spite of Paul's talk about the works of the spirit, let us suppose the natural world is all there is. If so, then any good that exists must arise from nature itself and so must any evil that exists. In that case, there is no mind or spirit except the brain itself. For instance, when an aneurysm ruptures, the blood begins to flood the brain, impeding its operation. The brain begins malfunctioning and may die. Then the mind simply disappears.

Or, when a certain kind of plaque begins to form in the brain, the electrical connections are not made. The brain again begins malfunctioning. Memory deteriorates. The power to speak falters. An inability to swallow may develop, and the brain finally stops telling the body what to do. So the heart stops beating, the lungs will not breathe, and the body dies, taking the mind along with it. That is known as Alzheimer's disease.

The problem with this is there is something else that is happening for which the brain has no responsibility. Think about this: A computer can do many things better than the brain can, like calculate and even appear to reason. They call it AI, or artificial intelligence. We can be sure, however, there is one thing a computer cannot do. It cannot become aware of itself like a human being can. It can be programmed to fix itself when certain things malfunction, but it does not know itself. Nor does the brain know itself.

This self-awareness is the miracle of "you" and "me." Therefore, not everything is matter. Not all is attributable to the natural world.

Of course, there is another theory that has also been around for a long, long time. Maybe everything is spirit! In that case, the source of evil has to be in the spirit, as well as any good that exists. And self-consciousness, with all its powers of thought, imagination, creativity, love, hope, hate, egomania, and so forth that are dependent for their existence on being self-aware, is all that exists.

In that case, the body and the natural world around us are a creation of the spirit's imagination. Seriously, there have been philosophers who have made such a claim. There have even been those who have tried to argue that there is only one mind or spirit and everything else that exists—nature and even other human egos—is a product of that mind's imagination.

Of course, the one who tried that argument would have to assume the only mind that existed was his own. Such people are called solipsists. There is a story about Professor Borden P. Bowne of Boston University School of Theology. One day, a student made the argument for solipsism. Bowne simply said, "Then what are you telling me for?" That seems to me to be a pretty decisive response. Obviously, the student simply did not believe his own argument.

Therefore, it seems inconceivable the body creates the self-awareness of mind. It seems equally inconceivable the natural world is simply a figment of some other mind's imagination or even of my own. So, it looks like we are thrown back on the old assumption that there exist both nature and spirit. The self-aware mind and the natural body, along with the earth and its beauty, both exist together.

Let us just look again at the list of bad stuff Paul cited. The first three are apparently sexual in nature: fornication, impurity, and licentiousness. The next two have to do with misdirected desires. Idolatry makes gods out of natural objects, and sorcery depends on magic to achieve one's ends.

There is also a whole series of divisive passions: enmities, strife, jealousy, anger, quarrels, dissensions, and factions. Paul claims all these are things of the world and the flesh. However, we know all such powers as these exist as negatives within our own spirits. Therefore, it is clear these evils are all undesirable products of the human spirit in which divisive and pathological powers are inevitably in constant struggle against the unifying and healing powers.

Other than such natural events as storms, volcanoes, and earthquakes, which popular mythology calls acts of God, evil is rooted in the human spirit, not in the natural world. Let us suppose that some self-aware mind that thinks, imagines, desires, and therefore has the power to create, decided to create the natural world with bodies and all the regularities that natural laws formulate. Then, suppose, out of herself, she gives birth to spirit minds like herself to inhabit the bodies she has also created. (You see, having given up our inherited masculine image of God, we are free to choose a feminine image of God.)

That would make those spirit minds a part of her own spiritual body, just like our physical organs are parts of our physical body. Just like our head knows what is right and good even while some of our organs may be diseased, and often dysfunctional, that original self-aware mind is in full possession of its unifying and healing powers while its self-aware parts are defective and need healing.

Perhaps we can see how the mind and the body are connected by the network of laws and regularities that allow the body to affect the mind and the mind to affect the body. When the body ceases to function properly according to the physical laws that determine its deterioration with age or disease, it must let the spirit or mind go.

That is why the natural world, along with our physical appetites and natural functions, is both necessary and good, as the Genesis story says. They are good because the Spirit who is God has made them and given them. They are good because they are the nest in which our own spirits were born, nurtured, and matured. They are good because they provide the delights and pleasures of our natural life. They are good because they make us thankful.

They are also ephemeral, temporary, and evanescent. They are often deceptive. They are deceptive when we rest on any of them for our security. They are deceptive when we come to think of them as permanently available. They are deceptive when we think they can give us a purpose for our life. They are deceptive when we mistake any of them for God himself.

How then do we keep a proper perspective on our natural life? That is, how do we resist the temptations of idolatry?

First, we can look the facts in the eye! The fact is that the natural world passes. The second fact is that physical pleasures will end. The third fact is that our bodies will one day fail us and will die. Finally, the fourth fact is that false gods will show their feet of clay.

Jesus spoke more often about money and possessions than about any other form of idolatry. Wealth and possessions will all pass away.

Jesus himself, who clearly loved his mother, yet insisted on keeping a loose hold on family. Family connections, as we know them in this life, will disappear.

Reputation, honor, and position are nice and feed our egos, but they grow dim and fade away. Jesus repeatedly insisted they are worthless compared to the value of one's own soul and he demonstrated it on the cross. These forms of idolatry he rejected out of hand.

Second, we need to resist the temptations of idolatry by internalizing this knowledge. That comes by getting used to the absence of the most tempting delights of our natural life.

Example One: Fast one day a week or one meal a day. Or try some other plan that will not damage the health of the body but perhaps even enhance it. Fasting was John Wesley's suggestion.

Example Two: Reclaim the old practice of Lenten abstinence, or set your own time. Try one month a year without sweets or other desserts, one month a year without sex, or one day a month or even every Monday without speaking. This last is an especially good discipline for the preacher.

As for family attachments, arrange to be separated for some period every year from your family. Treat it as a spiritual discipline, not a sacrifice.

Honors and reputation credits need not be accumulated as though they were the source of your personal value. Put the certificates and the clippings away in a drawer for six months.

Tithing should not be seen simply as a means of raising money or even of resourcing our charities. It is not a virtue to be pled before God in exchange for his mercy. Rather, its primary role is to loosen our hold on our money.

However, here is a quick warning: These disciplines are not religious duties to be fulfilled. They are personal spiritual disciplines that you yourself determine to undertake. Of course, self-discipline is tough. It is almost as tough to let go our grasping as it is to pass through the eye of a needle. But, with God's help, all is possible.

As means of grace, the whole purpose of the self-disciplines I have just suggested is to break down those internal barriers that inhibit the grace of the Great Spirit who is God from impregnating our own spirits with his grace and power, his reconciliation and healing, and his own harmony and peace. They are intended to loosen our grasp on those things that must finally be let go when we enter into that perfect communion with God who is our true home.

Amen.

O Great Spirit,
   You who glorify our bodies by your presence within them:
I am so tightly bound to this body
   that I can scarcely imagine life without it.
The pleasures of my flesh,
   eating and drinking,
   playing games and celebrating special occasions,
   loving and embracing and touching,
   are all so delightful and so beautiful,
   that I forget it is I, a creature of spirit,
   who does the enjoying,
   who experiences the pleasure,
   who feels the ecstasy.
Help me to hold these blessings loosely,
   these blessings which arise from the flesh,
   as gifts to be thankfully received,
   reveled in, shared, and then freely released.
Then may I revel in and share the blessings of the spirit,
   unity, love, and peace.
Amen. Saf

Sermon 11
The Greatest of These
I Corinthians 13:1–13

Comment:

Of all the gifts of the spirit, Paul wrote, the greatest is love. No other word than love more frequently characterizes God's nature in Wesley's sermons. Wesley also provided numerous descriptions of spiritual perfection, all of which included the presence of love in some manner or other. For him, the ultimate expression of holiness was love for God and fellow man. The love chapter in I Corinthians is a natural reference for this sermon.

In our image of God, the ultimate purpose of his self-awareness is seen to be the overcoming of all alienating and divisive powers by the powers of reconciliation and unity. All other powers are good or bad as they are used in the service of the unity the Great Spirit seeks. Some appear to be categorically inimical to unity, such as hatred, revenge, and resentment. Others seem to be neutral in themselves, for example, creativity, calculation, and even the power to hope. Trust, when directed toward untrustworthy objects, such as possessions or appearances, can have a destructive and alienating result. Even love as care, when directed toward the wrong purposes, can create an undesirable product. However, love as a unifying or reconciling power can serve as the sine qua non *of holiness, perfection, or, as I prefer to think of it, human spiritual maturity.*

This sermon is intended as the keystone in our sermonic treatment of what Wesley called sanctification. That is, it sits at the apex of the arch. Without it, the arch falls.

What universal human needs are served by a sermon like this? Clearly, the need for a firm hope, both in the short- and the long-term, can be met by the promise that love is stronger than hate and that its effects can often be seen almost immediately. Moreover, it results in a clearer understanding of the way God's unmerited love as grace is immediately available, awaiting nothing more than the breaking down of our internal barriers. That is, if God's grace is in fact unmerited, then there is no need for merits provided by Jesus' death to make it available. That leaves his death free to be what it was, a manifestation of the possibilities for unmerited love to take possession of our own human spirits, thus effecting a perfect reconciliation of our spirits with the Spirit who is God. This produces internal peace of mind and spirit.

Given these roles of the sermon, it should also serve our needs for connection, guidance, and meaning.

◆   ◆   ◆

> The love of God is greater far
> than gold or silver ever could afford.
> It reaches past the highest star,
> and covers all the world.[16]

How amazing! How totally incredible that love could ever be so free of conditions, so completely without strings, that it covers all the world!

Don't we approach that when we love our children so absolutely no matter what? That is the part that makes it so amazing. That is what grace means.

> Amazing grace, how sweet the sound
> that saved a wretch like me!
> I once was lost but now am found,
> was blind but now I see.[17]

On the other hand, that does not seem quite fair either, does it? What about all the bad people? What about those who do not care anything for God; who hurt their fellow human beings with impunity; or whose greed for power, prestige, or wealth takes precedence over any shred of human decency they might still possess? They have no right to the grace of God! They have only earned a just condemnation, haven't they?

That is just the point, isn't it! Of course, they have no right to unconditional love or grace. But that is just exactly what makes it grace.

So here we are, caught in a bind between grace and justice. Evil must be punished, right? At the same time, grace is a gift of God's power that has no strings attached whatsoever. The problem is that we have always assumed God judges and condemns us and then punishes the wrong we do or think. Yet he forgives, endlessly forgives. Isn't that what Jesus called on his disciples to do, forgive seventy times seven, that is, endlessly?

How can we have it both ways?

Well, here is one way we have tried. Remember how the Hebrews dealt with this puzzle early on? Because God was a lawgiver and a judge and a prosecutor and executioner, what hope did the poor Hebrews have? Well, the old Law called on them to offer sacrifices of all kinds, a different sacrifice for nearly every kind of disobedience. They all called for the pouring out of the blood of some animal or other, so the slaughtered animals were the ones who paid the price for the sins of all the people. Once the price was paid, God was free to forgive and have mercy.

When Jesus died, the early Christians just substituted the blood of Jesus for the blood of the old sacrifices. That way, God could both punish and have mercy. But mercy, grace, or the love of God still had to be purchased. So it was no longer grace or unconditional love. This theory simply does not work.

There were also those in the early church who tried something else. Some of them said, "Because God is gracious and forgives, we can go ahead and sin all the more." It was sort of like saying, "It is God's business to forgive; so let's give him some business." Well, Paul saw to it that they did not get away with that silliness, that is, grace without judgment. With the kind of lawmaker God he had inherited from his Jewish background, you cannot abandon judgment, even if you lay it all on Jesus.

So what's left? Sounds like judgment and no grace. Now, that is the worst alternative of all. However, we are stuck with it as long as we cling to God as the lawmaker and judge. There goes the last shred of hope for the human race! God will just have to send another flood to wipe us out. A nuclear holocaust might also serve his purposes.

There is still one thing left for us. A new vision of God! The old image of God as lawgiver, judge, and executioner just will not do. No, God is pure spirit! Therefore, within both God and us are the negative counterparts of grace, including the powers of revenge, one-upmanship, hate, violence, and destruction.

He does not make moral and religious laws for people to obey. It is in the very nature of spirit to be in a struggle between the positive and the negative powers. God is seeking to give all of us power to overcome the negatives in ourselves. That is grace, free grace—unconditional love. From the very beginning, when God first breathed spirit over the waters and brought order out of chaos, love and harmony were his purpose. When God first gave birth to human spirits, obedience to rules and the threat of punishment for disobedience as a means of enforcement were not his way.

Unity and peace were his purpose from the beginning. Wherever there is division and strife to be found in us and among us, the Great Spirit strives to give us what we need more than anything else in all the world, the unifying power of love! This is his generosity. And generosity, just like grace, does not demand repayment.

Our task is to find ways to allow God to give us the power he seeks above everything else to give, the power to love, reconcile, and unify. Every other gift takes its value from the contribution it makes to peace and harmony. Every power that cannot be used toward a world of peace and harmony is to be crushed beneath our feet.

But that creates another problem, doesn't it? As long as there has been religion, even the Christian religion, we have been tempted to force our religion on one another. Just look at the horror and suffering our religious wars have caused!

All in the name of Christ, Rome invaded northern Europe, and northern Europe's Crusaders invaded the Holy Land. In Ireland, Protestants and Catholics were at war with each other for decades, both in the name of Christ. The Muslims of Pakistan and the Hindus of India have been fighting each other for years in the name of their respective religions. In the Balkans, Muslims and Orthodox Christians still kill each other. Today, terrorists wage orthodox holy wars against the imperialist West. The West's invasion of Iraq has been no less self-righteous. Again, those who live by the sword are dying by the sword. How then can the powers of love and peace put down and crush the forces of division and hatred?

By more hatred and division? Do we fight fire with fire? Is that the idea? That worked on the western prairies when grassland fires threatened homesteaders' shanties, but it has never worked in the affairs of men and women. How clearly did our Jesus see that! He had a whole history of religious wars behind him in the story of his own country.

He knew religions at war appeal to the righteous judgment of God under the assumption that God has given us laws by which he is judging us and whose infractions justify punishment and even execution.

However, what his story demonstrates is that, in his life, death, and resurrection, love defeats hatred, reconciliation bridges division, peace pulls the teeth of violence, hope defeats fear, trust overcomes distrust, and amazing grace outlasts gaudy self-righteousness.

Everything that opposes or blocks the creative power of love in the human spirit stands in stark opposition to the spirit Jesus taught, the life he lived, and the death to which he submitted himself.

The touchstone of all morality is the harmony and unity that reconciliation and love make possible. We are responsible for making the terrible decisions about how to use our powers of thought, imagination, creativity, trust, hope, and patience to contribute to the practical application of love. Even anger and impatience may occasionally be powers we can exert in support of unity, but they must neither be exercised in hatred nor on the assumption we are punishing anyone for breaking some rule.

Simple? No! Easy? Never! It was not for nothing that Paul wrote, "Work out your salvation in fear and trembling."[18]

The power of love is the greatest power in the world. Love never ends. As for warm fuzzies, they will dissipate like the fog. As for good manners, they will come to an end. As for the compatibility of like interests, it only makes us comfortable. As for the community of social class or ethnic identity, it will only make us proud.

Paul said it,

> Love is patient; love is kind; love is not envious or boastful or arrogant or rude. It does not insist on its own way; it is not irritable or resentful It does not rejoice in wrongdoing, but rejoices in the truth.[19]

The power of love is the power to care for the other, nurture his spiritual growth, and help break down the barriers that inhibit the Great Spirit from accentuating his positive powers and eliminating his negatives. It is the power and the wisdom to resist the destructive forces in society by exalting the creative and the unifying. And it is tough to do!

However, the greater the love poured abroad in our hearts by the Spirit who is God, the easier it becomes.

Charles Wesley, John's younger brother, wrote a hymn of which Isaac Watts, another great hymn writer, said he would exchange every hymn he ever wrote for this one hymn by Charles.

Based on Jacob's wrestling with the angel, it reads:

> Come, O thou Traveler Unknown,
>   whom still I hold, but cannot see!
> My company before is gone,
>   and I am left alone with thee.
> With thee all night I mean to stay,
>   and wrestle till the break of day...
> Who I ask thee, who art thou?
> Tell me thy name and tell me now...
> Speak or thou never hence shalt move,

and tell me if thy name is Love...
'Tis Love! 'tis Love! Thou diedst for me,
I hear thy whisper in my heart,
The morning breaks, the shadows flee,
    pure, Universal Love thou art.
To me, to all, thy mercies move,
    thy nature and thy name is Love!"
Amen.[20]

> *O You, Great Spirit,*
>   *whose nature is love,*
>   *who by that love seeks to overcome*
>   *the powers of hate and revenge and pettiness:*
> *Make me honest enough to acknowledge*
>   *the negatives that burble up from the cauldron*
>   *of my own spirit,*
>   *courageous enough to confront and reject them,*
>   *to put in their place the powers of pardoning love,*
>   *of reconciling grace and of healing balm.*
> *And never let me forget that your spirit of love,*
>   *pressing already within me,*
>   *waits for me to open.*
> *Amen.* saf

11

Choosing the Future—Sermons on Glorifying Grace

SERMON 12
FEAR NOT

Luke 12:32–40

Comment:

Wesley wanted to know the way to heaven, but what he ended up describing was the way to live right now. On his deathbed, his joy was not in the expectation of heaven. It was in the assurance that "The best of all, God is with us."

Still, what he had found was also what he had started out to find. It was not really possible for him to separate the hope of heaven from the care of the soul.

Therefore, in Wesley's scheme, this sermon would be a kind of bridge sermon, linking sanctifying grace with the grace of glory. I prefer to think of it as a bridge that connects growing up as a human being in this life with a second chance at becoming complete after the natural body can no longer support our presence. The latter interest is developed more fully in the sermon that follows this one..

The biblical reference is a group of words attributed to Jesus in which he encourages preparation for the coming kingdom, but I interpret it against the background of a different image of God. It is one that, in itself, could never suggest the need for fear.

The universal needs addressed here are guidance, meaning, and hope. The understanding involved again rests on the foundation of our new spiritual image of God.

◆　　◆　　◆

There's an urgency in the air! You've heard it said, "The kingdom is coming! So be ready! Don't be caught unprepared! What if the time has got away from you? Maybe you've lost track of it and it is later than you think!"

You've heard it before! And it goes back a long way—all through the Old Testament when they expected the coming of the Day of the Lord! But the urgency was never there like it is in the New Testament. It just is not possible to read the Gospels, the letters of Paul, and the Revelation of John and miss the urgency.

So what's the hurry? Well, the urgency does not come from fear. The story says Jesus announced its coming. Here is how he did it, "Never fear, little flock," he said, "it's the Father's good pleasure to give you the kingdom."[1]

First, he says it is not something to be afraid of. He needed to say that because the very idea of God was enough to cause a good Jew some anxiety. Second, it is not something down the road in the future. Rather, it is great good news for today! The Father, that is how Jesus spoke of God, is giving it to you right now!

Even so, the times still are urgent! So where's the urgency? The real clue to the urgency is found right after Jesus announces the coming of the kingdom. He says, "Sell all you have and give it away, for where your treasure is there shall your heart be also."[2] In other words, the urgency must come from the heart, not from the fear of losing something you treasure.

You must find this kingdom in your own heart. It is not a matter of sitting around waiting for the doorbell to ring and God to show up someday with the kingdom in his hands. It is finding the kingdom where he has put it. Remember? Jesus had also said, "The Kingdom is within you."[3] That is where the Great Spirit has put it."

It is an unfinished kingdom. It is the kingdom of the Spirit of which your spirit is a part. The urgency is there because you are the finisher. It is like the builder did the framing and even built the roof and walls. Yet, you have to finish the inside, do the trim, paint the ceiling, lay the tiles, sand the floors, and buy the furniture. You also really do not have a lot of time to do it.

Of course, you do not have to work alone. The builder provides the tools and the materials. He even has the design in hand, and he is right there to help. You are in partnership with him. You are really working together on the project in which you are building the kingdom within. You are sharing in the work of the Spirit who is God.

I want to tell you a story about how I came to understand something about all of this. My wife had died very recently, and I was beside myself. I seemed to have lost any sense of what I now needed to do with my life.

One day, a friend of mine said, "Think of your favorite name for God. Then think of the one thing that is most important to you in your life right now."

Then he said, "Now put those two things together in a prayer."

So I did, and I wrote down, "Father, show me a sufficient purpose for the rest of my life." That is when it dawned on me that the purpose of my life really had not changed at all. When I was engrossed in my work and consumed by Anita's care, I was still doing the same thing. I was doing what every single person has to do, no matter what his or her circumstances. I was trying to make a life.

That is what we are all trying to do, whether we are living in the worst poverty and our main concern is survival or whether we are highly paid professionals or CEOs of huge companies. What we are trying to do is make a life. That is what I had been doing, and that was what I still had to do.

The other thing I have come to see is, when I make a life or create myself, I find, by far, the greatest fulfillment does not come when I am turned in upon my own loneliness, frustration, or even my own happiness. It is when whatever I am building involves other people and my relationships with them. Because I am really nothing except for my relationships with other people, my children, my spouse, my coworkers, and my friends. I build myself and make a life when I nurture my loves and friendships and when I create networks, not just of associations, but of caring and sharing.

God is not some giant lawgiver, judge, prosecutor, and executioner I have to fear or whose blessings I have to earn. He is the whole world of spirit and exists wherever spirit exists, including every human spirit who has such powers as creativity, thought, passion, love, hope, and joy. When I make a life by nurturing my relationships with others, I am also linking myself to God for all eternity and finishing the kingdom he has given me.

That is why the times are urgent! The hour is always late! It is because time flies by so fast in this life. It is like driving down the highway and watching the telephone poles fly by *fft, fft, fft, fft!*

We are called to participate in the making of the kingdom of the spirit within and fulfilling the possibilities of the human spirit! However, the opportunities to participate fly by too fast, and we miss most of them. This kingdom of the Spirit is built by deeds of compassion that soften the hardness of the heart, voices raised against injustice that drown out the small voices within that are always demanding our own rights, and acts of forgiveness that refuse to cling to old hurts. It is sharing our wealth with those less fortunate, keeping our eyes always open for someone who is hurting instead of always nursing our own wounds, and listening for the cries of the suffering and going where they are instead of holing up in our own dens.

This kingdom of the spirit within is built by disciplines of self-control, refusing to pass by on the other side, refusing to participate in the accumulation of unnecessary wealth at the expense of others, and refusing to exploit the earth at the expense of future generations.

It is built by a million little things, such as giving a few hugs when hugs are needed, speaking a "thank you" or a "please," and perhaps surprising a stranger.

The opportunities come by so fast! They come and go, and we hardly see them. Maybe there is not enough sensitivity in our spirits for us to notice. Maybe there is not enough energy and we just cannot move fast enough. Maybe there isn't enough money. The letters come too fast in the mail, and the opportunities to build the kingdom are too expensive.

Now it is so late! We are running too far behind! No way can we ever catch up! The opportunities to bless, love, and care outrun all of us. The faster we go, the further behind we get! The urgency gets greater as the days and the years go by.

Still, the powers of division and destruction, revenge and resentment, and selfishness and insensitivity live there within our spirits and inhibit the powers of imagination and creativity, love and compassion, and wholeness and unity.

So, is it hopeless? This bind we are in?

No! No! Never! It is never hopeless! It is never too late for the kingdom of the spirit because it is never too late for God who is nothing other than the world of spirit!

The kingdom finally does not depend upon us. This piece of the kingdom we are is already a part of God, you see. Not even our smallest deed of kingdom-making will ever be lost because, of course, it becomes part of the kingdom of the Spirit who is God.

We who are already spirits are a part of it, becoming more and more complete! The kingdom is here in us. It is also coming every day all through God's creation, wherever there is a human spirit to be found. He gives it to us a bit more in every deed of compassion we do, every word of forgiveness we speak, every helping institution we aid in building, every penny we give, every kind word we speak, and every act of reconciliation in which we engage.

Oh, I have seen it coming! I have seen it in the tent villages of the Sioux Indians where they gathered outside my hometown to pick potatoes. It is where my father entered those tents to speak God's grace and baptize those babies.

I have seen it coming in the land of Brazil where the word of grace is announced and received. It is where whole communities have been renewed and hope has been reborn.

I have seen it in Kenya where ancient tribal hostilities have been overcome at the common table in remembrance of the integrity and courage of a man in whom God the Spirit lived in his fullness. It is where rainwater is captured off the roofs and brings life. (Before, it simply washed away the soil.)

We have seen the kingdom coming whenever somebody has seen the possibilities and has chosen to participate in its making. There forgiveness overcomes hostility, compassion alleviates pain, and hope replaces despair.

Sometimes, even in the most unlikely places, the kingdom can be seen a-building. We saw it in the midst of the terror, blooming out of the rubble of the World Trade Center when firefighters and police officers gave up their lives for the sake of those trapped and labored beyond the point of exhaustion in the search for survivors. There we saw the grace and beauty of the human spirit, which is part of the world of Spirit, at work. We saw it in the tears shed all across this land and around the world for those who had suffered such terrible losses. We saw it in the outpouring of volunteers and money in the overwhelming task of rebuilding a great city and restoring a wounded nation to health and peace. We have heard its echoes in the voices of those who plead for the safety of innocent Arab-Americans and speak against retaliation and vengeance. They call for new ways of establishing justice instead. So, God in whom we live has not given up on us because he is in us and we are in him.

The opportunities still come every day and every night, faster than we can ever expect to grasp them. The time is still urgent as long as we have breath. Either we will help build it by destroying the negative powers in our own spirits or we will tear it down by feeding the negative powers in our spirits. We are either builders, or we are the termites in the foundation. However, the greatest blessing of this life is to share in the work he is doing, the work he is doing in us, the work he is doing through us, and the kingdom he is already giving us.

This is that spirit world, which even now gives meaning to all our days, which gives meaning to the struggles of peoples and nations, which gives meaning to the history of the world and creation itself.

At the last, an even greater blessing will be ours when we enter into the fullness of the kingdom he has promised us and feast there at his table. Nobody knows just what the feast in the kingdom of the Great Spirit who is God will look like. We only know that, "now we see in a mirror, dimly; then we will see face to face. Now (we) know only in part; then (we) will know fully, even as (we) have been fully known."[4]

Amen.

> *Sometimes, O Lord, I've wondered where You were hanging out*
> > *when I couldn't see you or hear You.*
> *What where you doing*
> > *when You were supposed to be taking care of things*
> > *and watching out for me and my loved ones?*
> *But if your kingdom is within me and in everyone else,*
> > *like Jesus said it was,*
> > *then I think I can begin to understand*
> > *why things don't always go just the way I'd like*
> > *or even the way You would like them to.*

There's so much negativity in me,
 and in just about everybody I know,
 that sometimes things aren't just right yet.
The things we want to happen aren't yet spiritually possible.
You are working at it,
 So I'll get with the program and be a part of it.
And in the end I do believe that what You have started,
 together we can finish.
Amen. Saf

Sermon 13
The Flower of Hope

Isaiah 11:1–3, 6–9, and I Corinthians 13:8–13

Comment:

Wesley referred to instantaneous sanctification as the moment in which the process of sanctification was completed. He tentatively suggested it may happen at the moment of death or even a moment before. However, the notion of instantaneous sanctification was more the logical consequence of his teaching that sanctification was a gradual process than it was the product of experience or observation. He did suggest this or that person might have come to the end of the process and might have actually come to embody the mind of Christ. Yet, he refused to make an issue of this suggestion.

In any case, he did not teach that perfection or holiness was an event like the experience of the warm heart of assurance had been for him. Nor had he taught justifying faith itself was necessarily the event of a moment. Later in his career, he largely abandoned in his preaching the very heavy demand for repentance for sin that marked his early career and had often issued in ecstatic behavior in his hearers.

Wesley addressed the long-term hope for a fulfillment beyond the death of the natural body through his teaching on sanctification, perfection, or holiness as a process. Instantaneous sanctification was the fulfillment of the process; it was the final goal. He did preach one major sermon, however, on the Last Judgment, but this was a sermon written by invitation and was preached to a congregation of judges and lawyers. It was called "The Great Assize." Clearly, the image of God as judge and lawgiver dominated that sermon.

The present sermon addresses the hope for full union with God when the space and time limitations of the natural body are removed by death. It thereby seeks to respond to our need for meaning and purpose, as well as hope. The union with God envisioned here is not that of many mystics in which two discrete entities become one. Rather, it is the reconciliation and harmony achieved between the intention and purpose of the self-aware head of the world of spirit, that is, God, and the human spirit, which is a cell in that spiritual body. Therefore, this is a somewhat speculative sermon, as must be the case when we move beyond our immediate experience.

My biblical references are two: the first is from an eschatological passage from Isaiah, and the second is from a strikingly spiritualized vision of Paul's.

◆   ◆   ◆

Pyramids, funeral pyres, flower-bowered tombstones. Prayers for resurrection to assure the dead shall rise again. Shovels of dirt symbolized the dissolution of the body and the rising of the spirit. Personal items in silk-lined caskets comforted the deceased in their new life beyond.

Among all races, tribes, and peoples and in all times and places, the universal hope of the human race for a longer life than this one, for some glimpse beyond, and for some power to control it has occupied human minds.

But long after the human race first peered so deeply into the future that it lost its sight in the peering, another tribe raised up a prophet who promised a more earthly future:

> The wolf shall live with the lamb, the leopard shall lie down with the kid, the calf and the lion and the fatling together, and a little child shall lead them. The cow and the bear shall graze, their young shall lie down together, and the lion shall eat straw like the ox. The nursing child shall play over the hole of the asp, and the weaned child shall put its hand on the adder's den. They will not hurt or destroy on all my holy mountain; for the earth will be full of the knowledge of the Lord as the waters cover the sea.[5]

Earthly it was. It was comprehensive and rich. Without a doubt, it seems a little bit more realistic than some dream world beyond death, beyond the veil where no one can see anything.

Besides, this picture painted by Isaiah was pretty enticing. Maybe it was a future that could actually be achieved right here on earth.

Of course, that hope was messed up pretty quickly. The desire for immediate gratification was simply never fulfilled. Then the people began to forget, and the vision became even more cramped and warped. No longer was the land they occupied devoted to peace and reconciliation. No longer was it a place hospitable to all. So the prophet's glorious vision faded.

However, the need to hope remains. Once again, it seems like the natural world is the most likely scene for a future of peace and beauty. Today, millions of people around the world believe and work for such a result. New prophets have arisen. Another dream forms, a world in which nature is sacred and respected, its blessings are enjoyed and cultivated, its resources are used wisely and well, and no one is hungry, no one is cold, and all are at peace and live in a community of equals. No one is permitted to grow rich at the expense of others, and people can trust one another because honesty is a way of life.

Can such a world satisfy our need for a new future? Think about it. It is still a world limited to those who survive that long. It is limited to only one piece of history. What about those who have gone before and will never have a chance at it? What about those who have already perished from old age, though they lived their long lives in hope? What about those who have been crushed under avalanches and mudslides or buried under buildings and bridges collapsed by earthquakes? What about those massacred in bloody genocides or slaughtered in futile and insane wars? What happens to their hope?

Those who hoped in this kind of future are like Moses who looked over the Jordan and saw the Promised Land, but was never permitted to enter. Such a world of our dreams is worth working toward. It must be sought for the sake of those who will be able to enjoy it. For the rest who will never enter, it will be a dream forever unfulfilled.

Still hope remains! Like the water behind the dike, when one hole is plugged in the dike, it finds another by which to enter. Paul certainly knew the promise of the prophet, but it was unsure, fleeting, and all quite unbelievable in the end. It could never satisfy the needs of the human spirit. That was very clear to him, as he writes to the Romans: "[T]he kingdom of God is not food and drink, but righteousness and peace and joy in the Holy Spirit."[6]

Now there is a hope for you! It is a hope more comprehensive than anything the prophet ever wrote or the crusaders for the earth envisioned. It is a hope for every man, woman, and child who ever lived or will ever live.

It is a more certain hope. It does not depend finally on a successful effort by people. No matter how well-intentioned, in this life, knowledge and especially wisdom, will never be perfect.

It is a more beautiful hope as well. Nothing in this world or out of it is so beautiful as a whole spirit, a spirit in which there is no stain of self-pride or self-righteousness. Nothing is lovelier than a spirit in which there is no self-serving boasting or competition, no anger or revenge, and no ugliness of the spirit that accompanies one who trusts in nothing but himself. It is the hope for a kingdom of righteousness in which peace, joy, and love rule. It is the vision of a life beyond our natural life in which our spirits can finally enter into a perfect harmony with the Great Spirit who is God.

Such a hope is for everyone. It is a hope for every human spirit ever born into a natural life. It is a hope for those who will never see a utopia on earth. It is a hope for those who die young and those who die old. It is a hope for all time and all seasons because the love of God is without conditions.

Pardon and new life have always been, are, and will be available.

What about the vile, cruel, vicious, and despicable man, in whom the spiritual powers are mostly negative, divisive, and destructive? What hope is there for him? Surely, he has to be judged and then punished.

I can only imagine what the fulfillment of this hope might be like. I can imagine him when his spirit first slips out of his ravaged, nonfunctioning body and he stands naked before his own eyes. There he is, and he is one surprised dude! And you know why! Because, "Now (we) see in a mirror dimly, but then (we) will see face to face. Now (we) know only in part; then (we) will know fully even as (we) have been fully known."[7]

He will see his own ugliness. He will see his ravaged spirit, his sickness, and his weakness. He will see the great powers of his own spirit turned shriveled and useless. He will see the wasted life he has lived and the kind of cancerous spirit he has become right in the midst of God in whom he has been all along living, moving, and having his being.

He will see all that because he will finally see the Godhead in all the beauty and glory of the pure spirit that he is in whom there is "no shadow of turning" and in whose own self-awareness no negative power is able to gain a hold. He will need no more judgment than that because he will see himself as he is. In God, he will see the light of his love and hear the sound of his voice saying, "Welcome home, son. Let's get you cleaned up and moving right." That is what I can imagine.

But what about you? You are not like that poor, wretched man. You have an excellent reputation. You have done well with the gifts you have been given. You are not the self-righteous or vindictive type at all. You truly care for your neighbor. You are kind and generous. You are even religious most of the time. Perhaps you teach Sunday School. You have accepted Jesus as your Lord and Savior. You do think Jesus is quite a remarkable individual.

Once in a while, you wonder if you are doing all right. You have been assuming you would make it into heaven, (wherever that is) when the time came. Maybe you are not quite sure just how good you have to be to make it. But you are hoping.

Here is what I imagine it might be like when, somewhere down the road, you shed this body and your spirit is free. You may be a little surprised, too! You will probably see yourself a little differently than you assumed. You may even remember Jesus again. You will see him a little differently, too. In fact, you will be so close to him that you simply cannot miss seeing all the little compromises with the truth you are in the habit of making.

I do not know what all you will see, but you will put yourself under your own judgment, just like the vile man does, because both of you have always been a part of God's spiritual body. So I think you will maybe hear the voice of God speak to you.

Here is what he will probably say:

> Hi there! Welcome home! You have a great start. You've tried to be honest with yourself and others about most things. You've been doing very well, but we have a little work to do because I want you for one of my saints. And I won't be complete until you are whole. You've still got some little secrets, and you still have a lot of love to learn. So you aren't ready yet.

Then, I think you might say, "God, I can see what you mean. I'm ready to go to work with you again. Just—just help me, please."

Well, of course, I do not know what it will be like after our death, but I believe you and I will have some such conversation within ourselves and another opportunity to harmonize our spirits with the Spirit who is God, just because it is his nature to love us and keep us within himself.

When I try to get my mind around the miracle of my beginning as a human being, that is when the flower of hope is born. Surely, he who gave birth to my spirit out of himself and kept me within himself while he connected me up with a human body will love and keep me when the natural laws by which my body lives have ceased to function.

Then my spirit will be set free, and I will see myself in the bosom of the one from whom I came and in whom I have always lived. There, he will help me continue to grow up until I am made completely whole and yet another part of him is healed. So I believe.

By the promise of that vision, you and I can live and die and—live some more. Amen.

> *I sing glory,*
>   *O You who breathed me into life!*
> *I sing glory,*
>   *O Spirit whom no corruption can destroy!*
> *Great Spirit,*
>   *You who bring me along my journey,*

who will never abandon me,
for my spirit is a part of You,
I rest in hope.
I do not know my time,
but I trust my destiny into your hands
into your hands,
for my destiny is with You.
Amen. saf

Sermon 14
Joyful, Joyful

Philippians 4:4–9

Comment:

It seems fitting this sermon on joy should fall under the heading of <u>Glorifying Grace</u> because joy is, in fact, as close as one gets to glory in this life. It is also an appropriate way to end this course of sermons. Perhaps it can serve as a kind of summation of the vision of God set forth in the earlier chapters and the elaborations which that vision suggests. As for Wesley's treatment of joy, it is largely incorporated in some of his descriptions of perfection.

<u>The gift of joy comes in two forms:</u> one of which arises from the decision to undertake the life of the spirit, and the other arises from contemplation of the possibilities that may follow after the death of the body.

The first is the exhilaration of the struggle against the destructive and divisive powers one finds in one's own spirit. The second is a sure expectation of another opportunity beyond this life to put down the negative powers and exalt the positives.

The biblical reference in Philippians is primarily an exhortation to rejoice always and is related to gentleness, thanksgiving, and peace.

Perhaps the universal needs targeted here include them all: connection, hope, meaning, guidance, and, as always, a certain degree of new understanding.

◆ ◆ ◆

You don't like very much to be exhorted by someone, right? Well, I don't either, especially when I'm exhorted to take a new attitude or change some emotion. Those usually are not things that are susceptible to control by a simple decision of the will.

But here's Paul, in his letter to the Philippians: "Rejoice in the Lord always: again I will say, Rejoice!"[8] But you want to say to him, "What if I don't feel like it? What if I've had a lousy day? My wife got on me about wearing the wrong tie with the suit I have on. My boss complained because I was five minutes late to work. I did not get to Danny's baseball game after school today. Why should I rejoice? It has been a bad day. If tomorrow is better, I'll rejoice then."

I think I could make a pretty good case for you. You have many reasons why you cannot just turn joy on like you turn on the water tap. It depends on so many things over which you have no control. Well, yes, you did have control over some of it today. You could have paid closer attention to the tie you picked. Yet, you were late for work because breakfast was late. You also missed the baseball game because your boss told you that you had to finish the report before you could go home. You could say all that, but blaming somebody else does not make you happy either.

Still, Paul will not let us go. He comes right back at us and tells us what to do, "Let your gentleness be known to everyone."[9] In other words, he says you can put on a good face. If you feel like shouting at someone, speak with a gentle voice. If you are down, look up. If you want to get even with someone, bite your lip, and do him a favor. Act like a decent person, and you will see how good it feels. Maybe you will become just a bit more decent than before.

If you smile and give someone a cheery "Hello!" it will do wonders for your spirit. You might even feel like rejoicing a bit. Obviously, a good piece of advice from Paul, "Act like it, and you'll feel like it!" That is not too bad a start, but, frankly, it doesn't always work.

However, his next advice is absolutely and always true, "The Lord is near."[10] That is advice, of course, only in the sense that he is forcing us to remember something we are inclined to forget. In fact, the Lord is so near that he is nearer than anything else we have. He is nearer to us than our toes certainly. But he is also nearer than our own faces. We live in him like a fish lives in water. Even closer than that, he who is spirit lives in us. In fact, he is the Spirit who is us. Therefore, our spirits are a part of the Great Spirit who is God. We cannot get any closer than that.

That is a pretty good reason to rejoice, and it is a reason that is always there, no matter what else is going on in our lives! Given that fact, Paul says, "Do not worry about anything," because you can never be destroyed. "But in everything by prayer and supplication with thanksgiving let your requests be made known to God."[11]

The hard part here is making our prayers with thanksgiving. Ordinarily, that would be as hard as obeying the injunction to rejoice. If we do not feel grateful, how can we make our prayers with thanksgiving?

However, if we remember that nothing in heaven or earth or over or under the earth can separate us from the Spirit who is God and of whom we are already a part, it would be easier to relax and be thankful in spite of the external things we do not really feel like welcoming. But is thanksgiving really what Paul means by joy? I am sure thanksgiving is sometimes accompanied by joy! But Paul has more to say.

He says, "The peace of God, which surpasses all understanding, will guard your hearts and your minds in Christ Jesus."[12] Then is the peace that surpasses understanding the same thing as joy? Not exactly! So I just do not think Paul quite succeeds here.

At least he does not leave us hanging with an exhortation to do something we cannot do just by deciding to do it. He has, at least, been trying to tell us how we can learn to rejoice.

But let me try something a bit different. Supposing your vision of God is that he is Spirit, not some ghostlike thing out there, not something that floats. Suppose he is not someone who sits on a throne or marches around snooping into our dark corners looking for things to catch us with. Suppose he is neither a judge behind his bench with his laws and gallows nor a Santa Claus intent on deciding who is naughty and who is nice so he will know which presents to bring. Suppose he is not a horse trader ready to make a deal with anyone who offers him enough in exchange. But suppose he is spirit, like we are spirits. In fact, suppose our spirits are part of his spirit.

Then suddenly our vision of God is that of the Great Spirit, of whose spiritual body the human spirit is a cell. When we see both of us are engaged in the universal struggle between the positive and negative spiritual powers, between the unifying, healing powers and the divisive, destructive powers, then the stage is set for joy.

Then every human spirit has the option of focusing his attention on the things of the spirit and of entering into the struggle with intention. Therefore, the joy is in the very struggle, in the strenuous, demanding effort to crowd out the negative, destructive powers and enhance and exalt the positive, creative powers.

All the means of grace must be brought to bear: prayer and prayer without ceasing, conversation and sharing with other struggling human spirits, meditation, and journaling. The sacrament as well can focus our eyes on the integrity and courage of the Spirit who was in Jesus, our ideal and hero. And, yes, the discipline of showing by our behavior, gentleness, patience, enthusiasm, and the deeds of compassion, even when we do not feel like it, nurtures our growth.

Day by day, week by week, year by year, we will grow into the kind of human beings who embody more and more the spirit that was in Jesus. Our negatives will grow weaker, and our positives will grow stronger. Moreover, rising out of the struggle and hovering all about us will be a song of joy.

It may sometimes carry the strains of pain like a runner in the weight room preparing. It may sound sometimes like the panting of a runner, straining toward the prize. It may be earthy like the runner's sweat. It may sound the momentary panic when the runner fears he is about to fall. Sometimes it only hums, but it soon sings like a mighty chorus sounding through the halls of our hearts.

Joy does not depend on all being right with the world. It does not depend on our having a good day. It does not depend on the success of our daily ventures. It does not depend on the approval of others. It does not depend on our reputation or the outward appearances of our lives.

Joy comes from seeing the world of the spirit. It comes from entering that world to run the race. It comes from the sweat and pain of training. It comes from the effort, the gasping for breath, the stretching of the legs for a few more inches of reach, and the vision of the finishing tape ahead.

It remembers it was "for the joy that went before him" that the one who is our ideal and our hero could endure the cross and thus show himself to be a true human being in all the power, beauty, and glory a human being is intended to have. It remembers, when a human spirit becomes perfect, he becomes divine as well.

That is the end toward which we run that cannot be denied us at last. For the Spirit who is God already struggles within us and for us, while we struggle in and for Him.

Therefore, "Rejoice in the Lord always: again I will say, Rejoice!"[13]
Amen.

> *I sing in the rain, O God,*
>   *and in the beauty of blue skies.*
> *I sing when the sun sets*
>   *and when it rises.*
> *I sing when the mist hides the hills*
>   *and when the mountains shine in majesty.*
> *I sing when the snow falls softly in the night*
>   *and when thunder rolls through the sky,*
>   *when disappointment sets in*
>   *and when success lifts me high,*
>   *when love waxes*
>   *and when it wanes,*

when the spirit quakes
    and when it overcomes.
I sing, O God, because I know You struggle with me,
    because I know You hurt with my hurt.
    You smile when I smile,
    and cry when I cry.
And I know every victory of yours is my victory,
    and all my victories are yours.
I sing, O my spirit!
I sing, O my God!
Amen. saf

Endnotes

NOTES ON CHAPTER 1: He Lived by Preaching

1. Albert Outler, ed., *The Works of John Wesley*, vol. 1, *Sermons*, vol. I, Nashville, Abingdon Press, 1984. 29.

Outler's work as editor of the first four volumes of the Bicentennial Edition of *The Works of John Wesley* has produced far and away the most thorough treatment of John Wesley's preaching to be found anywhere. That includes his "Introduction" in Volume 1 and the introductions and footnotes to each of the sermons in the first four volumes.

2. Ibid. 2.

3. Ibid. 33.

4. Ibid.

5. Reginald Ward and Richard Heitzenrater, eds., *The Works of John Wesley*, vol. 23, *Journal and Diaries*, vol. VI. Nashville, Abingdon Press, 1995. 105.

6. "Justifying faith" is the term St. Paul used in his letters to describe the faith by which a person comes to trust the sacrifice of Jesus as the basis for his acceptance by God. Theologians variously describe justification. For Wesley, it meant that first act of trust by a person in his/her forgiveness by God's grace made available by Jesus' sacrifice. It is only a part of his doctrine of salvation.

7. Romans 8:16.

8. Ward and Heitzenrater, vol. 18, vol. I. 1988. 249.

9. Outler. 4.

10. Ibid.

11. Ibid.

12. Ibid. 405.

13. Ibid.

14. Outler. 13.

15. W. L. Doughty, *John Wesley, Preacher,* London, The Epworth Press, 1955. 109.

16. Outler. 16.

17. Ibid.

18. Ibid.

19. Ibid.

20. Albert Outler, ed., *John Wesley,* New York, Oxford University Press, 1964. 5.

21. Richard P. Heizenrater, *The Elusive Mr. Wesley,* vol. 2, Nashville, Abingdon Press, 1984. 85.

22. Doughty. 108.

23. Outler. 115.

24. Ibid. 38.

25. Ibid. 18.

26. Ibid. 20.

27. Ibid. 10.

28. Ibid.

29. Thomas Jackson, ed., *John Wesley's Works,* vol. XIII, Grand Rapids, Michigan, Baker Book House, 1979 (Third Edition). 36.

30. Outler. 353.

31. "Antinomianism" refers to the position that, once a person is saved, the Law has lost its force, that is, anything goes. St. Paul encountered this attitude in the early church and responded to it in Romans 6:1–4.

32. Outler. 6.

33. Henry D. Rack, *Reasonable Enthusiast,* Nashville, Abingdon Press, 1993 (Second Edition). ix.

34. Richard P. Heitzenrater, *Wesley and the People Called Methodists,* Nashville, Abingdon Press, 1993. 318

35. Ibid. 132.

36. Albert Outler, *The Works of John Wesley,* vol. 4, *Sermons,* vol. IV, 1987, Appendix A. 422.

37. Outler, vol. 1. 14.

38. Ibid. x.

39. Ibid.

40. Ibid. 13.

41. Ibid.

42. Ibid. 14.

43. Ibid. 103.

44. M. H. Abrams, ed., *The Norton Anthology of English Literature,* vol. 1, New York, W. W. Norton and Co., 1993 (Sixth Edition). 1123.

45. Outler. 103.

46. Ibid. 105.

47. Ibid. 107.

48. Ibid. 97.

49. Jackson, vol. X. 485.

50. Heitzenrater. 164.

51. The words law, laws, and Law will appear frequently. Therefore, it is wise to distinguish the several uses to which they are put. The words law and laws may refer either to natural or spiritual laws. These are laws formulated by humans to describe observed regularities in the natural and spiritual worlds respectively. On occasion the words law and laws are used less precisely to refer to the regularities themselves, whether formulated or not. They may also be used to refer to laws formulated by humans to prescribe behavior, such as moral or ethical laws. The capitalized word Law refers to the laws found in the first five books of the Old Testament, or the Torah, though Wesley did not always follow this convention. These usages may be distinguished from one another by the context in which they are used. The term "natural law" is also used by the Roman Catholic Church as the name of moral laws that exist in nature and upon which human laws ought to be based. (This usage does not occur in this book.)

52. Jackson, vol. XI. 486.

53. Outler. 15.

54. Heitzenrater, *The Elusive Mr. Wesley*. 83.

55. Doughty. 110.

56. Ibid. 115.

57. Outler. 13.

58. Ibid. 10.

59. Ibid.

60. Ibid.

61. Ibid. 7.

62. Doughty. 112.

63. Theodore Gill, *In the Steps of John Wesley,* London, Lutterworth Press, 1962. 149.

64. Outler. 8.

65. Ibid. 2.

66. Ibid. 11.

67. Ibid. 17.

68. Ibid.

69. Ibid.

70. Jackson. 486.

71. Ibid.

NOTES ON CHAPTER 2: Deep Were the Roots

1. Albert Outler, ed., *The Works of John Wesley*, vol. 1, *Sermons*, vol. I, Nashville, Abingdon Press, 1984. 68.

2. Ibid. xii.

3. Thomas Jackson, *John Wesley's Works*, vol. X, Grand Rapids, Michigan, Baker Book House, 1979 (Third Edition). 481.

4. Outler. xii.

5. For example, see "The Almost Christian" in which he follows a common practice among the Puritan preachers by ignoring the clear meaning of that text.

6. Outler. 69.

7. Ibid. 70.

8. Scott Jones, *John Wesley's Conception and Use of Scripture*, Nashville, Kingswood Press (Abingdon imprint), 1995. 104.

9. Outler. 69.

10. Jones. 110.

11. This discussion of the seven rules of interpretation I owe completely to Scott Jones' discussion from 110–126.

12. Outler. 57.

13. Ibid. 105.

14. The Council of Nicea was convened by Constantine in May of AD 325.

15. Ted. A. Campbell, *Wesley and Christian Antiquity*, Nashville, Kingswood Books (Abingdon imprint), 1991. 9.

16. Ibid. 7.

17. Ibid. 2.

18. Ibid. 4.

19. Outler. 74.

20. Outler, *John Wesley*, New York, Oxford University Press, 1964. 9.

21. Outler, *The Works of John Wesley*, vol. 2, *Sermons*, vol. II. 1995. 600.

22. Karen, Armstrong, *A History of God*, New York, Ballantine Books, 1993.109.

23. Gerald R. Cragg, ed., *The Works of John Wesley*, vol. 11, *Appeals to Men of Reason and Religion and Certain Related Open Letters*, Nashville, Abingdon Press, 1989. 509

24. Outler, vol. 1. 75.

25. *The United Methodist Hymnal*, Nashville, The United Methodist Publishing House, 1989. No. 880.

26. Outler. 80.

27. Ibid.

28. Robert Burtner and Robert Chiles, eds., *A Compend of Wesley's Theology*, Nashville, Abingdon Press, 1954. 21.

29. Outler, vol. 2. 587.

30. Ibid. 588.

31. Jackson. 480.

32. Ibid.

33. Ibid. 598.

34. Ibid. 591.

35. Outler, vol 1. 273.

36. Ibid.

37. Walter Klaiber and Manfred Marquardt, *Viver a Graça de Deus, Um Compêndio de Teologia Metodista,* São Paulo, Editeo and Editora Cedro, 1999. 19.

NOTES ON CHAPTER 3: Saved by Grace

1. Albert Outler, *The Works of John Wesley*, Vol. 1, *Sermons*, vol. I, Nashville, Abingdon Press, 1984. 104.

2. Robert Burtner and Robert Chiles, *Compend of Wesley's Theology*, Nashville, Abingdon Press, 1954. 23.

3. Colin Williams, *John Wesley's Theology Today*, Nashville, Abingdon Press, 1960. 16,17.

4. Elaine Pagels, *Beyond Belief,* New York, Random House, 2003. 34.

5. Outler, vol. 4, 1987. 42.

6. Ibid. 62.

7. Outler, vol. 2, 1985. 384.

8. Karen Armstrong, *A History of God,* New York, Ballantine Books, 1993. 111.

9. Outler, vol. 1. 187.

10. Ibid. 188.

11. Ibid.

12. Ibid. 189.

13. Ibid. 194.

14. Burtner and Chiles. 16.

15. Thomas Moore, *Care of the Soul*, New York, Harper Collins Publishers, 1992. Cover text.

16. Albert Outler, ed., *John Wesley*, New York, Oxford University Press, 1964. iv.

17. Outler, vol. 2. 156.

18. Outler, vol. 3, vol III, 1986. 203.

19. Outler, vol. 1, 405.

20. Romans 1:20.

21. Outler, *John Wesley*. 251.

22. Ibid.

23. Ibid. 184.

24. Ibid.

25. Burtner and Chiles. 201.

26. Outler, vol. 1. 351.

27. Ibid. 201.

28. Ibid.

29. Ibid. 190.

30. Ibid. 187.

31. Outler, vol. 2. 598.

32. Outler, vol. 1. 192.

33. Ibid. 181.

34. *The United Methodist Hymnal*, Nashville, The United Methodist Publishing House, 1989. 361.

35. Burtner and Chiles. 182.

36. Ibid. 183.

37. Outler. 414.

38. John 17:20–21.

39. Burtner and Chiles. 207.

40. Ibid. 206.

41. Ibid. 209.

42. Philippians 2:5.

43. Thomas Jackson, ed., *John Wesley's Works,* vol. XI, Grand Rapids, Michigan, Baker Book House, 1979 (Third Edition). 442.

44. Outler, vol. 1. 407.

45. Jackson, vol. X. 442.

46. Outler. 408.

47. Ibid. 364.

NOTES ON CHAPTER 4: In Search of a New Vision

1. Albert Outler, ed., *The Works of John Wesley*, vol. 1, *Sermons*, vol. I, Nashville, Abingdon Press, 1984. 16.

2. Paul Edwards, ed., *The Encyclopedia of Philosophy*, vol. 4, "Kraus, Karl Christian Friedrich," New York, Macmillan Publishing Co. Inc., 1972. 363. Edwards, vol. 2, "Emanationism." 473.

3. John Shelby Spong, *A New Christianity for a New World, Why Traditional Faith is Dying and How a New Faith is Being Born*, New York, Harper Collins Publishers, 2001. xxi.

4. Morris West, *The Navigator,* Mandarin, 1976. 249.

5. Outler, vol. 4, 1987. 61.

6. John 11:37 and John 11:40.

7. Luke 13:1.

8. Karen Armstrong, *A History of God*, New York, Ballantine Books, 1993. 107.

9. Philippians 2:6–8.

10. Romans 5:9.

11. Acts 17:28.

12. Ephesians 2:8.

13. Thomas Jackson, ed., *John Wesley's Works*, vol. XIII, Grand Rapids, Michigan, Baker Book House, 1979 (Third Edition). 34.

14. Outler, vol. 1, 10.

15. Elaine Pagels, *Beyond Belief,* New York, Random House, 2003. 40.

16. Armstrong. xxi.

17. Ibid. xx.

18. Ibid. xxi.

19. Outler. xxi.

20. Outler, vol. 2, 1985. 568.

21. Jackson, vol. XIV. 354.

NOTES ON CHAPTER 5: Spirit Is God

1. Albert Outler, *Quarterly Review,* 1988, Summer, "Spirit and Spirituality in John Wesley." 40.

2. Elaine Pagels, *Beyond Belief,* New York, Random House, 2003. 54.

3. John 3:16.

4. Ephesians 2:8,9.

5. Outler, ed., *The Works of John Wesley*, vol. 1, *Sermons*, vol. I, Nashville, Abingdon Press, 1984. 323.

6. Outler, vol. 2, *Sermons,* vol. II, 1985. 576.

7. George McMichael, ed., *Anthology of American Literature,* New York, Macmillan Publishing Co., 1980. 1044.

8. Romans 12:4,5.

9. Thomas Jackson, ed., *John Wesley's Works*, vol. XII, Grand Rapids, Baker Book House, 1979. 232.

10. Karen Armstrong, *A History of God*, New York, Ballantine Books, 1993. 108.

11. John 1.

12. Thomas Moore, *Care of the Soul,* New York, Harper Collins Publishers, 1992. xiii.

13. Brooklyn Tabernacle Choir, "I Bowed on My Knees and Cried Holy," track 8 on *Live...Again*, Word, Inc., 1989. On compact disc.

14. I Corinthians 13.

15. T. S. Eliot, *The Varieties of Metaphysical Poetry* (see discussion of emotion and intellect), New York, London, Harcourt Brace & Company, 1993. 50.

16. Genesis 2:7.

17. Romans 7:15.

18. Outler, vol. 2, *Sermons*, vol. II. 377.

19. II Corinthians 5:19.

20. Philippians 2:8.

21. Hebrews 12:2.

NOTES ON CHAPTER 6: Things of the Spirit

1. Albert Outler, ed., *The Works of John Wesley*, vol. 1, *Sermons*, vol I, Nashville, Abingdon Press, 1984. 13.

2. Thomas Jackson, ed., *John Wesley's Works*, vol. VIII, Grand Rapids, Michigan, Baker Book House, 1979 (Third Edition). 331.

3. My use of the feminine pronoun in this context seemed appropriate. Otherwise, I have used the masculine pronoun, which is one of those tag ends of theism with which I have not found a way of coping.

4. *The United Methodist Hymnal*, Nashville, The United Methodist Publishing House, 1989. 378.

5. Theodore Runyan, ed., *Wesleyan Theology Today, A Bicentennial Theological Consultation*, "With the Eye of Faith" by Rex Matthews, Nashville, Kingswood Books (Abingdon imprint), 1985. 406.

6. Outler. 418.

7. Ibid. 317.

8. Ibid. 335.

9. Romans 8:6. Here, we must understand Paul to mean by the "flesh," not necessarily gluttony or sex, but all the natural goals and ambitions that vanish when the flesh decays.

10. John 3:3 and 5.

11. Outler, vol. 3, *Sermons*, vol. III, 1986. 528.

12. It should be remembered that Wesley did not profess to understand how the Atonement worked to make grace available, but he did deal quite extensively with how faith in the Atonement worked to justify the believer. However, the transactional nature of his thought on the Atonement remains.

13. Acts 4:12.

14. Outler, vol. 4, *Sermons*, vol IV, 1987. 174.

15. Galatians 5:22.

16. Jackson. 299.

17. *The United Methodist Hymnal.* 386.

18. I Corinthians 15:35–36, 42–44.

19. I Corinthians 13:12.

NOTES ON CHAPTER 7: Addressing the Universal Needs

1. T. S. Eliot, *The Varieties of Metaphysical Poetry,* New York, London, Harcourt Brace & Company, 1993. 53.

2. Ibid. 54 and 61.

3. John Shelby Spong, *A New Christianity for a New World, Why Traditional Faith is Dying and How a New Faith is Being Born*, New York, Harper Collins Publishers, Inc., 2001. 41.

4. Bill Gaither, "Where No One Stands Alone," track 4 on *I Do Believe,* Spring House, Inc., 2000. on compact disc.

5. Albert Outler, ed., *The Works of John Wesley*, vol. 2, *Sermons,* vol. II, Nashville, Abingdon Press, 1985. 87.

6. Ibid., vol. 1, *Sermons*, vol. I. 274.

7. A remembered quote from the television production of *Contact* by Carl Sagan.

8. Thomas Jackson, ed., *John Wesley's Works*, vol. VII, Grand Rapids, Michigan, Baker Book House, 1979 (Third Edition). 386 and vol. XI. 1.

9. *The United Methodist Hymnal*, Nashville, The United Methodist Publishing House, 1989. Nos. 57, 287, 384, 386.

10. John Wesley, *Explanatory Notes on the New Testament*, New York, T. Mason and G. Lane, 1837. 638.

11. Eliot, 54.

12. Romans 8:12.

13. Colin Williams, *John Wesley's Theology Today,* Nashville, Abingdon Press, 1960. 74.

14. Proverbs 29:18.

15. Dante, *The Divine Comedy,* The World's Great Classics, Danbury, CN, Grolier Enterprises Corp., (no date). 11.

16. Outler, vol. 1. 17.

17. Hebrews 12:1.

18. II Peter 1:4.

19. Brooklyn Tabernacle Choir, "I Bowed on My Knees and Cried Holy," track 8 on *Live...Again,* Word, Inc., 1989. on compact disc.

20. Outler, vol. 1, 299.

21. Philippians 2:12.

22. Robert Burtner and Robert Chiles, *Compend of Wesley's Theology,* Nashville, Abingdon Press, 1954. 24.

23. Ibid.

NOTES ON CHAPTER 8: More Than Natural—Sermons on Prevenient Grace

Sermon 1

1. Genesis 1:1–5.

2. Morris West, *The Navigator,* Mandarin, 1976. 249.

3. Dag Hammarsjold, *Markings,* New York, Alfred A. Knopf, 1964. 214.

Sermon 2

4. II Peter 1:4.

5. Bill Gaither, "Where No One Stands Alone," track 4 on *I Do Believe*, Spring House, Inc., 2000. on compact disc.

6. John 17:21,22.

7. John 3:17.

Sermon 3

8. Martin Luther King, Jr. in Washington on August 28, 1963.

9. Galatians 5:1.

10. Galatians 5:13.

11. Galatians 6:15.

NOTES ON CHAPTER 9: Coming Home—Sermons on Justifying Grace

Sermon 4

1. Genesis 20:1,2.

2. Genesis 20:18–20.

3. I John 2:1.

4. *The United Methodist Book of Worship*, Nashville, The United Methodist Publishing House, 1992. 42.

5. John 3:17.

Sermon 5

6. Bob Herbert from an undated column clipping.

7. Hebrews 11:1.

8. Hebrews 11:13,14.

9. Hebrews 11:13.

10. Martin Luther King, Jr. in Memphis on April 3, 1968.

11. Philip Burton, ed., Augustine's *Confessions,* New York, Toronto, Everyman's Library, Alfred A. Knopf, 2001. 5.

Sermon 6

12. Romans 8:2.

13. John 3:6 essentially.

14. James Baldwin, *If Beale Street Could Talk*, New York, Dial, 1974. 3.

Sermon 7

15. Robert Bolt, *A Man for All Seasons*, New York, Vintage Books (a division of Random House, Inc.), 1990. 159.

16. Ibid. xii.

17. John 12:32.

18. *The United Methodist Hymnal*, Nashville, The Methodist Publishing House, 1989. 171.

19. John 3:16.

20. *The United Methodist Book of Worship*. 98.

21. Ibid. 39.

22. Thomas Jackson, ed., *John Wesley's Works*, vol. XIII, Grand Rapids, Michigan, Baker Book House, 1979 (Third Edition). 36.

23. John 12:32.

24. Mark 8:36.

25. Romans 5:8.

26. John 1:29 and 36.

27. Hebrews 12:2.

28. John 12:32.

29. *The United Methodist Hymnal*. 171.

NOTES ON CHAPTER 10: Growing Up—Sermons on Sanctifying Grace

Sermon 8

1. Mark 11:23.

2. David Bevington, ed., *Hamlet*, Toronto, New York, Bantam Books, 1980. 87.

3. This prayer was copied from a sermon I preached in1964 in Schroon Lake, New York, source unknown.

4. *The United Methodist Hymnal*, Nashville, The Methodist Publishing House, 1989. 492.

Sermon 9

5. Luke 11:13.

6. Romans 7:15–17.

7. Romans 7:24.

8. Luke 11:8.

9. Luke 11:9.

10. Luke 11:13.

Sermon 10

11. Matthew 19:24.

12. Galatians 5:17.

13. Galatians 5:19,20.

14. Galatians 5:22,23.

15. Genesis 1:30,31.

Sermon 11

16. Bill Gaither, "The Love of God," track 9 on *I Do Believe*, Spring House, Inc., 2000. on compact disc.

17. *The United Methodist Hymnal*. 378.

18. Philippians 2:12.

19. I Corinthians 13:4–6.

20. *The United Methodist Hymnal*. 386.

NOTES ON CHAPTER 11: Choosing the Future—Sermons on Glorifying Grace

Sermon 12

1. Luke 12:32.

2. Luke 12:33.

3. Luke 17:21.

4. I Corinthians 13:12.

Sermon 13

5. Isaiah 11:6-9.

6. Romans 14:17.

7. I Corinthians 13:12.

Sermon 14

8. Philippians 4:4.

9. Philippians 4:5.

10. Ibid.

11. Philippians 4:6.

12. Philippians 4:7.

13. Philippians 4:4.

Index

A

"Address to the Clergy," 32, 46, 52
à Kempis, Thomas, 123
Aldersgate Street, 6, 7–8, 10, 49, 63, 72
"Almost Thou Persuadest Me," 12
"Amazing Grace," 129
Anglican Church, 12, 28, 34
Ante-Nicene period, 38, 125, 161
antinomians, 8, 18
Apocrypha, 34, 35
Archbishop of Canterbury, Thomas Cranmer, 9
Aristotle, 4, 168
Arius, 40, 42, 43, 44, 59, 124, 125, 139
Arminianism, 28
Arminian Magazine, 17, 19, 66
Armstrong, Karen, 96–97, 100
Articles of Religion, 38–39, 63
The Art of Speaking, 25
Athanasius, 42, 43, 58, 59, 121, 124, 125
Atonement, 7, 37, 41, 43, 44, 45, 50, 54, 55, 56, 58, 59, 60, 61, 64, 66, 67, 68, 70, 71, 72, 81, 85, 91–94, 96, 102, 103, 117, 121, 125–126, 131, 132, 134, 136, 140, 152, 157, 170, 184, 211, 217, 220, 221
"The Attributes of God," 178
Augustan England, 38
Augustine, 208
Aulen, Gustav, 157

B

Babcock, Samuel, 27
Baldwin, James, 214
Basil, 41, 50, 51
Bishop, Mary, 92
Blackstone, William, 13
Boehler, Peter, 7, 10
Boleyn, Anne, 218
Bolt, Robert, 218
Bonhoeffer, 83
Book of Common Prayer, 9, 35
Book of Homilies, 8, 38, 45, 55, 63, 74
Bowne, Borden P., 240

C

Calvin, John, 16, 63, 94
Calvinists, 17, 18, 24, 28, 45, 62, 63, 64, 65, 72, 93, 94, 95, 127, 160, 167, 191
    Toplady, Augustus, 73
    Whitefield, George, 3, 10, 12, 14, 63, 69, 159
Campbell, Joseph, 123
Campbell, Ted, 38
Candide, 143
Candomble, 99
Cappadocian Fathers, 41, 50
Care of the Soul, 111
"The Case of Reason Impartially Considered," 46
Castle at Oxford, 23
Catholic Church, 3, 36, 202, 219
"Catholic Spirit," 34
"The Character of a Methodist," 39
Charter House School, 4, 13
Christ Church College, 4
Church Fathers, 37, 38, 39, 40, 41, 43, 47, 62, 74, 205

Church of England, 3, 4, 8, 16, 17, 25, 43, 54, 62, 63, 97, 151
"Circumcision of the Heart," 6, 9, 10, 14, 44, 74, 76, 127
Clark, Adam, 27
coded diaries, 4, 6
Compendium of Natural Philosophy, 55
Constantine, 42
Contact, 153
Council of Nicea, 42, 43, 58, 96, 102, 121, 124
Cranmer, Thomas, 9
Crusades, 88, 247

D

Dame Summerhill, 27
"The Danger of Riches," 20, 238
Dante, 158
Dark Ages, 38
"Death and Deliverance," 5
de Melo, Sergio, 212
Directions Concerning Punctuation and Gesture, 25
"divine mystery," 89–90
"Divinity School Address," 104
dogma, 41
Donne, John, 23, 155
"The Duty of Reproving One's Neighbor," 20

E

Edwards, Jonathan, 8
Eliot, T. S., 117, 149
Emerson, Ralph Waldo, 104–105
Enlightenment, 38, 39
"enthusiast," 41
Epworth, 4, 5
ex nihilo, 83, 109, 145

"extraordinary ministry," 4
"eye of faith," 41, 47, 50, 51, 56

F

"A Farther Appeal to Men of Religion and Reason," 69
Fleet Marston, 5
"folk-theologian," 3, 15, 24
free will, 106
fundamentalists, 34, 80

G

Gaither, Bill, 151
Georgia
    formation of Methodist groups, 11
    mission to the Indians, 63, 151
    Moravians, 6, 7
Germany, 151
    Moravians, 8
glorifying grace, 77, 144, 263
Gospel of John, 95, 103, 125, 135, 187
Gospel of Thomas, 95, 102, 125
"The Great Assize," 147, 257
Great Awakening, 8
Great Bible, 35
Great Evangelical Revival, 11
Gregory, 41

H

Hammarsjold, Dag, 178
Hartshorne, Charles, 83
Haweis, Thomas, 29
Havel, Vaclav, 160
Heitzenrater, Richard P., 20, 21, 27
Henrik, Johan, 28

Henry VIII, 218
Herbert, Bob, 206
A History of God, 96
Hoffman, Abby, 195
Holland, Bernard, 69
Holy Club, 5, 10, 11
Hopkey, Sophy, 7
Huntington, Lady, 152

I

If Beale Street Could Talk, 214
"The Image of God," 5
The Imitation of Christ, 123
imparted righteousness, 19
imputed righteousness, 19
Incarnation, 41, 42, 50, 54, 55, 58, 61, 82, 85, 90–91, 95, 96, 102, 121, 122, 123–125, 126, 170
Inquisition, 88

J

Jeremiah, 212
John (the apostle), 103, 110–111, 133
Johnson, Samuel, 38, 152
Jones, Scott, 35
Justification, 6, 8, 9, 18, 45, 49, 56, 59, 63, 65, 68, 69, 70, 71, 72, 73, 74, 84, 93, 128, 131, 133, 134, 138, 143, 196, 205, 225
"Justification by Faith," 59, 73
justifying grace, 68, 133, 137, 138, 159, 199, 217

K

Kardecism, 99
Kazantzakis, 120
Keen, Sam, 61-62
Kennicot, Benjamin, 13

kerygma, 41
Kierkegaard, 163
King, Martin Luther, Jr., 193, 208, 212
Klaiber, 52
Knox, Alexander, 30
Kraus, 83

L

Last Judgment, 147
Law, William, 45, 74
"Letter on Preaching Christ," 26
Lincoln College at Oxford, 4, 5, 27
Lincoln College of Divines, 4
Locke, 4
"The Lord Our Righteousness," 19
Luther, Martin, 63
"lutron," 157

M

Macarius the Egyptian, 40
A Man for All Seasons, 218
Marquardt, 52
"means of grace," 139
Methodist Episcopal Church
    formation in the colonies (1784), 12
Methodists
    the Holy Club, 5
"Model Deed," 128
Montanism, 28
Moore, Henry, 30
Moore, Thomas, 61, 111
Moravians, 6, 7, 43, 50, 62, 72, 139, 159
    Boehler, Peter, 7

More, Thomas, 218
"mystical writers," 5, 44, 74
mysticism, 207

N

"National Sins and Miseries," 20
Navigator, 178
Nelson, John, 28
"The New Creation," 167
New Testament, 34, 35, 37, 51, 103, 125, 126, 136, 157, 251
Nicene Creed, 42, 89, 90
Nicodemus, 70, 133, 135, 211–215, 217
Nonconformists, 3
Notes upon the New Testament, 128

O

Old Testament, 26, 34, 37, 126, 136, 158, 166, 181, 194, 199, 201, 221, 251
"The Omnipresence of God," 57
"On Divine Providence," 20, 167
"On Dress," 20
"On Eternity," 20
"On Faith," 20
"On Obedience to Parents," 20
"On Perfection," 19
"On Predestination," 19
"On Redeeming the Time," 20
"On Riches," 238
"On Sin in Believers," 19
"On the Education of Children," 20
"On the Omnipresence of God," 20
"On the Trinity," 20, 58, 178
"On Working Out Our Own Salvation," 19, 66
ordo salutis, 60, 64, 127
Origen, 83, 109

original sin, 56, 66, 68, 135
orthodox theism, 57
Osborn, George, 29
Otto, Rudolph, 168
Outler, Albert, 5–6, 9, 10, 14, 18, 20, 21, 25, 27, 32, 35, 37, 40, 41, 44, 48, 50, 52, 53, 60, 62, 67, 73, 81, 102, 127, 159
Oxford University, 4, 12, 27, 127
    Christ Church College, 4

P

Pagels, Elaine, 102, 125
pan-en-theism, 83, 145, 146
Paul (the Apostle), 63, 67, 70, 92, 104, 107, 114, 115, 120, 124, 133, 135, 137, 142, 145, 146, 154, 165, 191, 193, 194, 196, 234, 239, 240, 244, 248, 259, 263–265
Pentateuch, 37
Pentecostals, 11
Peter (the Apostle), 161, 227
A Plain Account of Christian Perfection, 75
A Plain Account of Genuine Christianity, 55
Plato, 41
Prayer Book, 23
"preaching-houses," 128
predestination, 63, 72, 179
prevenient grace, 66, 67, 68, 70, 128, 129, 131, 132, 137, 159, 160, 165, 179, 184, 191, 205, 225
Protestant
    Reformation, 36
    theology, 67
Puritans, 15, 23, 24, 36, 59, 62, 64

Q

Quakerism, 28
Quietism, 28

R

Rack, Henry, 20
Reily, D. A., 52, 225
Revolution for the Hell of It, 195
"Rock of Ages," 73
Roman Catholic Church, 3, 36, 202, 219
Rutherford, Dr., 98

S

sacramentalist, 15
Sagan, Carl, 153
Salem witch hunts, 88
sanctification, 65, 70, 71, 72, 73, 74, 76, 93, 128, 137, 138, 140, 144, 162, 184, 217, 232, 244, 257
Saviors of God, 120
"Scriptural Christianity," 13
"The Scripture Way of Salvation," 19, 65
Separatist, 15
"Serious Thoughts Occasioned by the Late Earthquake in Lisbon," 151
Sermon on the Mount, 217
Sermons on Several Occasions, 14, 17, 18, 21, 24
A Species of Madness, 69
"Spirit and Spirituality in John Wesley," 102
Spirit, Son and Father, 122
Spong, John Shelby, 83, 88, 117, 150
St. Irenaeus, 42
St. Mary's Church in Oxford, 5, 6, 8, 12, 13, 14, 27
substitutionary atonement, 59
"substitutionary theory," 91
Synod of Dort (1619), 64

T

Thomas (the Apostle), 103
Tillich, 96
Tories, 4, 5
Transcendental Meditation, 99
Trinitarianism, 89, 92, 94, 102, 122, 123, 178
Trinity, 41, 42, 43, 50, 54, 55, 56, 58, 82, 85, 88–90, 95, 96, 102, 121–122, 123, 124, 126, 170, 178, 181
TULIP, and the sovereignty of God, 64

U

unitive mysticism, 39
"The Unity of the Divine Being," 20, 57, 85
"The Use of Money," 20, 238

V

Van Dusen, Henry, 122
Vazeille, Mary
    marries John Wesley (1751), 16
Voltaire, 143

W

Watts, Isaac, 248
Webb, William, 10–11
Wesley, Charles, 5–6, 16, 30, 35, 39, 69, 154
    hymns, 154, 248
Wesley, Emily, 28
Wesley, John
    banned from the pulpit, 27
    childhood, 3, 4
    definition of sin, 18
    dies (1791), 21
    marries Mary Vazeille (1751), 16

ordained priest, 4
orthodox theism, 57
at Oxford University, Christ Church College (1720–1724), 4
salvation by grace through faith, 6–7, 9, 19, 60, 63, 65, 68, 94, 128–130, 238
St. Mary's Church at Oxford, 5, 6, 8, 12, 13, 14, 27
trip to Georgia (1735–1737), 6

Wesley, Samuel, 4
Wesley, Susanna, 4, 39
Wesleyan movement, 3, 10, 21, 27
"religion of the warm heart," 49
"Wesleyan Quadrilateral," 24, 48–49, 50, 51, 53, 225
West, Morris, 84, 178
Western theism
early image of God, 56
"Where No One Stands Alone," 151
Whitefield, George, 3, 10, 12, 14, 63, 69, 159
Whitehead, Alfred North, 83
Williams, Colin, 55
will-mysticism, 39
"The Witness of the Spirit II," 19

Z

Zen, 99

978-0-595-34656-1
0-595-34656-1

Printed in the United States
44847LVS00006B/37-45